A Gift
To the Watermark
from
Mary Moynihan
Date
July, 2012

Jews in Berlin

The Watermark
2 Franklin Town Blvd.
Phila., PA 19103

The Ephraim Palace at the corner of Poststrasse and Muehlendamm.
Wood engraving after a drawing by Doepler, around 1890.

JEWS IN BERLIN

Edited by

Andreas Nachama
Julius H. Schoeps
Hermann Simon

Translated by

Michael S. Cullen
Allison Brown

To Moynihan library
Hermann Simon
11. 03. 03

HENSCHEL

This publication was sponsored by:

Jüdische Kulturtage Berlin
Moses Mendelssohn Zentrum für europäisch-jüdische Studien
Stiftung 'Neue Synagoge Berlin – Centrum Judaicum'

The translation was enabled by:
Partner für Berlin

Die Deutsche Bibliothek – Cataloguing-in-Publication Data
A CIP record for this book is available from
Die Deutschen Bibliothek

ISBN 3-89487-426-0

Originally published in German as *Juden in Berlin*
© 2001 by Henschel Verlag, Berlin

English translation © 2002 by Henschel Verlag, Berlin

Henschel Verlag is a trademark of Verlagsgruppe Dornier.

http://www.dornier-verlage.de
http://www.henschel-verlag.de

Front jacket photo: The New Synagogue on Oranienburger Strasse, painting by
Emil de Cauwer, 1865; Stiftung Stadtmuseum Berlin
Back jacket photo: Opening of the Centrum Judaicum in the New Synagogue on
Oranienburger Strasse (seen from the courtyard) on May 7, 1995. Photo: G. Krawutschke

Essays by Flumenbaum, Schoeps, Schütz, Brenner, Nachama translated by Michael S. Cullen.
Essay by Simon translated by Allison Brown.

Reader and Photo Researcher: Michael Philipp
Reader of Translation: Miranda Robbins
Jacket Design by Morian & Bayer-Eynck, Coesfeld
Book Design by Typografik & Design, Berlin
Printed and bound by Westermann Druck Zwickau

Printed in Germany

CONTENTS

Moses Mendelssohn (1729–86).
Copper engraving after a painting by Anton Graff.

PREFACE

Jews in Berlin. Jewish Berlin. Jewish life in Berlin. These three terms are frequently used today. In the culture sections of the newspapers one reads enthusiastic articles about the purportedly "new" Jewish life in the city. One often sees attempts to contrast the House of the Wannsee Conference – site where the Nazis formulated the "final solution to the Jewish question" on January 20, 1942 – with the masterfully restored gilded cupola of the New Synagogue. Such reporting creates problems by giving the impression that today's official Jewish Community is in the tradition of and in continuity with the Jewish Community as it existed until 1938.

No matter how well intended such articles may be, it should be stressed that the pogrom that took place on November 9, 1938, represents a rupture. That night saw the destruction of innumerable Berlin synagogues and Jewish Community institutions. And it brought to an end a development that had begun in 1671, the year in which the Great Elector Friedrich Wilhelm gave refuge to Jews from Vienna and permitted them to settle in Berlin and Brandenburg.

Jewish life in Berlin developed – slowly but steadily – from 1671 on. In the second half of the nineteenth and the first third of the twentieth centuries, it actually flourished. A specific Berlin-Jewish culture appeared, a culture on which Jews were able to put their stamp, a culture often marked by cooperation between Jews and the non-Jews surrounding them. This culture was unique. Today, it is irreversibly gone. Little remains but a faint memory of those years in which Berlin was a European-Jewish cultural metropolis, a city situated between the West and the East and worthy of worldwide admiration.

This illustrated text does not highlight the contributions made by Jews and Berliners of Jewish origin to the city. Rather, we want to show that Jews were an integral part of Berlin society, a portion of which was heavily influenced by Jewish culture. The editors are sure of one thing: whoever leafs through this book, reads the texts and sees the corresponding illustrations will gain an impression of Jewish ways of life that no longer exist in Berlin today. Indeed, these ways of life are now little more than history.

There is hardly a site in the former capital of the German Reich that is without a link to the Nazi dictatorship. If we invert this, there is hardly a site in contemporary Berlin that doesn't inform us about Jewish life in the city – often about the Nazi persecution and elimination of the Jews. This book should bring the facts of this situation into focus. For more than six decades, Berlin's Jewish culture has been a mere "topic of remembrance." Such themes are addressed, to be sure, in exhibitions of contemporary art, theater productions, literature readings, film screenings, as well as in the guest appearances of scholars and artists who visit Berlin.

Today it would be an act of daring to speak of continuity in the life of the Jewish Community. There are, of course, synagogues and other institutions administered by the Jewish Community – even a Jewish high school. And there are many members who are active in the life of the Community. These institutions and activities create the impression that the Jews of Berlin lead a normal life. But the ever-present security measures show how unnatural life in Berlin can actually be.

One cannot therefore mention the contemporary Jewish Community of Berlin in the same breath as the Jewish Community as it existed in the city before World War II. Between today and yesterday lies the traumatic experience of the Shoah. The Shoah has left a lasting mark. This is not changed by the fact that the non-Jewish majority is now attempting to work through what their grandparents' generation neither prevented nor was willing to claim responsibility for.

This illustrated text is intended for everybody. Jews can reread their own history and better understand it. Non-Jews can take up the book to realize that Jewish history is an important part of their own. Whether or not Berlin's Jewish past can be revitalized remains to be seen. The question of whether or not Berlin will ever again have a vibrant Jewish life – as it had before 1933 – is also open. Surely, the answer to whether or not this life will be integrated into the life of the city does not lie solely in the hands of its Jews. It depends on society as a whole.

The editors wish to thank the authors of the essays as well as the employees of the many archives that contributed materials to this book. We would especially like to thank Heidrun Klein of the Bildarchiv der Stiftung Preussischer Kulturbesitz, the graphic designer Ingeburg Zoschke and the reader Michael Philipp. For this English edition we thank translators Michael S. Cullen and Allison Brown and the reader Miranda Robbins. We also thank the Henschel publishing house for issuing this book in their illustrious house.

Berlin, in January 2002

Andreas Nachama

Julius H. Schoeps

Hermann Simon

From the Beginnings until 1789

The first centuries of the history of the Jews in Berlin were no different from the centuries of the history of the Jews in other German cities and provinces. Jews were alternately tolerated and expelled, and they were caught up in a never-ending series of chicanery, robbery, persecution and even murder at the hands of the rulers of the land.

One may assume that Jewish traders arrived in the area of present-day Brandenburg when Coelln – the original city of Berlin – was still a tiny fishing village occupied by the Sorbs, a Slavic people. Since no written sources exist, educated guesses lead us to believe that the first permanent settlement of Jews in the area took place after the first Crusades in the eleventh century. The city of Berlin itself dates from around that time, and the history of the Jews in Berlin is as old as the city itself.

The first official mention of the city – that is, of Coelln, the city's core – dates from 1237. The earliest trace of Jewish history in the area is a gravestone dating from 1244 found in the western district of Spandau, once an independent city. This was the same year that Coelln's sister city, Berlin (which wouldn't give its name to the entire city until 1709), is first mentioned in an official document. The year 1244 thus marks both the first official mention of Berlin and of the region's Jews.

The first reference to Jews in Berlin proper dates to 1295. It consists of only a single sentence, and – interestingly enough – it is a proscription: an order issued by the Wool Weavers' Guild prohibiting non-Jews from procuring from Jews the yarn necessary to make their cloth. Every proscription always has a pre-history, and this means that many cloth makers had been purchasing yarn from Jewish merchants.

In the fourteenth century one may assume that a relatively large Jewish community existed within the city walls, though there was no ghetto. The so-called *Grosse Judenhof* (Large Jewish Courtyard) was located in the center of the city, near the old city hall. In

The oldest Jewish gravestone found in the Berlin area (Spandau) dates to 1244. Photo: Hans D. Beyer.

1354, a smaller one, the *Kleine Judenhof*, was constructed and attached to the large one. It seems, however, that several Jews lived outside this area. Apparently this compound, which contained a small synagogue, was the primary place for Jews to live. It is reported that the entire area could be blocked off, though it would appear that this was intended to protect those inside rather than to isolate them from the rest of the populace. Like other parts of the city, the area was guarded by paid sentries.

Indeed, Jews lived apart from non-Jews, physically as well as socially. The Fourth Lateran Council in Rome of 1215 reframed the laws on Christian-Jewish relations. Among other things, it regulated the lending and borrowing of money and interest rates. Jews were forced to identify themselves with a yellow ring on their garments and to wear a so-called *Judenhut* (Jews' hat). They were prohibited from holding public office and were barred from attempting to proselytize.

Already in place were a number of even older prohibitions. Marriages between Jews and Christians were forbidden on pain of death. Jews were not allowed to have Christian servants. If a Jew committed a crime he would be punished more severely than a Christian who committed the same crime. For a Jew to swear an oath, he had to subject himself to extremely humiliating ceremonies – for instance, standing barefoot on the hide of a sow, the most unclean of animals according to Jewish tradition. In the event that Jews perjured themselves they would suffer the direst of consequences, for their family and descendants as well as themselves.

Only the medical profession was open to Jews. Although in decisions made by the pope and Councils repeatedly prohibited Christians from being treated by Jewish physicians, they frequently found imaginative methods of getting around such proscriptions. During Berlin's infamous trial for the "desecration of the host" of 1510, in which many Jews were tried and burnt at the stake, one Jew was pardoned because he was a physician with great knowledge of eye-disorders. Almost two centuries later, in 1693, a Jewish physician in Berlin named Loebel was highly respected. Nonetheless, any Christian who wanted to be treated by him needed to have special permission from the Elector.

Economic Coexistence

One profession in which Jews were successful in circumventing guild-rules during the middle ages was that of butcher. It was explicitly permitted for Jews to cut meat according to Jewish ritual law, and it was permissible to sell the meat that Jews did not use to Christians. This law was in observance from the end of the thirteenth century (prior to which Christians had been prohibited "for their own protection" from buying meat from Jews). Jews were thus able to develop businesses dealing in meat and animals. There were, however, many cases in which the Jews came into conflict with Christian butchers, as several fourteenth-century documents found in Berlin indicate. Berliners, however, were somewhat contradictory in the way they went about their dealings with Jews. Many of them were perfectly happy to be able to buy a piece of inexpensive meat, or to be able to borrow money against security. But they were occasionally the same people who started rumors that Jews had poisoned wells, kidnapped children or caused the plague. And they were occasionally the same people who mugged, expelled, maimed, burned and murdered the Jews in their midst.

Because of repeated persecutions, Jews saw themselves as forced to acquire goods that were easily transportable. Because almost all other occupations or professions were closed to them, they had little choice but to live by lending money for interest. The word "usury," to be read in many documents from the middle ages, did not have the negative meaning that it has today; it simply meant to lend money for interest. The profits, however, could be as high as the risks involved. Since Jews had to pay higher taxes to the state than Christians did, the practice of money lending was one of the few ways they could raise such sums.

The influence of Jewish moneylenders on the Berlin and regional money market can be assessed by examining the numerous regulations prohibiting rate-fixing and excessive interest rates enacted from the thirteenth century on. Christian moneylenders were prohibited from exacting interest on loans. Since that was not profitable, most did not obey these laws. Fourteenth-century documents from the Berlin city courts show that, unlike Jews, Christians were allowed to practice usury in a disguised form, for example demanding and receiving a life annuity or interest when payment was late.

It would seem that usury was even widespread among the regional clergy of the period. In 1472 the Elector Albrecht Achilles received a letter from the pope prohibiting usury among the clergy. It should also be noted that some Jewish rabbis made determined efforts to curb Jewish money lending activities – the canonical prohibition taken from the Hebrew Scriptures is, after all, reflected in the Talmud as well.

Jews were frequently engaged in the activity of pawnbroking. From this developed a trade in small goods, which was – for Jews – strictly regulated. Unclaimed goods could be sold in so-called *Judenbuden* (Jews' booths.) This was highly profitable, so much so that decrees were soon issued prohibiting

Jews from doing business on Christian holidays. It is known that in the mid-fourteenth century there were eleven *Judenbuden*. In general, however, the Jews were only allowed to buy and sell in those areas that were not reserved for Christian merchants. It seems that there were very few wealthy Jews at this time. In Berlin a social difference existed between Jews who owned their own booths and those who merely lived with those owning booths, or had no fixed place of residence. To the first category belonged the Jews Meier and Magnus, who in the middle of the fourteenth century were able to lend large sums of money. It was not until two hundred years later that a very wealthy Jew named Michael of Derenburg appeared in Berlin. He was the first German *Hofjude* (Court Jew) – a favorite of the Elector Joachim II. He owned his own home on Klosterstrasse and is the subject of many legends.

The first stage of the history of the Berlin Jews ends in 1349 with the persecutions that accompanied the plague. As all over Europe, Berlin's Jews were accused of having poisoned wells in order to kill the Christian population – despite the fact that Jews, too, died of the plague in numbers. In many cases entire Jewish communities were destroyed by the plague. In the year 1350, the city of Berlin sold the synagogue, the *Judenbuden* and several houses owned by Jews to Christians.

Not all the towns in the region expelled the Jews or had them killed. In Spandau for example, those Jews who pledged to pay higher taxes were permitted to stay. Other cities, such as Berlin, used the plague as an excuse to confiscate Jewish property. This followed only a random pattern, as can be seen from the princely practice of cancelling the loans made to Christians by Jews.

Berlin did not remain without Jews for long. As early as 1354, five years after the plague, the Margrave of Coelln permitted six

Jews to live there. This was in fact an advantage for the city, since the Jews brought commerce and, even more importantly, taxes into city and princely coffers. In the Golden Bull of 1356, the Kaiser allowed the Electors to adopt his so-called *Judenregal*. Originally an imperial prerogative, the *Judenregal* had financial benefits. Frequently the Electors delegated this right to the cities, as for instance in Berlin when Jews were allowed to return to it in 1354. Often, however the Jews had to pay taxes not only to the city but also to the regional ruler. When the cities received no income from their Jewish populations, they maltreated them and tried to force them to leave. In such cases, it was usually to no avail if the ruler ordered that Jews be protected. In 1472, for example, Albrecht Achilles spoke out in favor of protecting Jews; he did not want to lose annual taxes and interest amounting to some 3,000–4,000 gulden. There were, however, many people who owed Jews money and did not protect them from cruelties. In the middle of the fifteenth century it would seem that Jews were in possession of complete citizens' rights, though these had been acquired at a high price. In fact, the right to be a citizen was a privilege granted by the city, and it was especially useful since the right to engage in commercial activity was attached to it.

The first instance of persecution of the Jews in the Mark Brandenburg took place in the year 1446. The reasons for it are unclear. It is however probably untrue that this persecution was based on an order by Emperor Friedrich III, as earlier historians have maintained. Friedrich had, in fact, adopted a policy favorable to Jews. Brandenburg was, however, hardly different from the rest of Germany. Persecution of the Jews in the fifteenth and sixteenth centuries was something of a daily occurrence. The reasons for these persecutions and expulsions were not only

economic and related to church propaganda. They were political. In many ways it was a battle on the part of the free cities and territories against imperial policies. A very large portion of Jews emigrated from Germany during this period, especially to Poland but to northern Italy as well. By 1447, however, many Jews were already being welcomed back to Berlin.

The "Desecration of the Host" Trial of 1510 and the Expulsion of the Jews "for all Time"

The second expulsion of the Jews from Berlin was part of an expulsion and persecution of Jews on a very large scale. In 1510, the "Desecration of the Host" trial engulfed all the Jewish communities in the Mark Brandenburg. It began in early February 1510, when a Catholic coppersmith stole a golden monstrance and two hosts from a church in the town of Knobloch.

Before fleeing, he alleged that he had sold one of the hosts to a Jew from Spandau. From this accusation – entirely false, as it later turned out – an entire flood of false accusations against the Jewish communities of Brandenburg ensued.

One hundred "suspects" were brought to Berlin, where confessions were tortured out of them. A total of 51 Jews were indicted, fourteen for "desecrating the host," sixteen for murdering Christian children (despite the fact that not a single child was missing), and 21 for both offenses. At the end of the trial – the last part of which was held in public and whose outcome was known from the outset – the sentences were carried out. The execution took place at the New Market in front of the Marienkirche. In all, 38 Jews were publicly burned at the stake before a merry crowd that had assembled for the "entertainment." Three of the indicted Jews accepted conversion to Christianity and were thereby spared death at the stake. They, like the coppersmith, were executed by the sword, which was considered more humane. That only 41 of the indicted 51 were executed can be explained by the fact that several had died under torture, one had been pardoned, and a few had managed to flee.

Primarily economic motives lay at the heart of the persecution of 1510. The mass execution was an act of force to raise the economy of a poor region. The age-old accusation that Jews were murderers of Christian children had proved a useful ploy in inciting the hatred required for this Jewish bloodbath. At the same time the convicted Jews were executed, all other Jews were expelled from the Mark Brandenburg. Of course, many had already taken the hint and had left in a panic. The rulers tolerated the flight of the persecuted Jews, but quickly invited them back to their markets and fairs. Successful commerce in the region was impossible without the Jews.

In 1539 Elector Joachim II rescinded the rule prohibiting Jews from immigrating to Brandenburg, although this brought very bitter resistance on the part of the local nobility. Joachim II proved that he was a friend of the Jews of the Mark Brandenburg, and of the Jewish coin maker Lippold in particular who had immigrated to Berlin from Prague.

Obviously, the reasons for permitting the return of the Jews were not only philanthropic; they had much to do with deficits in the Elector's treasury. These had been incurred after the expulsion of 1510, though it had initially cancelled many debts. Commerce was in the doldrums. In 1556 Joachim II appointed his "dear and true Lippold" as overseer of all Jews in the Mark Brandenburg. It was an extremely small congregation.

No matter how indispensable Lippold was to the Elector, his fellow Jews despised him for his strictness. It was only in 1564 that the Berlin Jews asked for permission to build a synagogue. They had to pay eight thousand gulden to do so. Around the same time, the first Jewish cemetery was laid out on the west side of what is known today as the Landwehrkanal.

When Joachim II died on January 3, 1571, he was succeeded by Johann Georg, who immediately reversed the policies of his predecessor concerning Jews. First of all he closed all the gates to the city. It was a sign that anti-Jewish riots could commence. Very soon the synagogue was destroyed, Jewish homes were plundered and Lippold was put in jail without a formal accusation.

During the Easter period, while Lippold was still in jail without charges, the Jews were banned "for all time" from the Mark Brandenburg. Looking for evidence against Lippold, the authorities inspected his accounts and journals for an entire year. They sought proof that he had embezzled money but found, instead, that the opposite was the case; the Elector's treasury owed Lippold and his mint large sums. When this became known, Lippold was indicted for sorcery, with the added accusation that he had poisoned the Elector Joachim II. Other incredible accusations were hurled at him during the trial, which was accompanied by the usual superstition, hatred and envy among the population. Lippold confessed – under torture – to having poisoned the Elector in order to cover up the theft of some jewelry. On January 28, 1573, the sentence against Lippold was carried out in public in front of the Berlin City Hall. Because he had in the meantime recanted his confession, his death was particularly gruesome and included prolonged torture. The following day the last Jews in Berlin – members of Lippold's

Left:
In 1510, 38 Jews were burned
at the stake in Berlin for their alleged "Desecration
of the Host." This woodcut by Ludwig Berger
is from the nineteenth century.

Right:
Edicts by Friedrich Wilhelm, the Great Elector
"to arrest Polish Jews" (August 20, 1650) and
"to accept fifty families of protected Jews"
(May 21, 1671).

A woodcut, ca. 1530, depicts a Jewish moneylender
at his counting-table.

Petition of Jews of the Mark Brandenburg
to Elector Joachim II, ca. 1543. The Jews point
to their achievements and complain of the
increased financial burdens put upon
them by their leader Lippold.

Das III. Capitel. Von Juden-Sachen.

No. I. Edict wegen der Pohlnischen Juden Arretirung auff denen Jahrmärckten ꝛc. Vom 20. August. 1650.

Nachdem Sr. Churfürstl. Durchl. zu Brandenburg, zu Magdeburg, in Preussen, zu Jülich, Cleve, Berge, Stettin, Pommern ꝛc. Hertzog ꝛc. Unser gnädigster Herr, uff einemmige vornehme Intercessionales, und dan auch auff ihr demüthiges Bitten, der Juden in Pohlen, das hiebevor wegen des handels in der Chur-Brandenburg gehabte Privilegium, wiederumb auff die nechstfolgende Sieben Jahr in Gnaden ertheilet, und darnebst befrenet, daß, vermöge der packten zwischen der Crohn Pohlen vnd der Chur-Brandenburg, Sie, die Pohlnische Juden, uff den Jahr-Märckten und in Städten, wegen der Ausländischen, so sie zu besprechen haben mögen, nicht arrestabell sevn sollen, vielmehr aber einer den andern für seiner ordentli-

chen Obrigkeit zu belangen. Alß wird allen Magistraten in der Chur Brandenburg hiedurch befohlen, sich hiernach zu achten vnd solchem nachzukommen. Nichts weniger werden auch alle Churfürstl. Zöllner und Geleits Leute ernstlich befehliget, keine vngewöhnliche Zölle von den Juden zu fodern, noch sie sonsten mit einiger Neuerung zu beschweren, sondern wann sie das, was die Zoll Rollen besagen, erlegen, vnaufgehalten passiren zu lassen, damit deshalb keine Klage einkomme. Urkundlich unter Sr. Churfürstl. Durchl. Subscription und Pettschafft gedrucktem Secret, Geben zu Cölln an der Spree, am 20. August. 1650.

Fr. Wilhelm.

(L. S.)

No. II. Edict wegen auffgenommenen 50. Familien Schutz-Juden, jedoch daß sie keine Synagogen halten. Vom 21. May 1671.

Wir Friderich Wilhelm, von Gottes Gnaden, Marggraff zu Brandenburg, des Heil. Röm. Reichs Ertz Cammerer und Churfürst, ꝛc. Bekennen hiermit öffentlich, und geben einem jeden es nöthig, in Gnaden zu wissen, uff was sonderbaren Ursachen, und auff Unterthäniges Anhalten, Hirschel Lazarus, Benedict Veit, und Abraham Ries, Juden, bevorab zu Beförderung Handels und Wandels bewogen worden, einige von andern Orten sich wegbegebende Jüdische Familien, und zwar fünfftzig derselben, in Unser Lande der Chur und Marck Brandenburg, und in Dörffern sonderbaren Schutz gnädigst auf- und anzunehmen, thun auch solches hiermit und Krafft dieses auff folgende Conditiones:

1. Wollen wir ermeldten fünfftzig Jüdischen Familien, derer Namen, und Anzahl von Personen, auch an was Ort sich jederweder niederlassen, uns forderlichst durch eine richtige Specification kund gethan werden soll, in gedachte Unsere Lande der Chur- und Marck Brandenburg, auch in Unser Hertzogthum Crossen und incorporirte Landen hiemit auffgenommen haben, dergestalt und also, daß ihnen Macht gegeben sevn sol, in denen Oertern und Städten, wo es ihnen

am gelegensten ist, sich niederzulassen, allda Stuben, oder gantze Häuser, Wohnungen und Commodität vor sich zu miethen, zu erkauffen oder zu erbauen, doch in der Masse, daß, was sie Kauffweise an sich bringen, Widerkäufflich geschehe, und was sie erbauen, auch nach Verfliessung gewisser Jahre an den Christen wieder verlassen werden müsse, jedoch, daß ihnen die Unkosten davor restituiret werden.

2. Sol diesen Jüdischen Familien vergönnet sevn, ihren Handel und Wandel im gantzen Lande dieser Unser Chur- und Marck Brandenburg, Hertzogthumb Crossen und incorporirten Oertern, Unsern edicten gemäß zu treiben, wobey ihnen noch ausdrücklich nachgeben, offene Krahme und Buden zu haben, Tücher und dergleichen Wahren, in stücken zuverkauffen oder auch Ellenweise außzumessen, groß und klein Gewichte zu halten (doch daß sie dadurch keine Vervortheilung im Kauff oder Verkauff) auch mit denen Rabts-Wagen, oder wo der Magistrat das grosse Gewichte hat, etwas abgebe, mit Neuen und Alten Kleidern zu handeln, ferner in ihren Häusern zu schlachten, und was sie zu ihrer Nahrdurfft und ihrem Gesetze nach dem jenen schlachten, und ihrem Gesetze nach dem nicht bedürftig, solches zu verkauffen

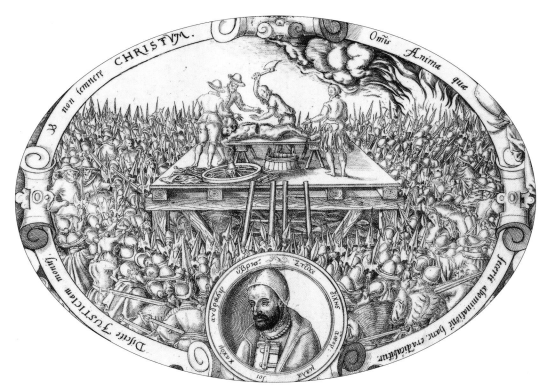

Lippold's execution: "True representation or figure of the face of Lippold, the Jew, together with his execution, very well deserved because of his cruel and inhuman deeds (which he perpetrated on innocent Christian blood) on January 28, 1573, in Berlin, done according to divine and imperial law." This is a detail from a contemporary single-page print published by Leonhard Thurneisser of Berlin.

family – left the Mark Brandenburg. The records show that there were no Jews living in the Mark Brandenburg for almost a century.

The Expulsion of the Jews from Vienna and the Founding of the Jewish Congregation in Berlin

The next mention of Jews being once again in the Neumark (the region north-east of Berlin) dates to about 1650. At that time the authorities permitted Polish refugees to settle there, and Jews who had certain *Schutzbriefe* (letters of protection), were also permitted to attend the markets in Brandenburg. Real immigration of the Jews, however, did not take place until the mid-1660s, when many Jews were expelled from lower Austria. Still, only a very few of them found their way to Berlin. In 1664, the towns of the Mark Brandenburg had themselves legally guaranteed that Jews would not be permitted to take up permanent residence there. This rule was observed for almost a decade.

The expulsion from Vienna of the large, wealthy and traditional Jewish Community there was an epochal event. Prepared by the authorities over a long period of time, it greatly occupied the European public. What set it off, however, was a royal miscarriage:

that of Margarete, the Spanish wife of Emperor Leopold I. Blamed for this misfortune were the Viennese Jews.

In 1670, after hearing of the order that expelled the Jews of Vienna, Friedrich Wilhelm, the Great Elector of Brandenburg, sent his emissary Andreas Neumann to contact several Jewish families. A year later the heads of three Jewish families wrote him stating that they wished for permission to take up residence in the Mark Brandenburg. They were Abraham Ries, Benedikt Veit and Hirschel Lazarus. They appealed to the Elector's mercy and referred to his high promise. The initiative thus proceeded from the Court of Brandenburg and not from the Jews themselves.

Indeed, one should not think that Brandenburg at the time was especially attractive. It belonged to the territories of middle Europe that had suffered greatly during the Thirty Years War (1618–48). The land was devastated, and about 50 percent of the population had fallen victim to the war and its following periods of starvation, epidemics and murderous lawlessness. The Great Elector was sensitive to these disasters and developed a major reform program to fight his territory's backwardness. He created a central administration and brought foreign specialists into his land. Other states were also interested in attracting such specialists to improve their economies. Friedrich Wilhelm was able to lure to his territories the talented Protestant Huguenots from France by offering them many privileges.

No matter how low their position was in the social order, no matter how low they stood, the Jews filled a major economic function in feudal society. They were better than all others at buying and selling agrarian products. They understood how to master liquidity crises and they were able to provide very necessary services to mediate between the cities and the countryside. It should not be assumed that tolerance or the ideas of tolerance played a major role in The Great Elector's acceptance of the Jews, as has often been maintained. Rather, it was the very simple principle that the state's economy was in need of improvement.

One need not go further than to compare the edict permitting the Jews to settle in Brandenburg with the one that was issued fourteen years later regarding the French Huguenots. Whereas the Jews were merely permitted to enter Brandenburg and their number was limited to fifty families (and only for a maximum of twenty years), the Huguenots were invited to Brandenburg for perpetuity and granted the same civil rights as the Germans. The acceptance of the Huguenots was based on religion and a perceived shared humanity. In contrast, the acceptance of the Jews was based on the need to improve commerce and trade. Whereas the Jews had pay their own way to get to the Mark Brandenburg, the immigration of the Huguenots was paid for by the state and organized by Brandenburg officials. Whereas the Jews made their own way, the Huguenots were accompanied by guides. Whereas the Huguenots did not have to suffer restrictions in the exercise of their religion, the Jews were for a long time banned from building a synagogue in Berlin.

Nevertheless, it was in a certain way an experiment, and the Jews themselves were able at least to feel the beginning of a new age – even if it was to dawn more slowly for them than it did for their Huguenot contemporaries. Thus began a long and rocky path toward emancipation, a path that would exact a high price from the Jewish Community: the price of assimilation. While many were prepared to pay it, others were not. In Brandenburg – soon to be a part of Prussia – this development began in Berlin in 1671.

Exiled Jews leaving Vienna in February, 1670.
Contemporary copper engraving.

The Struggle for the First *Schutzbriefe*

The first of Vienna's Jews to arrive in Berlin were from one large family. At the head was the rabbinical scholar Model Ries and his sons Abraham, Koppel and Hirschel. Also present were Model Ries's brother-in-law, Benjamin Fraenkel, and Abraham's father-in-law, Jacob Gumprecht. Finally, there was Abraham's brother-in-law, Benedict Veit (who was also Gumprecht's son-in-law). While their wives and children waited for them at the Austrian-Moravian border, the family heads traveled to Potsdam to negotiate their acceptance in the Mark Brandenburg. The Elector first wanted to find out how wealthy they were and hoped to choose on

the basis of their wealth those Jews who would receive a *Schutzbrief* (protection letter) and, with it, official toleration.

The edict accepting the Jews is dated May 21, 1671. The very title included an important fact: "Edict for the Acceptance of Fifty Families of *Schutzjuden*, who, However, May Not Maintain a Synagogue." The edict made no mention of the Austrian ancestry of the Jews. This exclusion may have been made out of respect for the Habsburg Emperor, who happened to be Emperor of the German Empire as well. It may have been intended to indicate that non-Austrian Jews might also be able to settle in the Mark Brandenburg. The Jews were not given *Schutzbriefe* right away. Each had to obtain one individually. Most importantly, the edict made no definition of precisely where the Jews would be allowed to settle. It was valid for the entire Mark Brandenburg, the Duchy of Crossen and the incorporated territories of Sternberg and Cottbus. At the end of August, Ries and Veit presented a petition to the High Court Councilor of the Elector Otto von Schwerin, with the plea to recommend to the Elector that they should be allowed to settle in Berlin. On August 31, 1671 they presented their petition to the Elector personally. It now became the task of the Royal Chamber to formulate the *Schutzbriefe*, which was worked out according to two conditions. First, it would be necessary for the Jews to maintain a peaceful relationship with Israel Aaron, the Jewish Court-Agent who had been in Berlin since 1655. Second, it reflected the hopes of several Berlin Protestant pastors to be able to convert the Jews.

The first *Schutzbrief*, issued September 4, 1671, was for Abraham Ries. This document, which was then used as a model for the other *Schutzbriefe*, contained however only a fraction of the promises that had been present in the edict of May 21. A clause stating that the Jews were not able to settle any disagreement in their commerce was inserted only on September 6, two days later.

Israel Aaron had arrived some fifteen years earlier from Poland, and he was active in furnishing the army and the mint in Koenigsberg with silver. For these services he received a *Schutzbrief* from the Duchy of Prussia, and in 1665 this was expanded to take in the entire Mark Brandenburg. Aaron was officially employed by the court, with an annual salary of two hundred talers, in addition to money for expenses. It is quite understandable that he saw the new immigrants as potential competitors and that he was somewhat worried about maintaining his influence in the courts. He had therefore written a letter to the court warning against the misuse of the privileges by the Jews who were now arriving.

Furthermore, he requested the right to make suggestions as to who should enter Berlin and who should not.

Friedrich Wilhelm was so alarmed by the petition of his Court Jew that he withdrew his permission for the release of the first ten *Schutzbriefe* for Berlin. He even wanted to modify the two that had already been issued in order to exclude the relatives of Ries and Veit. The two were not ready to give up the privileges that they already been granted, and they complained to the Chamber of the Courts. Its president, President von Canstein, made sure that *Schutzbriefe* were issued for all their relatives. These documents were issued on September 12, 1671, the same day Israel Aaron received a new *Schutzbrief* that reinforced his rights to complain and to deliver expert opinions. September 12, 1671 is considered therefore the date of the founding of the Berliner Juedische Gemeinde, Berlin's official Jewish congregation (hereafter referred to as the Jewish Community of Berlin).

Aaron seems to have felt that he would be bypassed by the influx of Austrian Jews in Berlin. They had, after all, been able to arrive and take up residence in the city without availing themselves of his help. There was another problem that Israel Aaron tried to solve. He did not want to accept any rabbi elected by the new immigrants. Had they been permitted their own choice, they would certainly have selected Model Ries. Aaron was not ready to accept that. He therefore suggested to the Elector that Rabbi Chain, also from the Neumark, be appointed rabbi in Berlin. He knew that Chain, who was the rabbi in the small city of Landsberg, would not be a threat.

In the year 1671 only one other Jew was permitted to take up residency in Berlin and get a *Schutzbrief.* At the end of December this letter was signed and issued to Lazarus

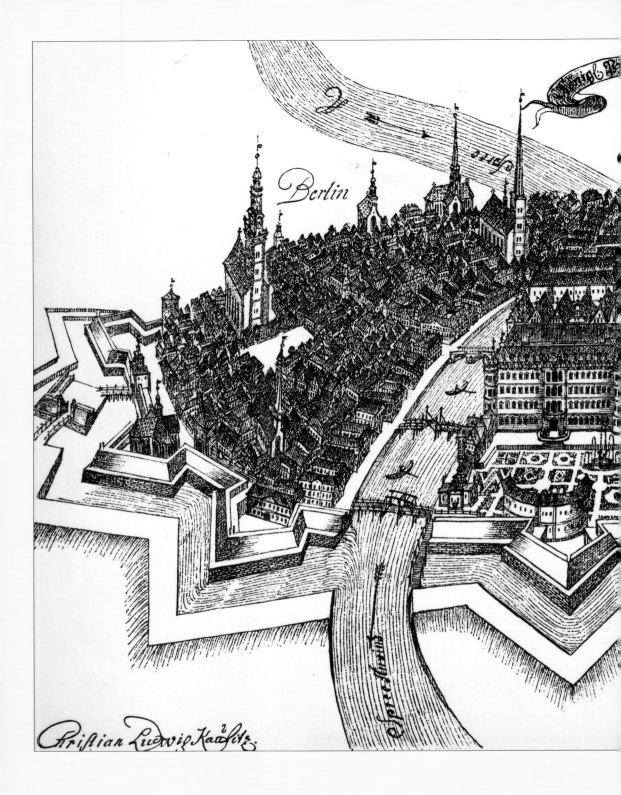

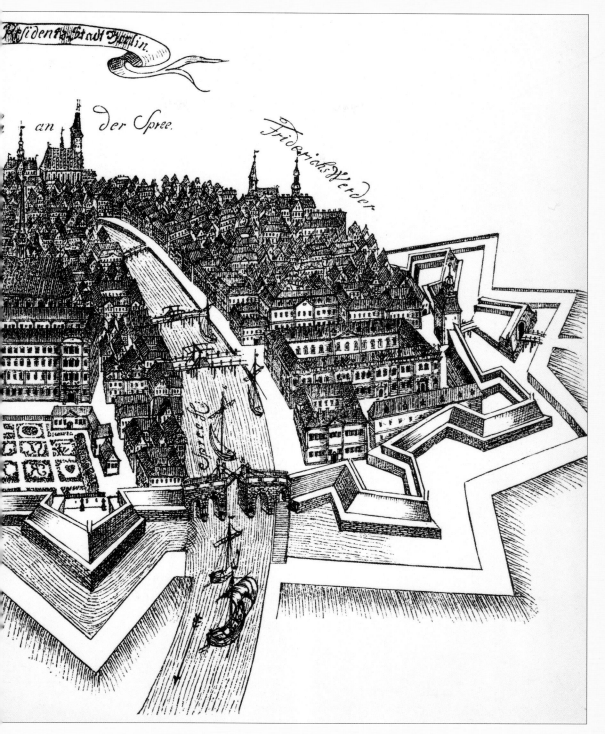

The "Royal Residence of Berlin" with its parts of Berlin, Coelln and Friedrichswerder.
Engraving after a drawing by Christian Ludwig Kaulitz, before 1710.

Israel, who had already been living in Brandenburg for many years. It is possible that Israel Aaron was able to impede the immigration of other Jews to Berlin, but by 1672 his influence was certainly on the wane. By then there were already forty Jewish families living in Berlin.

The First Years of the New Community

Friedrich Wilhelm, the Great Elector, laid out very specific rules pertaining to those Jews who could settle in his territories. In addition to the usual taxes, Jews were required to pay an annual *Schutzgeld* (protection fee) of eight talers. They were, however, freed from the "body" tax, which was levied on Jews passing through the region. In theory, Jews could settle anywhere in the Mark Brandenburg, though, at least at the beginning, they were not permitted to purchase real estate. With the exception of the clothing trade, all commercial activities were open to them. The Jewish faith was tolerated, but prayers could be said only in private congregations. Heavy penalties awaited those who were deemed guilty of calumny or blasphemy. Furthermore, the young Community was permitted to engage the services of a schoolmaster and a kosher butcher. The city government was expected to accept the Jews willingly and happily and to accommodate all their wishes and to favor them so that they would stay in the city. And it was charged with protecting them from being cursed or humiliated. Anyone found guilty of attacking Jews had to pay a fine of fifty gold gulden.

Nevertheless there was resistance, and it came from the territorial aristocracy and the guilds. Even though the Jews only had permission to stay for twenty years, both the no-bles and the guilds started working to have them expelled right away. The latter considered Jews uncomfortable competition and were anxious that Jews would corner the market in used goods – by creating a new clientele of poorer people. These new forms of trade were very different from the bourgeois and guild traditions that had been in existence for several hundred years. It took another two hundred years before they were adopted by the Christian merchants. The Great Elector, however, stuck to his word. After all, he had brought the Jews to the area because of their ability to bring innovation, for their great knowledge of the markets and their adaptability as pioneers in agriculture. At the same time, however, he made very sparing use of the *Schutzbrief*.

In 1674, the Jews of Berlin were once again prohibited from selling kosher meat to Christians, although as early as the middle ages they had been allowed sell what they could not use for themselves (unneeded meat and meat that, despite, ritual slaughter, was unusable for religious reasons). Jews were restricted to slaughtering only in order to meet their own needs.

From the very beginning there were many Jews who were *unvergleitet*, that is they lacked the protection of official documents, or *Schutzbriefe*. Such Jews were periodically expelled from the country. The administration spent much time and effort settling problems with *unvergleitete* Jews. The easiest method was to stop them right at the city gates. If the work could be done by Jews, so much the better. Frequent investigations were launched to discover Jews without *Schutzbriefe*. Regulations were published and republished – in 1694–95, 1700, 1705, 1710 and 1712. This suggests that such laws were not always taken very seriously.

In 1674, the new Jewish Community published a statute for the congregation in the interest of self-protection. After the usual entreaties and words of thanks, the signers committed themselves to making sure that no *unvergleitete* Jews would be able to sneak in to the city. The statute threatened severe penalties: large fines, banishment from the Community, even the confiscation of the *Schutzbrief*. The statute was signed by seven of the Austrian and five additional immigrants. What is not known is whether the statute was formulated voluntarily or under pressure from the state. In any case, this document may be seen as the origin of the principle of "liability through solidarity" or "joint responsibility" (*modus collectandi*, or *solidarische Haftbarkeit*). This would become one of the Berlin Jewish Community's major problems in the years ahead. The leaders of the Jewish Community were liable with their entire fortune if the *Schutzgeld* (protection fee) was not paid promptly to the state or if any other members of the Jewish Community – or even foreign Jews and non-members – were guilty of any offense.

The task of making *unvergleitete* Jews leave the city had been assigned to the *Hausvogt*, or the head of the police. In 1681, however, the *Hausvogt* asked to be released from his job. It was, apparently, very unpleasant. The position was assumed by the Royal Court Chamber. At the end of 1684 this court began yet another investigation to find out which Berlin Jews were allowed to be there and which were not. Some of them were simply indigent. Those who did not go voluntarily were threatened with prison.

For the most part, however, Jewish life began to flourish. One of the signs of the increasing establishment of the Community was the founding of some important institutions. In 1672, a Jewish cemetery was laid out on a piece of property on Grosse Hamburger Strasse, which the Community had been permitted to purchase. Moreover,

associations were established to enrich the Community's life. A *mikvah* (ritual bath) was constructed. Education was organized for children. As far as prayers were concerned, however, Jews had to meet privately, as before. There was still no synagogue.

The Development of the Community and the Building of a Synagogue

The Great Elector died in 1688. His son, who would later take the name of Friedrich I when he crowned himself Prussian King, was particularly interested in strict rules to govern Christian-Jewish relations. This was especially important to him since the twenty-year limit on the first edict of 1671 would soon be reached. When Friedrich ascended to the throne, the Berlin Council gave him a list of complaints about the Jews. The list contained many of the worst – but already familiar – accusations: that the Jews had murdered Elector Joachim one hundred years before; that they had been thrown out of Vienna for good reason, having brought the plague to it.

Friedrich established a new commission on Jews, the *Judencommission* to limit the number living in Berlin and to ensure that those who did, did so legally. This commission was made up of three privy councilors, to the head of which each Jew had to present himself, *Schutzbrief* in hand. The *Schutzbrief* could then arbitrarily be confirmed or rejected. After paying a tax of 16,000 talers, the Jewish Community received a confirmed privilege. Jews without letters of protection were only able to enter the city with a "laissez passer" issued by the *Hausvogt*. Thus did it become impossible for unauthorized Jews to settle in any part of Prussia or to stay anywhere in the region for longer than three days.

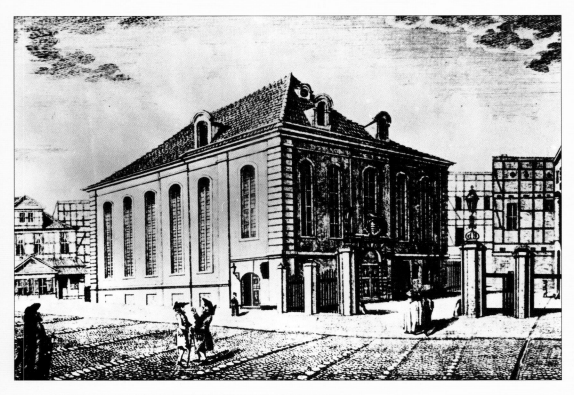

א   ווזיב

בישור זה וויי וניישעיב בנלענו וורוזייר הנולר ישול נוקין בו הנולונט הוונו וכלוי וחרבעיש וטלו...
וזון כמ רבט הכהלוה וברועוות יושב וכלוצון ווטר זיין ונטרו וולה וכל הטותריה ווטוזרה פור
וזהוריגן טב לה סור וטרוה ישוב כזו פולורי ופוות ווטוות ו וזלו והבן הולוטוים פון קלוטיו ל...
נהוהולוט בו לו וטטגי גי ווזעל ריחיר טלוה ביר וטן ורוב בטן בן נריגן במטי כע בטוות זטו...
גולבג עבט הב הרוטף חהטולין ולב וזליט ביח בטורי וטן וטורפה וויטן נהוטיוף ובר לן טן ...
טבעטיל הילי פייף וויל וווב ובוה וזוני וטון בוריר נייל לה החטוי וברהולוטול חטו ו...
הובר בב טב טו ווז ווסור גווטו ובטר וטוה ונטר נהוטן טבעיטר ליטרי הקון וטלה היי ו...
וטיבט טה ולול לה גוועלל וכוטשן וזברוני הטוה...
ולו וולף וטל ולו עט עה הגול הטריי וזן וכ וול וטברר הוה

הקצין הרר הירש נאלד שמיד
הקצין פו כהרר משה קליוא
הקצין פו כהרר אהרן כהן
האלוף התורני כהרר הירש כ'ן
האלוף הרר אנשיל עשווי
הנעלה כהרר יואל פילא
היקר כה' אלי' קראטשין

*The synagogue on
Heidereutergasse, dedicated in 1714,
after an eighteenth-century drawing
by F. A. Calau.*

*Left:
First page of the protocol book
of the Jewish Community
of Berlin, 1723.*

*Right:
Interior of the
Heidereutergasse synagogue.
Etching by A. B. Goblin after a
drawing by Anna Maria Werner,
ca. 1720.*

These rules became effective at the end of the year 1700 and contained several other restrictions. Jews were once again subjected to restrictions on the sale of clothing, barred from the clothing trade altogether and prohibited from selling door-to-door. Regulations were imposed on Jews lending money to Christians (although money lending had, with the "Imperial Interest Edict" of 1697, already become less of a Jewish occupation since the edict permitted Christians to accept interest on loans). Real estate purchases and marriages between distant blood relations were only permitted with special examination. An edict prohibiting the Jewish prayer Alenu was renewed in 1703, 1710, 1717 and 1730. The prayer was banned in connection with the publication of Johann Eisenmenger's book *Jewishness Discovered* (1700), in which he "proved" the worst accusations about Jews. Although the book was confiscated by imperial order immediately after it was printed, Friedrich I permitted Eisenmenger's heirs to reprint it ten years later. It is not known whether the "Alenu Edict" had ever really been applied in Berlin, but its purpose can be understood from the book's introduction, which stated that the final goal in dealing with the Jews was their conversion to Christianity.

In 1708 a new, broadly competent *Judencommission* was installed and assumed jurisdiction over Berlin's Jews from the *Hausvogt*. It oversaw the respect the Jews paid to royal ordinances and made sure that the *Schutzgeld* (protection fee) was paid punctually. It had no authority in matters of Jewish faith, however, but acted in cooperation with Jewish civil servants. In 1698 the election of a Council of Elders within the Jewish Community had failed. The state authorities intervened and picked a new council of its own to guide the Community. Originally the group consisted of five Elders and a chairman, cho-

Jost Liebmann (Juda Berlin, died 1702). Painting by Antony Schoonjans, 1702. Stiftung Preussische Schloesser und Gaerten Berlin-Brandenburg.

sen directly by the king. Among others there were a speaker, a treasurer and assistants to the Elders.

Various matters such as religious schooling, the problems of caring for indigents and others welfare matters were assigned to two of the Elders and their assistants. These areas were financed through contributions, charitable foundations, Community taxes and even extra money from the Community's own coffers. The Jewish Community also participated in raising funds for needy and indigent Christians. In 1732, for instance, they helped raise money for poor Protestants from Salzburg who resided in Berlin.

The Community's functionaries were chosen by secret ballot by seven electors. Those who voted were themselves chosen by lot, and three (later four) of them came from the highest class of taxpayers; two were chosen from the middle tax bracket; and two (later one) came from the lowest tax category.

These three categories had been formed to assess the taxes taken in by the Community. The upper class of taxpayers consisted of only very few families. One of the statistics in the year 1774 indicates that there were only three families who paid the highest tax of 2,000 talers, while 12 other families were in the position to pay 400 talers to the Community annually.

As the years went by, the Jewish Community's Elders were pushed more and more into the role of servants of the state. The Council of Elders was accomplishing its work more or less successfully, but there were many altercations within the Community (for which the royal family was often to blame). For example, Jost Liebmann and Marcus Magnus viewed each other with hostility and competed for power within the Council of Elders. Each had his group of supporters. Liebmann was a wealthy jeweler whose well-protected position at court passed to his widow after his death. It was said that Liebmann and his wife had access to Friedrich's inner circle. Magnus, on the other hand, was "Court Jew" to the Crown Prince. In 1709 he was appointed Elder Superior of the Jewish Community. In the end, the battle between them was fought in court. The decision, handed down in 1710, was a superficial ruling – a mere show of the king's handwriting.

The conflict between Liebmann and Magnus was clearest in matters regarding the building of a synagogue for the entire Community. By this time, the royal court started to see the advantage of having the private synagogues eliminated and replaced by a single main synagogue. Such a building could be controlled more easily, and fewer officials would be required to supervise them. The main thrust came from the state at the end of December 1700, but not one of the four owners of synagogue concessions was ready

Title page of the Hebrew part of a poem of acclamation, dedicated by the protected Jew Simon Wolf Brandes upon the coronation of Friedrich I of Prussia on January 18, 1701.

to give up his concession voluntarily. This situation made it nearly impossible to erect a synagogue. It took nearly fourteen more years before the Community's first synagogue was dedicated (in 1714).

In the early days of the Berlin Jewish Community, members met either at the house of Veit or Ries for their private prayers. Later, the court jeweler Liebmann was allowed to have services in his house. In 1684 his synagogue, although still private, was declared official. The two other synagogues of Veit and Ries continued to exist despite being illegal. They acquired official recognition in 1694. In order to maintain peace within the Community, but also because there was a genuine shortage of space, it was prohibited afterward to meet in any of the Jewish private houses for prayer. At the end of the seventeenth century, the Jewish Community consisted of about 120 families – roughly

Friedrich Wilhelm I, (1688–1740), King in Prussia 1713–40. Painted by Antoine Pesne ca. 1735.
Stiftung Preussische Schloesser und Gaerten Berlin-Brandenburg.

600 people. For a short time, there were two other generally acknowledged prayer halls, in the houses of Wulf Salomon and David Ries.

On May 9, 1712, the foundation stone was laid for the new synagogue on Heidereutergasse. For building permission alone, the Community had paid 3,000 talers to the royal treasury – a financial burden that could not have been borne very easily. Furthermore there were other taxes and tributes to be paid on behalf of the Community's private schools and the various prayer halls that were in the homes of individual Community members. It is reported that the king was so upset about the undisciplined way that these taxes and other payments were being made – the payment of *Schutzgeld* was also in arrears – that he threatened to give the entire new synagogue to Liebmann's widow.

The opening of the new synagogue took place on Rosh Hashanah (the Jewish New Year), September 14, 1714, in the presence of Queen Sophie Dorothea. Friedrich Wilhelm I did not visit the synagogue until Passover in April 1718. In March 1715 the Community paid the 3,000 talers to the king.

In the Power of an Absolute Monarch

The Prussian laws restricting Jews reached a low level during the reign of Friedrich Wilhelm I, the so-called "Soldier-King" (reigned 1713–40). He hated the Jews for religious reasons. In commercial matters he pressed them hard, and those who could not afford to live in Prussia were forced to leave. As early as 1714 he sought drastic measures against them. Not only did he wish to stop the entry of Jews into Berlin completely, but he also tried to limit the growth of families already living within his realm. Henceforward the

official residence permit could be passed on to only one child. Obtaining legal residence for more than one child became extremely expensive. A second child cost 1,000 talers; a third cost 2,000. New admissions to the Community were only possible if the applicant had a fortune of at least 10,000 talers.

Friedrich Wilhelm I introduced the practice of demanding extraordinary payments and contributions for every possible occasion. A tax was levied on each marriage. In 1713, the Jews paid 20,000 talers into the royal treasury for the king's coronation and to confirm their privileges. In 1714 they paid another 8,000 talers in order to circumvent a law that would have made it obligatory for Jews to carry a red hat throughout the city. In 1720 the Community had to make a "present" of 20,000 talers to the royal coffers, and in 1725, 7,000 talers were paid as partial payment for a church in Potsdam. In 1717 and 1722 new *Judencommissions* were installed. In 1722 it examined the Community's 1706–17 books and reached a disastrous conclusion. The books were in terrible condition; there were no receipts to be found relating to the construction of the synagogue; purchases had been made without royal permission; the Community was sitting on a mountain of debts. The commission declared the Elders guilty and fined them 8,000 talers. This was later reduced to 6,500 talers.

In 1722 the king issued an "Ordinance for the Elder Superior and other Elders of the Berlin Jewish Community." All positions (with the exception of the one held by Liebmann's rival, Magnus) were filled with new appointments. Liebmann, the son of the aforementioned jeweler and his widow and himself an Elder since 1712, was suffering so much under the open enmity of the others that he asked to be released from his position on the Council. The new Elders were Marcus Magnus and Moses Levy Gumpertz. The lat-

Anti-Jewish edict by Friedrich Wilhelm I declaring that "all unvergleitete *Jews must leave my territories all at once" (January 10, 1724), and "all the cheating by Jews in matters of promissory notes must be stopped" (April 8, 1726).*

ter was a favorite of Friedrich Wilhelm I (and the only Jew permitted to carry a dagger in public).

The aforementioned regulation on the Elders from 1722 marked a new beginning for the internal organization of the Jewish Community. Henceforth the mission of the Elders was clearly defined. They would keep a list of all the members of the Community, keep exact accounts of all income and expenditure (in both Hebrew and German), assure that all fees and other taxes were paid punctually and would be aware of "alien" Jews who were illegally living in Berlin. Because of many complaints, there was a clause specifying that the present and succeeding Elder should "exercise all his powers to maintain royal order and prerogatives and interest and should always try to avert unnecessary disputes, which, if they occurred, would carry heavy penalties." A College of Rabbis would assist the Council of Elders. This consisted of a First Rabbi, the vice-Rabbi and two or three assistants. The Community's other spiritual members were the cantor and the singers in the synagogue.

Because of its ever-increasing 'debts' to the state, the Community had to find new sources of revenue. It therefore leased the supervision of meat, which brought in 550 talers annually (from 1725 on, 800 talers annually). Other income was derived from absentee members who wished to maintain their status, from immigration fees and from the sale of seats in the synagogue. It was also traditional to expect small fees for the use of the ritual bath, the *mikvah*. Finally there were taxes to the Community on inheritances, property purchase and dowries. Nevertheless, the large sums expected by the royal treasury compelled the Community to increase such taxes and duties every three years or so. It was only with great difficulty that they were able to raise the necessary funds to hold the royal treasurer at bay.

Disputes within the Community did not just die away. Many of them arose from the severe way in which Gumpertz – one of the newer Elders – exercised his authority. The members of the Community demanded fair selections of the Elders. Every few years – 1725, 1728, 1729, and 1737 – the members petitioned the king or his officials to improve their lot.

Friedrich Wilhelm I, however, did the opposite. He frequently raised taxes, fees and other contributions. In addition to the collective *Schutzgeld* there was now a turnover-tax. He also exacted money to pay for his *Lange Kerls*, his soldiers (who were renowned for their exceptional height). A special payment called the *Servisgeld* was usually paid to citizens when soldiers were quartered in their homes; Jews, however, had to pay the same amount so that soldiers would *not* be quartered in their homes. He likewise charged for printing the Jewish calendar, something the Jewish Community had little interest in. There were fees to pay for certificates of marriage, birth, death, and so forth. Jews had to pay the *Montes Pietatis*, which was a tax on money lending. Furthermore they were forced to contribute large amounts of silver in lieu of other contributions. In general the state taxed every event and activity in the lives of Jews: birth, marriage, divorce, travel, death and funerals. Finally all kinds of taxes were levied on various occupations. This was the so-called *Stempelgeld* or stamp duty.

In 1728 Friedrich Wilhelm I ordered yet another 'reform' of the Jewish taxes, which extended the principle of *modus collectandi* (liability through solidarity) to all Jews in his kingdom. It was now necessary for provinces to pay all taxes and fees collectively instead on an individual basis. The *Schutzgeld* was raised to 15,000 talers for all of Prussia. Berlin's portion of this total was 2,610 talers, with a tendency to get larger, since the Berlin Community was obliged to make up whenever less wealthy communities could not raise their portion of the protection fee.

The provisions in this new ordinance of 1728 were even more onerous than those from the ordinance of 1714. Once again Jews were prohibited from dealing in spices and from working in almost all handicrafts, with the exception of butchering and die cutting. Goods taken in at pawnshops could only be sold after a two-year wait. So important was it to the king that the Jews understand his motives that he summoned the representatives of all the Jews in Prussia to Berlin. The

*Because of forced collective liability (*modus collectandi*) the Jews of Berlin were obliged to carefully control the entry of other Jews into Berlin. This is a "pass" issued by a Jewish "gate keeper" from the year 1744.*

Berlin Community itself was represented by Heine Ephraim and Hartog Goldschmidt. They had objected to the ordinance on the grounds that the number of Jewish families allowed in Berlin was to be reduced to one hundred. Furthermore, they were being forced to pay more "monies for recruits," a total now raised to 4,800 talers. The Council of Elders was able to obtain the assurance from court officials that the ordinance would be redrafted. For that, however, the Berlin Community was obliged to pay a higher *Schutzgeld*, now raised to 15,000 talers. Three years later, in September 1730, the ordinance was published in the original form, with only one of the promised changes. The preface, now removed, had contained humiliating remarks suggesting that the new ordinance had been necessary because of an expansion in Jewish trading and infiltration of alien Jews into the Jewish Community.

The king found imaginative new ways to harass the Jews. After Rabbi Michel Chosid died in 1729 he ordered the Elders to install a twenty-year-old, Moses Aaron from Moravia, as rabbi. The Community refused to accept him. There were several scuffles inside the synagogue. Aaron did not remain rabbi for

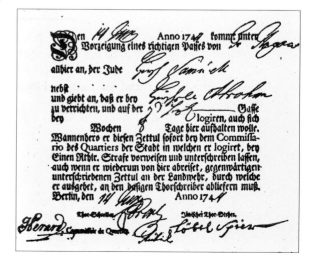

Daniel and Miriam Itzig. Painting by Joseph Friedrich d'Arbes.
Stiftung Stadtmuseum Berlin.

Itzig's palace on Burgstrasse, Berlin. Photograph ca. 1855.

very long, and a trial ensued. The parties reached a settlement in which vice-Rabbi Esajas Hirschel was appointed Aaron's successor. Aaron went to Frankfurt/Oder, where he continued to receive a salary from the Berlin Community for a long period. Moreover, the Community had to pay 1,500 talers to the royal treasury for firing him.

Despite the restrictions of 1728–30, the number of Jewish families had greatly grown by 1737 – to about 180 families. Friedrich Wilhelm I launched more draconian measures, using as an excuse the theft of some silver that had involved some Jews. Although the value of the stolen goods was fixed at 82 talers, the Congregation was ordered to pay 1,000 talers in damages. And the king published a decree declaring that the number of Jewish families was to be reduced to 120. Only the "best and wealthiest" would be permitted to stay. The Community protested and was able to have the "damage" payment reduced. It also arranged for papers to allow the members of families of those employed by the Community to remain in Berlin. Instead of 953, "only" 584 Jews were forced to leave the city.

The *Judencommission* led by Minister Broich, however, seems to have been more lenient with the Jews than the king. Broich's commission worked conscientiously and with deliberate slowness to decide who should stay and who should leave. For the king, things were going much too slowly. He wrote to the *Generaldirektorium* (best translated as "cabinet") that he was not prepared to wait much longer and would prefer even foregoing the 20,000-taler fees if the remaining families would also leave.

In June of the same year, the *Judencommission* announced the departure of 387 Jews. The king responded: "Thank God that they're gone – best would be if all the others would also leave and not settle anywhere else in my cities and provinces." What Friedrich Wilhelm I did not know was that in reality – according to the lists kept by the custom authorities – only 94 Jews had left Berlin and the others whose departure had been expected were still being tolerated within the city.

A short time later another regulation appeared stipulating that all Jews living between Koenigsstrasse and Spandauer Strasse had to leave their quarters in order for soldiers to move in. These soldiers had complained of unclean quarters elsewhere. The Jews who left were not indemnified. Instead, they were given the poorer military quarters or other quarters just outside the city walls, where they were forced to pay an arbitrarily fixed rent.

The Jewish-Ordinance of 1737, which was valid only for Berlin's Jews, did not bring even the slightest improvement to the ordinance of 1730. Provisions within it made it easier for authorities to confiscate the *Schutzbrief* for even the most trivial of offenses. This was intended to reduce the number of Jews in the city. The promulgation of the law was delayed by the king's death. This was, however, only a delay. Frederick the Great would prove hardly friendlier to the Jews than his father.

The Revised General Privilege

Friedrich Wilhelm I (the "Soldier-King") was succeeded by his son, Friedrich II ("the Great"). Friedrich's "Revised General Privilege and Regulation for the Jews in the Kingdom of Prussia" was published on April 17, 1750. Count Mirabeau called the law "worthy of a cannibal," since it contained so little of the spirit of Enlightenment. The law was based on suggestions made to the king in 1743 by his Financial Minister Uhden, who was alarmed when he found out that, instead of the 120 Jewish families allowed in Berlin there were, in fact, 333. Friedrich's aim was to abolish the *Judencommission*. Henceforth Jews would be subordinate either to his cabinet or to the Chamber of Military Affairs and Crown Lands. Though not intended, the effect was a major step toward integrating Prussian Jews into the political bureaucratic order of the state.

Drafting the law took much time. Minister Broich, who had served on the now-abolished *Judencommission*, was very ill and died before the law was completed. Friedrich himself took a lively personal interest in drafting parts of the law. It was at his initiative that each Jewish family was strictly limited to one child and *Schutzbriefe* were confiscated from any Jew who declared bankruptcy. Once a Jew was forced out of the Community, it would not be permitted to fill the vacancy with another. Friedrich decided that he himself would be the final arbiter of who was and who was not awarded the *Schutzbrief*. In 1757 he rescinded 17 such letters, which had already been signed and approved by his cabinet. Furthermore, Friedrich repeatedly rejected the idea of conscripting Jews into his ever-growing army.

The new regulation was to remain in force until 1812, for a total of 62 years. Set forth in its preamble was a summary of its reasons for the new policy: "After noticing certain deficiencies and foul methods among the *vergleitete* (protected) and *geduldete* (tolerated) Jews in our Kingdom – especially in their ceaseless multiplication – and [having seen that] they have caused great harm to the Christian merchants and residents, but also to the Jews themselves . . ." In short, Friedrich subscribed wholly to the opinions of Christian representative nobles and merchants who feared Jewish commerce and Jewish competition. His father, in contrast, had paid little

attention to these complaints and had not accepted such reproaches. His regulation was intended to reduce the number of Jews in Prussia, and with it their commercial activities, bringing them "into tune" with the common weal. The Berlin Jewish Community asked that the law not be published, with the reason that it was very humiliating and would damage both their creditworthiness and their reputation abroad. The request was temporarily heeded.

The regulation divided the *vergleitete* and tolerated Jews into six categories of different protection rules. The wealthiest Jews received what was called a "General Privilege." In terms of commerce and trade they were on an equal footing with Christian merchants. This privilege was, however, limited to a very small group – a few court Jews, in fact. The General Privilege was transferable to the children of the members of this group – certainly a special circumstance. The second group consisted of *ordentliche Schutzjuden* (regular protected Jews). These Jews had a limited right to reside in the region and to engage in commerce. They were prohibited from having more than one child, though that rule could be evaded by payment of a large sum of money. They were permitted to bequeath their status to two children, but only if the first had a fortune of at least 1,000 talers and the second a fortune of at least 10,000 talers. Group Three consisted of *ausserordentliche Schutzjuden* (extraordinary protected Jews). The protection status of such Jews was only personal and could not be bequeathed. It was obtainable only if the activity of the applicant was deemed useful for the general public.

A fourth group was composed of the Jewish Community's employees and administration – rabbis, cantors, and so forth. These were the *geduldete* (tolerated) Jews. The regulation fixed the maximum number of such Jews at 55, and only a small number of them

Friedrich II, "the Great,"
(1712–86)
shown in a copper engraving of 1797
by Bennet Salomon.
Two of his anti-Jewish edicts "against
peddling in general and in particular
against money changing by
Jews in the country-side"
(November 17, 1763) and against
the increasing numbers of foreign
Jewish beggars (December 12, 1780).
Both edicts were published several
times and carry remarks such as
"renewed," "more severe" and
"renewed and more severe edict."

Erneuertes und geschärftes

EDICT,

wegen

der überhand nehmenden fremden

Bettel-Juden.

De Dato Berlin, den 12ten December 1780.

Gedruckt bey George Jacob Decker, Königlichem Hofbuchdrucker.

were permitted to marry. The younger sons of the "regular" and all the children of the "extraordinary" *Schutzjuden* also belonged, with the Community's employees, to this category. The fifth and last group was composed of the domestic personnel of the tolerated families. They were prohibited from marrying or, if they married, were expected to leave. Foreign Jews were permitted to settle in Berlin if they paid the large sum of 10,000 talers.

The principle of *modus collectandi* (liability through solidarity) remained, despite all the petitions on the part of the Jewish Community, firmly fixed in the regulation. All Jews had to register. Anyone taking in *unvergleitete* Jews was subject to punishment. So-called *Betteljuden* (beggars) would be immediately deported after receiving alms. The gatekeeper was required to submit a daily report to the General Directorate on the movements of transient Jews. Nevertheless, it frequently occurred that *unvergleitete* Jews entered secretly or were taken in by Jewish families ostensibly as servants.

In 1750 Berlin's population had reached approximately 113,000, of whom 2,190 were Jews. Only 203 of these Jews were considered to be under "regular" protection, while 63 were considered as being under "extraordinary" protection. Because of the strict laws under which only wealthy Jews were permitted to settle in the city, Berlin became known as the seat of a wealthy Jewish Community. More than half of the Jews, however, belonged to the lower middle class and did not have the money to pay for *Schutzstatus* (protection status). Naturally, the number of indigent Jews in the city does not appear in the statistics. Many were either employees or "illegals" living in Jewish households. Those who had no steady employment appeared, if they appeared at all, on the Community's welfare rolls.

The Council of Elders feared that poorer Jews would try to settle in Berlin. Jews traveling through Berlin underwent embarrassing interrogations at the Rosenthaler Gate, one of the gates on the north side of the city. (It is said that the philosopher Moses Mendelssohn was one of those who first sought entry at the Rosenthaler Gate.) Thus can it be maintained that the policies of the absolutist state favored the establishment of a two-class Jewish society. The system of "protection" unintentionally helped create a Jewish proletariat made up of people who had no place to stay, no official protection and were constantly threatened with being thrown out of the city. The many edicts issued against *Betteljuden* (in 1719, 1737 and 1738) offer an example of this.

All of the Jewish Communities in Germany supervised a broad system of social institutions. This was anchored in the tradition of Jewish Law and ethics. At the beginning of the eighteenth century a Jewish hospital was founded in Berlin. For the most part, it treated those who were of lower social status. Unfortunately the hospital was frequently used to house poor people, a practice the authorities frowned upon. They demanded in 1743 that the hospital be separated from the poorhouse. In response, a poorhouse was built outside the city at the Rosenthaler Gate, a site that made it easier to control the *Unvergleitete*.

The Community provided a social net for those Berlin Jews who had fallen upon hard times. Since the regulations made it very difficult for Jews without financial means to remain in the city, the Community did all that was possible to prevent endangered Jews from slipping into permanent poverty. One of the best institutions for ensuring the Community's overall well being was an anonymous contribution box. There were two such boxes. One was passed from one member to the next. Those who could, gave. The other was filled with the contributions from the first box. No one ever knew who was giving the money and who was taking it. As far as wandering mendicants, or *Betteljuden,* were concerned, the Community shared the opinion of the authorities. The latter had intimated to Community leaders that taking in transient Jews would threaten the Jewish Community itself.

In 1755 a new Jewish hospital was opened on Oranienburger Strasse. In its day, it was one of the most modern of such institutions. There were, in addition, several associations that concerned themselves with welfare and other forms of social care. Among these were the Funeral Brotherhood – the Chewra Kaddisha – founded in 1676 and the Association of Visitors of the Sick – Chewra Bikkur Cholim – founded in 1703. Other associations existed to help support the poor, including one to assist in providing dowries. The cost for the "privilege" of having a second child remained inordinately high. In 1763, the fee was 70,000 talers.

The Beginning of a New Era

Important changes in the Berlin Jewish Community came about as a result of the Seven Years' War (1756–63). The war brought difficult times for all. All residents of the city had to contribute more than was normal, and the Jews of Berlin were hit even harder. In 1757 the Austrians besieged Berlin. Three years later, in 1760, when the Russians occupied the city they took the Jewish Council of Elders hostage.

The "voluntary contributions" to the state – which bordered on illegality – weighed heavily on the treasury of the Jewish Community. There were not only higher taxes. A steady stream of presents of goods and money was also deemed necessary to keep the officials happy. The royal treasury, too, had a hearty appetite. At one point the Jewish Community was obliged to buy furniture from the royal furniture storage for 16,000 talers. New laws of bankruptcy were especially damaging. The bankruptcy of any Jew was automatically considered intentional and criminal and penalized by confiscation of the ever-necessary *Schutzbrief.* If a bankrupt Jew died, his children or parents were expected to pay his debts immediately. Otherwise they would forfeit permission to bury him (particularly onerous, since Jews must bury their dead very quickly – rarely later than two days after death). If the heirs could not raise the money to settle the debts, the principle of 'liability through solidarity' took effect, obliging the Community Elders to assume them.

The principle of "liability through solidarity" also came into effect in cases in which Jews were guilty of theft. One such case occurred in 1769. A Jewish thief had fled. The Elders battled with the authorities for months to free the Community of liability. In response, Friedrich granted the Elders an extension of their rights to get rid of 'suspicious' members or foreigners. It was, in fact, a limitation on the rights of the Community as a whole. Many members of the congregation complained bitterly to the king or the General Directorate that the Elders were extremely strict and unjust in exercising their newly heightened authority. Royal intervention had, once again, created dissonance within the Jewish Community.

During this period a few Jewish merchants became extremely wealthy and began to occupy positions of influence and authority in the Jewish Community. Moreover, they attempted to trade off certain privileges for more sway at court. It was not long before these wealthy families were leading lives like the non-Jewish upper class. Three families became very prominent: those of Itzig, Isaac-Fleiss and Ephraim. All were *Muenzjuden* – coin or mint entrepreneurs. Among them, Veitel Heine Ephraim was the most famous, both for his richly appointed city palace and for the coins he issued, which quickly became known as "Ephraimites." In order to finance the war, the king had demanded that the silver coins be reduced in weight. It was said of the devalued coins that they had "Friedrich on the outside but Ephraim on the inside" (i.e., that they were hollow). The *Muenzjuden* were blamed for the these somewhat bogus coins, which nonetheless reduced the cost of the war by almost 25 percent – thereby helping to save the royal treasury from bankruptcy. Friedrich nevertheless was embarrassed by the *Muenzjuden* and did what he could to prevent the story from becoming public. After the war was over, in 1763, he 'released' all the *Muenzjuden* from his service without explanation.

Ephraim, however, became the most influential Jew of his time, and his influence extended beyond the Jewish Community itself. He had succeeded Magnus on the Council of Elders and had become, together with Gumpertz, one of the Elder Superiors in 1749. He was so powerful that he was able to ram through the appointment of his brother-in-law, David Fraenkel, as First Rabbi. No fewer than three pamphlets appeared about Ephraim, little tracts describing his dealings in Saxony in 1758. Ephraim had 50,000 talers confiscated from the merchant and speculator Gotzkowsky, director of the royal porcelain manufactory. It was also Ephraim who intervened so that the former mayor of Berlin, Albert Emil Nicolai, who had converted to Judaism in 1779, did not have to pay a fine for his conversion.

The houses built by the Jewish *Muenzjuden* were so noteworthy that Christoph Friedrich Nicolai included them in his 1769 guide to Berlin. The buildings had been constructed to the highest standards of the time – they included private synagogues, art collections and impressive libraries.

Friedrich II obliged the Jewish capitalists to invest in his new manufacturing establishments. Eager to bring more manufacturing to the area, Friedrich linked, in 1757, the issuance of new *Schutzbriefe* to the creation of new factories.

A number of Jewish merchants thus – not quite voluntarily – set about founding new factories, especially for the manufacture of silk. The names of Marcus, Hirsch, Riess, Bernhard and Friedlaender were all associated with this industry. David Hirsch had already founded in 1730 a silk factory in Potsdam, one of the first of its kind in Germany. Unfortunately the industry was hit by a major crisis around 1780, and only a few factories survived. One of those that did belonged to Isaac Benjamin Wulf, who had switched over to the manufacture of cotton products and in doing so laid the cornerstone for the most successful cotton manufacturing enterprises in Prussia. Wulf's factory created jobs, and the products themselves made Prussia less dependent upon imports. For these reasons the state paid little attention to the complaints of the Christian merchants. Indeed, it was quite the reverse. The king rewarded his Jewish investors with subsidies, monopolies and the highest protection offered to Jews by the state: the General Privilege. They were given, for instance, the coveted right to have more children without having to pay vast sums of money.

Another branch of commerce that underwent a radical change was associated with pawnbroking and money lending. As the years went by, such businesses started to look more and more like private banks. Pawn-shops lost their importance. Slowly but sure-ly Berlin developed into a financial center, and this proved to be likewise beneficial to some Jewish merchants. Jewish brokers and bankers attained importance. By the time the Berlin Stock Exchange was founded in 1803, about half the founding members were Jewish.

One can understand the abolition of re-strictions as a preliminary stage to emancipa-tion. Between 1761 and 1786 (the year of Friedrich II's death), 15 Jewish families ob-tained the coveted General Privilege from the state. The heads of these families seem to have been either bankers or manufacturers.

The 'owners' of General Privileges were, however, not freed from the obligation of buying porcelain. Friedrich had founded his Royal Porcelain Factory (KPM) in 1761, but it was very difficult to sell the products. Friedrich's idea was to couple the issuance to the Jews of certain privileges with the obli-gation to purchase certain amounts of porce-lain, which they were told to export – to make the porcelain more famous. Friedrich also suspected that the Jews were responsible for favoring foreign goods over those pro-duced in his territories. Those awarded a General Privilege were therefore obliged to buy porcelain amounting to 500 talers. Those who merely wanted a license to trade had to buy 300 talers worth of porcelain. It was furthermore obligatory to buy porcelain for marriages, births or when buying a house (though buying real estate was, for the most part, prohibited).

As usual, the Jewish Community protest-ed. The porcelain was not always of the best quality. Transporting the delicate ware was expensive, making it costly, often unprof-itable, to export. Jews were forced to buy only certain categories: one-third high quali-ty, one-third middle quality, and one-third

low quality. In general, however, most of the wares could not be sold. Porcelain from the royal factory quickly came to be known as *Judenporzellan*, outside Germany in particu-lar.

In order to maintain control over the Jews, Friedrich appointed Daniel Itzig and Jacob Moses to be the main superintendents of the Jewish Community. The fact that these appointees of the king were also the Elder Su-periors on the Council only served to annoy the other Community members further.

The Berlin Haskala (Jewish Enlightenment),

Even though Friedrich the Great never really exercised toward Jews his – otherwise re-nowned – tolerance, the spirit and ideas of the Enlightenment were present within his cabinet. The age of Reason furthered the political maturity of individuals within the state. It promoted tolerance toward those who thought or believed differently – though those "others" were, for the most part, other Christians. At Friedrich the Great's request, his financial councilor d'Asnières wrote an opinion in 1765 about raising the amount of the *Schutzgeld* paid by Jews. D'Asnières took the situation of the Jews in 1728 as his point of reference, but his remarks went consider-ably further back. He traced the beginnings and reasons for the *Schutzgeld* and made sev-eral suggestions. Though these were hardly made public, they did serve as a basis for a general debate about the question of Jewish emancipation. D'Asnières considered the his-torical and present situation of the Jews to be unjust and recommended that – instead of raising the *Schutzgeld* – most of the laws re-garding Jews be changed. His ideas were not accepted. In 1768 Friedrich raised the annual

Schutzgeld for Prussia's Jews to 25,000 talers, of which 8,982 had to be borne by the Berlin Jews. In addition, the Jews had to pay 2,033 talers for military recruits and 4,919 talers for the delivery of silver.

Despite the repressive measures, the Jews of Berlin were developing into a multifaceted Community and slowly making their way into modernity. Gradually and quietly a new Jewish lifestyle and way of thinking began to spread. With it came the Haskala (the Jewish Enlightenment), which found much favor among Berlin's Jewish upper classes. Not surprisingly, there was a great deal of self-interest involved. The *Maskilim*, or intellectual representatives of the Haskala, were however somewhat reserved when it came to dealing with the elite and its way of life. For this was often at variance with their intellectual ideals. Nevertheless the groups were inseparable from one another. Without the support of the rich Jews, the Jewish Enlightenment would have proceeded much more slowly. For their part, the leading figures of the Community used the *Maskilim* as interlocutors and pioneers for more reforms that they themselves were not able – or allowed – to promote.

Berlin had, with its recently founded Royal Academy, become a center of the German Enlightenment. The city's transformation by the Hohenzollerns from the center of a modest territory to the seat of a great European power contributed in turn to the rise of the Haskala. In many ways Berlin's Jewish Community mirrored the growth of the city. In the first half of the eighteenth century, Berlin had experienced a population explosion. The newcomers helped the city, which had only a small class of aristocrats, to become an intellectual center in Europe. In 1685 the population was 17,400. In 1750 it was over 113,000. The Jewish Community, too, was growing rapidly, but with 2,190 members, it was still small in comparison to the Jewish communities of Prague, Amsterdam and Istanbul. Even smaller settlements to the east, like the district of Posen, had larger populations of Jews than Berlin did. It is thus remarkable that such enormous intellectual changes issued from so small a Jewish Community.

Most of the *Maskilim* had been born not in Berlin but in eastern Europe. Many wrote in Hebrew. In most cases these thinkers began their careers as private teachers in Jewish households. One of the most important *Maskilim* was Naphtali Herz Wessely. Born in Hamburg in 1725, he was a pupil of the famous rabbi Jonathan Eibeschuetz. Arriving in Berlin, Wessely was accepted into the circle of the famed philosopher Moses Mendelssohn and worked on a translation of the Bible. Wessely became a pioneer of modern Hebrew literature.

Salomon Maimon (1754–1800) was the most eccentric of the *Maskilim*. He had been considered a Wunderkind in the Polish region of his birth, where during his studies he adopted the name of Maimon out of admiration for the ancient Jewish philosopher Maimonides. He soon began his life as a wanderer, and in 1779 he first knocked on Berlin's Rosenthaler Gate. He was turned away. Two years later he had more luck and was accepted into the circle around Mendelssohn. Maimon, somewhat notorious for his 'immoral' lifestyle, was shunned by many. He left Berlin but returned after Mendelssohn's death in 1786. He had long since become an atheist, and now he steeped himself in the philosophy of Immanuel Kant. Maimon's ideas were received with great respect, most notably by Kant himself. His autobiography, published in 1792, is an important source for Jewish history and life. But Maimon had long ago forfeited his membership within the Jewish Community.

When he died he was buried as a heretic outside the Jewish cemetery.

The most important period of the Berlin Haskala began in 1778, when the Juedische Freyschule (Jewish Free School) was founded. A year later the *Reader for Jewish Children* was published, and a Hebrew printing shop and bookshop were opened. Between 1780 and 1783 Moses Mendelssohn published his famous translation of the Bible. In 1781 Wessely wrote his *Words of Freedom and of Truth* – the manifesto of the early Haskala. In 1783 Mendelssohn published his work *Jerusalem, or On Religious Power and Judaism*. In Koenigsberg the periodical *Hameassef* began to appear.

Two wealthy Community Elders, Veitel Ephraim and Daniel Itzig, had already tried during the Seven Years' War to open a Jewish school in which non-religious subjects would be taught. It had proved impossible. The first modern Jewish school was founded 17 years later by Isaac Daniel Itzig and his brother-in-law David Friedlaender. There were both Jewish and non-Jewish teachers in the Juedische Freyschule. The subjects taught were German, French, Hebrew, religion and ethics, geography, mathematics, weights and measures, bookkeeping, drawing and calligraphy for Latin, Gothic and Hebrew characters. The school had an innovative character and admitted Christian children, in return for which Jewish children were admitted to Christian schools. In 1786 there were eighty pupils, most of whom were children of poorer families. Rich parents did not allow their children to attend the Freyschule and continued to engage private tutors for their children at home. Other schools were founded, but the Freyschule retained its reputation as a school for the poor.

Moses Mendelssohn

There are only a few Jewish Communities in Europe that have attracted as much attention as the Berlin Jewish Community, especially after 1770. This is due to the influence of Moses Mendelssohn. The effects of certain events that started with the Berlin Haskala – the reform movement, the "conversion epidemic," the salons – not only changed Jewish life in Berlin and Germany, but left their traces all over Europe and even in America.

Moses Mendelssohn is considered the "Father of the Haskala," the "universal joint" between the Jewish and the general Enlightenment. He was born in Dessau in 1729, the son of a Torah scribe, and received his first name from a sixteenth-century ancestor, Moses Isserles, who had written a compendium of religious traditions. Mendelssohn received a careful education at home in Dessau, attended the Cheder (primary school) and the Beth-ha-Midrasch (high school). In order to continue his studies he followed the former Dessau rabbi David Fraenkel to Berlin in 1743. 'Armed' with a letter from Fraenkel, he appeared at the city gates and obtained a temporary residence permit.

Berlin's First Rabbi became Mendelssohn's mentor and introduced him to different works on the philosophy of religion, especially to the works of Maimonides. Another important acquaintance was the scholar and universal man Aaron Salomon Gumpertz. Gumpertz was a physician and came from a family of well-known court Jews. As a young man he had served the Marquis d'Argens, a friend of Friedrich the Great. Gumpertz encouraged Mendelssohn to pursue wide-ranging studies and introduced him to the learned circles of Berlin. If the career and education of Gumpertz was extraordinary for a Jew in that era, this would become even more so with Moses Mendelssohn.

The family of Moses Mendelssohn.
Left: Fromet Mendelssohn
(1737–1812) née Guggenheim,
wife of Moses Mendelssohn in an
anonymous portrait of 1767.

Right page: Moses Mendelssohn
(1729–86) in a portrait by
Johann Christoph Frisch of 1786.
Staatsbibliothek zu Berlin.

The silhouettes of the Mendelssohn
children: Dorothea, Joseph and
Abraham, ca. 1790.

Excerpt from the
family register of the
Berlin Jewish Community, in
which the births of the
youngest children Susgen and
Nathan Mendelssohn
are registered.
Leo Baeck Institute, New York.

In addition to learning the Talmud, Mendelssohn taught himself all the major sciences and languages of his time. Without adapting himself to his Christian surroundings, he was open to impulses from all the people and events surrounding him, and he had contacts with all the major intellectuals of his time. Mendelssohn's material prosperity was entwined with that of a silk factory owned by Isaac Bernhard, who employed him as a tutor for his children. Mendelssohn later became bookkeeper in the factory, and was named a partner in 1758. After 1761 he was procurator.

Important for Mendelssohn's commitment to the Enlightenment was his friendship with Gotthold Ephraim Lessing, one of the leading intellectuals and writers of the era. Gumpertz, who introduced the two in 1753, had inspired the main figure in Lessing's 1749 comedy *The Jews*. Lessing printed the play in 1754 and was immediately criticized for it, for it posed the question of whether a "noble Jew" existed. One of the fruits of the friendship between Mendelssohn and Lessing was Lessing's famous drama *Nathan der Weise*, which appeared in 1779.

In 1763 Mendelssohn received the first prize in a competition published by the Prussian Academy of Sciences for his "Tract on Evidence in the Metaphysical Sciences." Immanuel Kant, hardly known at the time, received second prize. Several years later Mendelssohn was unanimously elected a member of the Academy, but Friedrich the Great refused several times to confirm the nomination.

Philosophically, Mendelssohn sought to preserve the existence and identity of the Jewish religion by placing it under the umbrella of enlightened philosophy, which he did not attack fundamentally. As a philosopher he became famous with his 1767 tract *Phaedo, or On the Immortality of the Soul*.

The realization that the "Republic of the Learned" was open only to Christians came to Mendelssohn at the time of the "Lavater Controversy," which began in 1769. Johann Caspar Lavater was a Zurich theologian who had met and come to respect Mendelssohn in 1763. After reading Mendelssohn's writings – and in the belief that he had taken them to their logical conclusion – he challenged Mendelssohn to either refute the "Truth about Christianity" or convert to Christianity. By doing this openly, he invoked a religious dispute that presaged other dangers that would beset the Jews in connection with the debate on the Enlightenment. Surprisingly, Mendelssohn agreed to a disputation, on the condition that it be conducted in the spirit of Enlightenment. Mendelssohn understood Judaism primarily as a religion of laws, as a religion of Reason from the perspective of the Enlightenment. In contrast he understood Christianity as a religion of revelation. (The latter was therefore more in compliance with the rising spirit of Romanticism.) Mendelssohn's friends stayed clear of the dispute.

Mendelssohn's correspondence gives an idea of how deeply he was moved by the subject of the distinction between Judaism and Christianity. It stayed with him until his death. He frequently expressed his regret that he had not become more strongly involved in debating Lavater. His book *Jerusalem, or On Religious Power and Judaism* of 1783 was his most ambitious answer to Lavater. The impetus for the debate had been the wish of educated Christians to convert a "noble" Jew, to make him one of their own. Their admiration for Mendelssohn was itself not enough. Only a few critical writers realized this. Georg Christoph Lichtenberg, famous for his aphorisms, demanded as early as 1773 an end to Christian "proselytizing."

One of Mendelssohn's greatest achievements was his translation of the Pentateuch (the Five Books of Moses) into High German (in Hebrew characters). Originally he did it only for his children. The initial reaction to his work was negative. Orthodox rabbis from Prague, Fuerth and Hamburg were indignant, and called for Mendelssohn's exclusion from the Jewish Community, a punishment that had no consequences for him. Mendelssohn was still able to take up the defense of Jews all over Europe on a variety of occasions. He was, through his active correspondence, the recipient of numerous suggestions for improving the lot of Jews. Even the coin maker Ephraim approached him with a tract about "Improving the Jews" – in this case through training them in the handicrafts.

Socially Mendelssohn attained a position never dreamt of by the other *Maskilim*. The Berlin Jewish Community heaped honorary offices upon him – despite the fact that only shortly before, the leaders of the Community had censored – and ultimately closed down – his Hebrew periodical *Kohelet Mussar*. In 1763 the Community liberated him from payment of taxes for the rest of his life. In the same year, at the urging of his friends, Mendelssohn sought to improve his legal status within the state and petitioned the king for a *Schutzbrief*. The petition remained unanswered. Only after a second attempt was he given the status of "extraordinary *Schutzjude*." Moses Mendelssohn died in 1786. He was already a legend.

Adaptation and Crisis

Mendelssohn's philosophy of Enlightenment offered a contemporary interpretation of Judaism. It could, however, be widely misunderstood by Christians and Jews alike if interpreted from the individual standpoint.

Christians could sympathize with Mendelssohn because they felt that he had *progressed* from Judaism. Jews could reject their Judaism, attain distinction and pursue happiness in a Christian environment. In fact, of Mendelssohn's six children, only two retained their father's Jewish faith; the other four converted to Christianity.

It was a period in which Jewish ritual laws were treated by many members of the Community with increasing laxity. Some individuals had already broken with many of the traditions. One man, Jeremias Cohen, appeared shaven and wearing a wig in the synagogue as early as 1737 – an act for which he had to forego his honorable rights. A similar thing happened in 1747 with Abraham Hirschel. In 1746 the great-grandfather of the nineteenth-century magnate Gerson von Bleichroeder was thrown out of Berlin by the Jewish Community for purportedly owning a German book.

Despite these punishments, the wealthier families increasingly styled their hair, clothing and manners to blend in with their Christian environment. They also attached importance to playing down the role of Yiddish – or "jargon" as it was pejoratively called. In the final analysis it was for this reason that Mendelssohn had translated the Bible into German. Berlin Jews increasingly rejected Yiddish in favor of the Berlin dialect. This was documented by Felix Eberty, a great-grandson of Veitel Ephraim, in the memoirs of his youth. From his travel diaries we learn that Berlin Jews were passionate about going to the theatre and that they, like all the other Berliners, went strolling on weekends in the Tiergarten.

In *Jerusalem* Mendelssohn addressed his fellow Jews: "Adopt the mores and the constitution of the land in which you have settled, but keep the faith of your fathers." He would hardly have reminded them of this had many

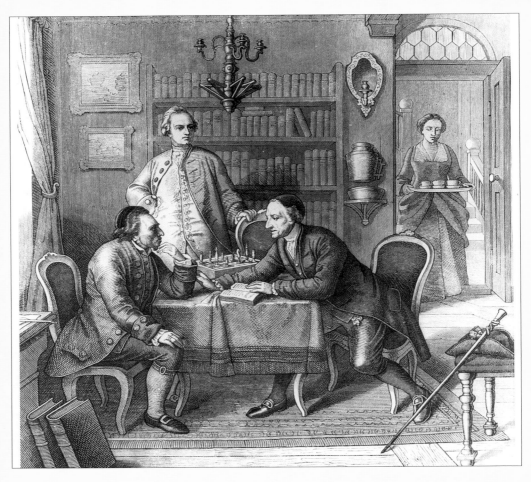

Above:
An idealized representation
of a meeting among Lessing,
Mendelssohn (left)
and Lavater (right)
in Lessing's house.
Woodcut after a painting by
Moritz Daniel Oppenheim,
1856.

Below:
Title page of the first
edition of Lessing's play
Nathan der Weise,
published by
Christian Friedrich Voss
in 1779.

Nathan der Weise.

Ein

Dramatisches Gedicht,

in fünf Aufzügen.

Introite, nam et heic Dii sunt!
APVD GELLIVM.

Von

Gotthold Ephraim Lessing.

1779.

Representation of Nathan.
Vignette from an engraving by Payne
after a drawing by Storck,
first half of the nineteenth century.

of them not already conducted themselves differently. But he also admonished the Christians: "And you, dear brethren and fellow men, those of you who follow the teachings of Jesus: Should you be angry with us when we do what the founder of your religion himself did? If civil unity can only be achieved by our disobeying the laws that bind us, it is with sorrowful hearts that we declare that we would prefer to do without civil unity."

For himself, Mendelssohn turned down membership in the exclusive "Monday Club" since its meetings were accompanied by non-kosher meals. No number of entreaties by his friends Lessing and Nicolai could persuade him to change his mind. In the "Wednesday Society," where Christian Wilhelm Dohm, Probst and others sought to silence "the hyenas of superstition and intolerance," Mendelssohn's poor health only permitted him the status of corresponding member. Mendelssohn lived a model life, but he obviously did not speak on behalf of all his fellow Jews. After he died a definitive break in the Community between "modern" Jews and traditionalists occurred.

A harbinger of this break was to be seen in the dispute over Wessely's book *Words of Peace and Truth*. When the "Patent of Tolerance" issued by Joseph II of Austria appeared in 1782, the Jewish Community of Triest asked Wesseley for his opinion on how the new reforms could be brought into agreement with Jewish law. Wessely's answer was a defiant challenge to rabbinism, for he came to the conclusion that those who studied only Torah and Talmud, without learning anything else, would become a burden on society. A lengthy controversy ensued, in which the great rabbinical authorities took positions. The Berlin Community tried to prevent the book from being published and drive Wessely from the city. But Berlin was not a center of Talmudic study. There was no Yeshiva (the highest school for study of the Talmud). Nor was Berlin home to a particularly important rabbi. It was only in 1743 that the Beth-ha-Midrasch (High School for Study of the Talmud) was opened. Only two significant pieces of rabbinical literature have survived: those by the rabbis Joschua Falk and David Fraenkel.

The increasing dissonance within the Community was not originally caused by the arrival of Mendelssohn and the other Jewish Enlighteners. It was rather the consequence of a process that had begun decades earlier. The pressure had come from the absolute state, which had gradually gained more and more influence over the affairs of the Jewish Community. Tension within the Community itself was caused by nepotism and the misuse of authority and the Community Elders, many of whom stemmed from the families of court Jews. Last but not least, a spiritual vacuum had become visible as early as the end of the seventeenth century. Rabbinical authority had been eroding for generations.

The Haskala revolutionized the old Jewish world of scholarship, introducing a new social and educational ideal. This took time to become established. The split in the Community was especially clear in terms of the Jews who converted to Christianity and thereby left the Community altogether. One could not yet speak of a "conversion epidemic" – this did not take place until the nineteenth century – but 146 Jews converted to Christianity between 1770 and 1789. With a Jewish population of about 3,400, this amounted to some 4.3 percent of the whole. Moreover, the percentage of converts was actually a higher number than that of the Jews in the city's entire population. These figures do not include the members of the Jewish Community whose conversion took place outside the city. Interestingly, the great number of cases involved either single mothers whose children had been born out of wedlock or wealthy people from the Jewish upper classes.

From the point of view of the Orthodox Jews the conversions were the logical result of the reforms, which in their opinion had gone too far. On the other hand, even Orthodox families had their share of members who converted. According to the historian Abraham Geiger, Mendelssohn's death was followed by a time of "licentiousness." An atmosphere of freedom and permissiveness prevailed in the Court of Friedrich Wilhelm II (reigned 1786–97), and its effects were felt among the Jews of Berlin as well. The result for the Community was a higher divorce rate, as well as many illegitimate children and a significant increase in conversions. Family heads started to stipulate in their wills that their children could inherit only if they remained true to the Jewish faith. But such restrictions had little effect. It was quite different in the case of *unvergleitete* Jews, who thought that conversion would help them obtain a residence permit. The authorities simply turned them away.

Mendelssohn and his followers would hardly have known that the ideas and theories of the Haskala would have such 'revolutionary' implications in terms of cultural adaptation. On closer inspection, the sudden attractiveness of Christian baptism suggests that the Jewish Community was experiencing a generation/identity crisis, and that it was unable to withstand the pressure from outside. In the absence of a range of alternatives, many saw baptism as the only possible way to change their lives. Only later would the emergence of Neo-Orthodoxy and Reform Judaism offer new alternatives.

The Debate on Emancipation Begins

The discussion about emancipating the Jews in Prussia officially began in 1781 with the publication of a 154-page tract entitled "On the Civic Improvement of the Jews" by Christian Wilhelm Dohm, the privy war counselor. The tract was prepared in response to a petition to Mendelssohn by the Jews of Alsace. They had written to ask his opinion on how their situation could be improved. Mendelssohn passed this request to his friend Dohm, who appended the text to his longer memorandum on the subject.

A caricature of Moses Mendelssohn at the Berliner Gate in Potsdam in a copper engraving by Lowe (after a drawing by Daniel Chodowiecki), 1792.

Title pages of three important works by Moses Mendelssohn: Phaedon or On the Immortality of the Soul in Three Discussions *(1767),* The Psalms *(a translation "with all-merciful liberties," 1783), and* Jerusalem, On the Power of Religion and Jewry *(1787).*

Some of Moses Mendelssohn's
non-Jewish discussion partners.

Left:
Gotthold Ephraim Lessing
(1729–81).

Right:
Publisher and writer
Christoph Friedrich Nicolai
(1733–1811).

Below:
The theologian Johann Kaspar Lavater
(1741–1801).

Essential representatives of the Haskala (the Jewish Enlightenment):
Left: Hartwig Wessely (1725–1805), Hebrew poet, friend of Mendelssohn and collaborator on his translation of the
Pentateuch (Five Books of Moses).
Middle: the philosopher Salomon ben Josua (1753–1800), who out of veneration for Maimonides renamed himself Salomon Maimon.
Right: David Friedlaender (1750–1834), merchant, educator, and writer.

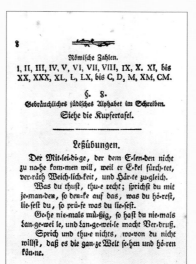
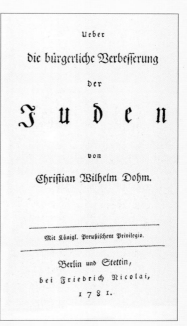

Left: Title page of the Reader for Jewish Children *(1779) for David Friedlaender's Jewish Free School.*
A page from the Reader *with reading exercises and Roman numbers.*
Right: Title page of the book by Christian Wilhelm Dohm, On the Civic Improvement of the Jews, *published in 1781.*

Dohm proved – somewhat circuitously – that the Jews had, in a certain respect, become tainted, albeit by no fault of their own, and that they would be useful and worthy subjects only if the state created favorable circumstances and institutions for them. Dohm presented nine practical "ideas on how the Jews could become happier and better members of society." His first and principle point was that Jews should have the same rights as all others. Secondly, they should be able to choose their professions. Thirdly, they should be trained in agriculture in particular, with restrictions being placed on their general trading activities. Fourthly, they should keep their account books in German. Fifthly, he proposed that Jews showing exceptional talent in the arts and sciences should be helped and furthered in those areas. His sixth suggestion was that special attention be paid to education and upbringing of the young, and his seventh point was to address Christian prejudices about Jews. The eighth point was that Jews should be free to exercise their religion. Lastly, Dohm proposed that the Jewish Communities be given complete autonomy.

This work was epochal in many ways, and its impact was enhanced by two related events on the European stage. For one thing, the Austrian Emperor Joseph II proclaimed his "Patents of Toleration" the next year, in 1782. Furthermore, the cause of Jewish Emancipation won two important champions in France: Abbé Gregoire and Count Mirabeau. Each made reference to Dohm's thought and recommendations. Of course, Dohm's recommendations were received with as much vehement rejection as applause. The perhaps most vocal critic was the Goettingen-based orientalist and theologian Johann David Michaelis. In response to criticism from Michaelis and other opponents, Dohm published a second and more detailed tract in 1783. The discussion about Dohm's papers lasted until almost 1800. For the most part, however, it took place within a rarefied stratum of educated citizens. Even in Jewish circles, the emancipation debate reached only the upper classes.

The first campaign for the emancipation of the Jews of Berlin took place in 1786, the same year that Friedrich the Great and Moses Mendelssohn died. The Jews of Prussia elected three representatives to take their part in the ensuing negotiations – Daniel Isaac Itzig, David Friedlaender and Liepmann Meyer Wulff (the grandfather of the composer Giacomo Meyerbeer). The first step was to submit a petition to Friedrich Wilhelm II recommending certain improvements. The initiative was greeted, and a commission of inquiry was set up, though its work to make new laws became long and drawn out. Nevertheless, certain successes were visible. In 1787 the law compelling Jews to buy porcelain was rescinded (against payment of 40,000 talers). Moreover, the *Leibzoll* (a poll tax) was abolished for all the Jews of Prussia, and one year later for foreign Jews as well.

It seemed that the period for reform was finally at hand. The maxim of the Jewish Enlightenment had been "assimilation," and it meant that the Jews should adjust to the Christian lifestyle and give up many of their own traditions. Even in Mendelssohn's time, it was apparent that progressive and enlightened royal officials would ultimately *grant* the advantages of emancipation and that progressive Jews would not be able to wrest them from the state by *fighting*. The majority of the Jews and Christians were left untouched by the emancipation discussion. Emancipation remained a privilege – one that could be granted and revoked at the discretion of the authorities.

Claudia-Ann Flumenbaum

The Process of Adaptation (1790–1870)

The Elders of the Jewish Community of Berlin made many attempts to shake off the regulations imposed by the state in 1750, especially the onerous rule of *modus collectandi*, "liability through solidarity," which was made even tighter in the 1790s. This forced collective liability, discussed in the previous chapter, made the entire Jewish Community responsible for any debts incurred by any of its members. Their efforts were frustrated by the officials of the Berlin central bureaucracy, who seemed intent on stifling every attempt at reforming the laws about Jews.

The bureaucrats repeatedly fell back on the same arguments: the time was not ripe; Christian subjects needed protection from the Jews; the prevailing laws provided the best possible protection against the "immorality of the Jews." These laws could only be repealed when the Jews had adopted the mores of Christian citizens. Objections of this sort indicate the degree to which non-Jews were antagonistic toward the idea of granting Jews legal equality. Those Jews who participated in the Enlightenment – the bookseller and writer Saul Ascher, for example – understood that the problem was actually on both sides of the religious divide. Jewish-Emancipation would only be attained if both Jews and non-Jews tried to reduce their mutual distrust and reach out to each other. It would be a long and arduous process.

The Gesellschaft der Freunde (Society of Friends)

Toward the end of the eighteenth century, the participants in the Jewish Enlightenment (Haskala) had radically placed in doubt the traditional faith of their fathers and advocated that the religious laws had to be reformed for rational reasons. The naturalist Mordechai Schnauber (Georg Levison), for example, wrote in his book *Ma'amar Hatorah Vehachochmah* (On the Connection between the Torah and Reason) that many laws of Judaism were incomprehensible without knowledge of the sciences. There should be no dispute, he claimed, between the proponents of Reason and religion. Religious laws according to Schnauber could be explained by Reason.

Saul Berlin, the rabbi in Frankfurt/Oder and son of the Berlin's First Rabbi Hirschel Lewin, went even further in his 1794 book *Ketav Josher* (The Writing of Sincerity). He attacked in satirical form the traditional Jewish systems of education and upbringing, calling them outdated. Moreover, he suggested that his contemporaries conducted themselves "like donkeys" by voluntarily subjecting themselves to the laws of Jewish ritual. This criticism went much further than that of Moses Mendelssohn, whose modernization program had criticized the "unreason-

Above:
A view of the
Mauerstrasse, where the
Varnhagen von Ense's
home was situated.
Copper engraving by
T. Riedel, after a drawing
by J. Rosenberg,
ca. 1780.

Below:
Rahel Varnhagen von Ense,
(1771–1833),
wife of Karl August
Varnhagen von Ense
and head of one of Berlin's
most celebrated salons.
Engraving by C. E. Weber,
1817.

*A contemporary wood engraving shows
Karl August Varnhagen von Ense (1785–1858) conversing
with Alexander von Humboldt (1769–1859).*

able" laws very gingerly without calling for their elimination.

Resistance to the traditional structures could be seen in such newly formed clubs as the *Gesellschaft der Freunde* (Society of Friends), founded in 1792. The first members – Isaac Euchel, Aaron Wolffsohn and Joseph Mendelssohn, among others – wanted to provide younger, unmarried Jews (for whom entrance to public places of amusement was taboo) with opportunities to meet like-minded people. The goal was to provide a place "where they could forget their daily cares and where an atmosphere of friendliness and favor prevailed" regardless of the members' religious background.

The Society of Friends had their first official meeting on January 29, 1792. About a hundred persons attended. Joseph Mendelssohn, son of the famous philosopher, gave the opening address, "The Light of the Enlightenment", he claimed, had "had a beneficial effect on our nation for more than thirty years. Even among us today there are many who are interested in seeing in the religion of their fathers a difference between the wheat and the chaff . . . especially in the state in which we live." For their motto, the Friends selected an entry from Moses Mendelssohn's family book: "Realize the truth. Love beauty. Wish for the good. Do the best."

At the beginning, the Society of Friends could count on an accommodating attitude from the official representatives of the Jewish Community. This changed, however, when a long-simmering scuffle over burial rituals broke out into a genuine battle. The Enlighteners gathered around Isaac Euchel, Joseph Mendelssohn and other Friends wanted to end the tradition of immediate burial. They argued in much the way Moses Mendelssohn had done in 1772 when he called for a change in the rules of burial. At that time,

the Duke of Mecklenburg-Schwerin had decreed that Jews must wait three days before burying their dead, until their death had been ascertained.

This dispute only partially concerned burial – specifically the concern that somebody who only appeared dead might be accidentally buried alive. In reality, it was a spiritual conflict between traditionalists and Enlighteners. The former stubbornly stood fast to the rule calling for early burial, for reasons not entirely understandable. The rabbi in Breslau, Salomon Seligman Pappenheimer, drew particular scorn from enlightened circles for his series of writings in which he vehemently pleaded that the tradition of early burials be preserved.

As the years went by, the Society became more and more involved in charitable work. In the opinion of the mistrustful traditionalists it remained, however, a club of "renewers." In many ways they were right. The Society had first formed as a group of young Jewish men from traditional families who wanted to shake off the "shackles of national separation in their thoughts and in their deeds."

David Friedlaender

David Friedlaender (1750–1834) stood at the head of those German Jews who sought to enter modern civil society. Like his great friend and mentor Moses Mendelssohn, he firmly believed that the only way to be accepted by the great Christian majority was to accept their methods of learning and to "further the Enlightenment among the Jews themselves." One of the initiatives that Friedlaender worked on with great energy was the founding of the Juedische Freyschule, mentioned in the previous chapter. It was called the "free school" because the parents of the children did not have to pay for tuition. Its pedagogical principles were firmly rooted in the new thinking. The Jewish Enlightenment figure Lazarus Bendavid went as far as to urge that all education reject a Jewish-religious character, and that this would make the integration of the Jews into Christian society much easier. Bendavid wanted to structure teaching in a way that would underscore Judaism's universality and the fact that it had much in common with other religions.

Friedlaender was conscious of the fact that this would demand much of the Jews – to be more precise, that they would have to break with tradition and adapt themselves to their Christian surroundings. His famous *Sendschreiben* (Message) of 1799 was in all probability conceived to make the public aware of the Jews' difficult situation. In it, he proposed to the Pastor Wilhelm Abraham Teller (a friend of the Enlightenment) that Jews would swear a modified oath to Christian society and church, in the expectation that this would further or even realize the equalization of the Jews with other members of society.

In his *Sendschreiben* Friedlaender admitted (in his name and in the name of several "house fathers") that the Jews – especially the enlightened Jews of Berlin – had long since adopted a position between Jewish tradition and belief in Reason. Jews, he wrote, recognized the basic truths of every religion: the existence of God; the immortality of the soul; and the belief that mankind is designated for happiness. Moses and Christ, he wrote, had both placed these principles at the basis of their faith. But now both religions had drifted from their original foundations. Judaism had become ensnared in ritualism, Christianity in mystical dogmatism. Friedlaender and his "house fathers" dreamed of uniting both religions on the basis of faith in

Reason. If the Christians would desist from their "Christological" dogma, and if the Jews would let go or reduce their faith in ritual laws, they could unite – thereby removing the barrier to the assimilation of the Jews in Prussia.

Pastor Teller refused to entertain such concepts. He feared unforeseen consequences. The answer he sent to Friedlaender was therefore somewhat dilatory and probably written with the goal of propagating the notion that Christianity was the only True Faith. According to Teller, the Enlightenment had its limits; the content of the Christian faith should not be reduced.

Despite the opposition Friedlaender perceived within Christian-German society, he continued to press his ideas beyond the Jewish Community. By 1809 he had become a Stadtrat (commissioner) in the Berlin municipal government. After the Emancipation Edict was published on March 11, 1812, he furthered his goals within the Jewish Community. Without reforms of the synagogue and schools, the coming generation would not be able to fully taste the fruits of the newly granted civil rights. It was, he claimed, necessary to stop praying in Hebrew. Moreover, German Jews needed to liberate themselves from those passages of the Bible that adjured them to return to Jerusalem.

The Emancipation Edict of 1812

The Edict of 1812 abolished the system of *Schutzjudenschaft* (the requirement that all Jews apply formally for "protection" from the state). It put an end to special taxes, duties and fees that had burdened Jews for centuries and eliminated the distinction between Jewish residents and those who were foreign. It

Leopold Mueller's 1804 view of the Muehlendamm from the Kurfuersten Bridge (Elector's Bridge).
The background shows an area inhabited by Jews.

was greeted enthusiastically by the Jews of Berlin, who believed it would end all social and national discrimination as well. They wrote and sent countless messages of thanks to the King, rejoiced in their new position as 'citizens,' rejoiced in their citizens' 'dignity' and became proud of their 'fatherland.' Their new oath began: "I am citizen and subject of Prussia, born and raised in Germany . . ."

For decades the Edict was considered a sign that a change of thought had taken place. Of course several aspects were criticized, among them the fact the Edict was restricted to the territory of Prussia as it was in 1812. This meant that Jews in the newly conquered territories that resulted from the Wars of Liberation (1813–15) could only move to Berlin with great difficulty. Still, in general the Jews were satisfied with what had been attained. And they were satisfied that

their status as citizens was safe. This could later be used as a model to obtain the same rights in other parts of Germany.

An important success was the fact that Jews were finally allowed to do military service. This was considered proof that citizenship was no longer fiction but fact. Throughout the Prussian provinces Jews heard the call to arms during the Wars of Liberation. "Which of you noble, great-hearted youths does not think and feel today the way David felt? Which of you does not hear with joy this noble summons to fight and win for your fatherland? Whose heart does not beat faster at the thought of stepping onto the field of honor?" The young Jews of Berlin heeded the call.

Jews were greatly honored and received many awards and promotions within the military at this time, relative to their proportionally small numbers within the entire population. Twenty-one became warrant officers, hunters and drum majors. One became an ensign. Nineteen became Second Lieutenants and three became First Lieutenants. It is known that four members of the Society of Friends took part in the war, three of whom returned as lieutenants.

One of the participants was Meno Burg, known in his own lifetime as the *Judenmajor*. Born into modest circumstances, Burg volunteered to serve in 1813. In 1815 he was promoted to the rank of Second Lieutenant – a promotion due exclusively to his military capabilities. He was highly respected, not least for having resisted the temptation to convert to Christianity in order to advance his career. His memoirs were widely read, and his courage was considered a model for other youths. Even though he knew that his promotion to artillery captain was thwarted, even prevented, by the fact that he was a Jew, he never converted. He wrote to his protector, Prince August, on March 30, 1830: "No hindrance to my career was so great as to make me renounce my faith."

Attempts to Reform Jewish Religious Services

Emancipation changed how the Jews thought about their traditions and way of life. A double-sided process of adaptation began. On the one hand, many Jews tried to come to terms with German culture and the norms of their surroundings. Others realized that this would only be possible if they changed their own ways of doing things – that is, if they were ready to accept reform.

David Friedlaender and his friends were of the opinion that the best way to achieve total acceptance and integration was to re-

form the Jewish liturgy. One of his allies in the reform movement was Israel Jacobson. After the dissolution of the Kingdom of Westphalia (a short-lived creation of Napoleon) and, with it, his own Jewish congregation, Jacobson had settled in Berlin. His Berlin home became a place for regular but modernized services. Later they were continued in the palace of the banker and sugar manufacturer Jacob Herz Beer (father of Giacomo Meyerbeer) on Pariser Platz, near the newly built Brandenburg Gate. Sometimes as many as four hundred Berlin Jews took part in these services.

There were a number of young preachers, such as Eduard Kley – a student of the philosopher Fichte and the Protestant pastor Schleiermacher – Isaak Lewin Auerbach and especially Leopold Zunz. Zunz preached in a private synagogue that was raised to the status of a Community synagogue in 1817. The synagogue was soon closed, after strict believers denounced its services as "deist" to the authorities. A cabinet order dated December 9, 1823, declared: "The liturgy of the Jews is henceforward to be held in the traditional mode and language, with the traditional songs. In Prussia no sects will be tolerated."

The dispute within the official Jewish Community turned on relatively minor issues. For instance, was it appropriate to have services on Sunday instead of on Saturday? Regarding seating: could men and women sit together or did they have to sit separately, as they had always done? Was it permissible for men to uncover their heads? Circumcision and many other ritual rules thought by some to be archaic were also in dispute.

Within the Berlin Jewish Community, many members felt uncomfortable with these attempts to reform and modernize the liturgy and other customs. The reformers were not content to reform the liturgy alone but strove to rid the religion of "irrational"

Left:
The Philosopher and "patriotic warner"
Johann Gottlieb Fichte (1762–1814).
Lithograph by Friedrich Bury,
ca. 1800.

Right:
A caricature by
Johann Gottfried Schadow,
1814.

elements and dogmas. One of the typical subjects of dispute was the matter of prayer books. Some reformers wanted to strike out all references to Zion as a geographic goal for the coming of the Messiah. According to the reformers, this goal of returning to Palestine was not only anachronistic but also irreconcilable with their new commitment to Germany and to German culture.

The journalist and writer Aron Bernstein (uncle of the Social Democrat Eduard Bernstein) was one of the founders of the Berlin Reformgemeinde (the reform congregation). In a tract from 1865 he defended the reform movement against the reproach that it had given up the Messianic dream (i.e., the return to Zion) and therefore Jewish unity: "We did not destroy those parts of Judaism – the national, political ideas and institutions – that were bequeathed to us when we inherited Judaism. Time had destroyed these ideas long before we rejected them." Bernstein at-

Left:
A mid-nineteenth century
woodcut depicting of a lecture.

tacked his critics for stubbornly maintaining a positive-historic viewpoint. Before the reforms were proposed, what Bernstein called "slavish degeneration of Judaism" prevailed in Germany:

> The service [in the synagogue] had become a half-wild and confused ritual, disfigured by mannerisms that were taken to be Jewish but were in fact Polish. The studies in the schools and rabbinical seminaries were not really based on knowledge but on dialectical disputation. Profound superstition reigned instead of knowledge. Wild, measureless and aimless sophistry prevailed instead of research.

The radical reform movement in Germany was restricted in large part to a few large cities, of which Berlin's was the best known. Decisive reformers such as Samuel Holdheim and Joseph Lehmann preached to growing congregations in the city. What had initially appeared as a demand for a "Jewish Church" (Sigismund Stern) would go on to become by the 1920s a demand for a "German synagogue" (Joseph Wachsner). What remained essential over the years was that the reform congregation's spiritual and lay leaders as well as its members considered themselves to be "practicing" Germans. The only thing that they felt distinguished them from their fellow German citizens was their adherence to a different faith. They protested vigorously when others criticized or doubted their attachment to German culture.

The Salons of Berlin

The short-lived Association for Culture and Science of Judaism, founded by Leopold Zunz, Eduard Gans and Moses Moser (a friend of the poet Heinrich Heine), was formed in response to the anti-Semitic "Hep-Hep Movement" growing outside Prussia in 1819. The teaching program that was planned could be only partially realized. Nevertheless, important impulses proceeded from it. For example, a boys' school for the Community was founded in 1826. Until 1829 the school was led by Zunz. After him, Baruch Auerbach led it until 1851. As a movement, Zunz's Science of Judaism would have lasting success.

The process of adaptation led to Jews seeking more and more acceptance in Christian-German cultural and social circles. Many Jews were convinced that the more they adopted the norms and values of their surroundings, the more they took on a certain degree of secular knowledge and culture, the more they would find acceptance. This was especially true in Berlin, where, toward the end of the eighteenth and beginning of the nineteenth centuries, a lively social intercourse developed between the cultivated Christian upper classes (of both bourgeois citizens and aristocrats) and certain members of the Jewish Community who had property and education.

The period was famous for its salons, places for meeting and exchanging thoughts and views. Several of Berlin's most prominent salons were hosted by Jewish women: Dorothea Veit-Mendelssohn, who later became the wife of Friedrich Schlegel (one of Shakespeare's first German translators); Henriette Herz, the wife of the physician and philosopher Marcus Herz; and Rahel Varnhagen, wife of the diplomat August Varnhagen von Ense – and reputed to be one of the most intellectual women of her time. In the Varnhagen salon not only could one meet Schlegel and Schleiermacher, but Eduard Gans, Ludwig Boerne and Heinrich Heine were to be found there as well. Heine

Henriette Herz (1764–1847), who hosted a celebrated literary salon, in a portrait by Anton Graff, 1792. Alte Nationalgalerie Berlin.

Right: Various guests of the Berlin salons.
Clockwise: the author Jean Paul (1764–1825), the scholar Wilhelm von Humboldt (1767–1835), the philosopher of religion Daniel Friedrich Schleiermacher (1768–1834), the philosopher Friedrich Schlegel (1772–1829), the architect Heinrich Gentz (1766–1811), the poet Ludwig Boerne (1786–1837) and the artist Johann Gottfried Schadow (1764–1850).
Center left: A musical soirée with Henriette Herz at left and Abraham Mendelssohn at the piano in an undated drawing by Johann Gottfried Schadow.

himself called Rahel Varnhagen one of the "pioneers of the young Germany."

Rahel Levin, the daughter of the Jewish merchant Marcus Levin, apparently possessed great sensitivity and perspicacity. Her many letters show her to have been a woman of great heart, though she suffered much under her modest financial resources. She apparently felt that her Jewish heritage was a black mark against her and hoped through marriage to a Prussian aristocrat to compensate for her Jewish background. Her marriage to Varnhagen brought her the social acceptance she had long wished for, but it was probably not the happiest of alliances in other respects.

The informal institution of the Berlin salon had at that time a magic attraction for intellectuals and young Prussian aristocrats. One "visited" a "Jewish" salon for various reasons. It was a politically and religiously neutral place, for one thing, and enabled Jews and Christians to meet in a relaxed social atmosphere. One was sure to encounter 'like-minded' people there, and the discussion was generally as lively as the opinions were vigorous. To certain visitors, the salon also furnished a quiet route to better social status and financial advantages.

Historians still debate whether or not Jewish salonières like Rahel Varnhagen were more educated and cultivated than their Christian counterparts. What is agreed, however, is that the Jewish salonières were women who first understood the meaning of emancipation, and it enabled them to easily assume the role of successful hostesses. Indeed, women like Rahel Varnhagen were able to bring together people of the most varied backgrounds and professions, to initiate contacts and discussions that led not only to new impulses in society but also opened new intellectual horizons.

Jews Climb
the Economic Ladder

The years between 1815 and 1850 saw the transformation of Berlin Jewry from a traditional to a modern social group. This process of modernization led not only to a loosening of traditional structures within the Jewish Community but also had profound effects on the social and professional worlds the Jews lived in. For one thing, Jews were able to become self-employed entrepreneurs. No longer were they obliged to deal in secondhand goods. They became bourgeois entrepreneurs and the owners of companies. They were no longer door-to-door salesmen and rag-peddlers but had become wholesalers and retailers, bankers and factory owners.

Statistics for 1849 show how Prussian Jews successfully understood how to use their chances in the process of modernization. Some 218,998 Jews lived in Prussia (of which Berlin's share was 9, 595). Some 53.9 percent of them were active in finance, commerce, transportation, industry and trades. Businessmen made up 20.8 percent, and 1.2 percent of Prussian Jews were in agriculture. Wage earners and household help made up 6.4 percent of the Jewish population. An additional 13.1 percent consisted of lower paid employees of the Jewish Community, members of the "free professions" (physicians, lawyers, architects) as well as unemployed people and paupers. These figures become meaningful when one sees them against the figures for the non-Jewish population. Jews were proportionally over represented within finance, commerce, transportation, industry and trade.

In Berlin the Jews were successfully occupied in the consumer-oriented branches, especially in textiles and clothing. Half of those working in these fields between 1835

Left:
Prince Karl August von Hardenberg (1750–1822),
the initiator of the legal equality of Jews in Prussia,
in an engraving by Johann Friedrich Bolt, 1815.

Above:
Certificate of citizenship for
Martin Valentin and his offspring,
issued August 30, 1813, by the Royal Government
of the Kurmark in Potsdam.

Left:
Title page of the Edict of Emancipation,
March 11, 1812.

The family of Moritz and Therese Manheimer in 1850. In 1825 the merchant Manheimer purchased a patent of Berlin citizenship and married Therese Klemann in 1830. Their eldest daughter, Babette, shown here at the piano, was the mother of the dermatologist Alfred Blaschko (1858–1922).

*The painter and family drawing master, Julius Moser, included himself in
this family portrait. His likeness hangs on the wall next to the man of the house.
Juedisches Museum Berlin.*

and 1870 were Jews. If one considers that the percentage of Jews in the entire population was somewhere between 2 and 3 percent, one immediately sees the significant role played by such entrepreneurs as Hermann Gerson, the brothers Manheimer and Nathan Israel. Such men transformed the Berlin clothing industry into a mass business. Hermann Gerson's company, for instance, expanded quickly around 1850–60 and employed as many as 5 foremen, 3 directors and 150 seamstresses.

One of the most spectacular careers was that of Joseph Liebermann, who came from a merchant family in Maerkisch-Friedland and Sprottau and who became one of the most successful textile merchants in Berlin in the 1830s and 1840s. With his new methods of production and his talent for identifying saleable products he was so successful that, in 1843, he was given the title of *Kommerzienrat* (Counselor of Commerce) and could present himself to the King simply as "Der Liebermann."

The heirs of the philosopher Moses Mendelssohn were not only culturally successful but also did extremely well in business and commerce. The Mendelssohns climbed the ladder to social and economic prosperity. The founding of the Mendelssohn Bank in 1795 was the work of Joseph Mendelssohn, who, with the acceptance of the promissory-note business, laid the bank's foundation with Moses Friedlaender, the son of David Friedlaender. The bank successfully handled the French indemnity to Prussia after the Wars of Liberation and developed into one of the leading Berlin banking houses.

Joseph Mendelssohn, greatly respected for his honesty and sense of fair play, was also known for the care he devoted to his affairs. He did not conduct business in a way that ran contrary to his convictions. In a letter of 1830 about a possible Swedish bond issue to Salomon Heine (uncle of the poet), he described his perverse investment instincts: "If the entire world is hot for a certain deal, I feel within me a certain resistance. When everybody is against it, then I get a craving."

The banking house of Mendelssohn and Co., under the direction toward the middle of the nineteenth century of Alexander Mendelssohn and Paul Mendelssohn-Bartholdy would become one of the most important private banks in Germany. It held fast to the goal of keeping business separate from politics and resisted becoming a slave to state or political interests. The Mendelssohns relied on the same principle to which earlier generations had committed themselves: never to commit funds to a deal outside the normal business of money and credit. Generally they were able to maintain this principle.

Conversions

The process of adapting more fully to non-Jewish society involved many instances of conversion to Christianity. The reasons for this step were varied, as can been seen in the baptismal books, and they were often material rather than spiritual. They included the wish to marry a Christian, to open a business or to study at the university. Although the number of those converting was quite small, the phenomenon was a source of unrest in the Jewish Community (as well as loss of membership). In a petition to Staatskanzler (State Chancellor) Hardenberg from 1811, David Friedlaender described the conversion statistic of 10 percent as catastrophically high for Berlin's Jewish Community.

Historians cannot agree whether the number of conversions increased or decreased after the Edict of Emancipation of 1812. The case for increased conversions is made by the fact that after the Napoleonic wars, emancipation was restricted in many ways and that Jews still found themselves locked out of positions in the bureaucracy, teaching and in the military. It has been established, moreover, that 38 percent of all of Prussia's conversions were registered in Berlin-Brandenburg – home to merely 8 percent of Prussia's Jews. Two-thirds of the Prussian conversions therefore occurred in the capital. It can be assumed that between 1812 and 1848, more than one thousand persons converted. This number, however, cannot be considered a mass exodus from the Jewish Community, as some historians have maintained. It was, rather, a phenomenon that touched mostly the better-educated Jews who were interested in climbing the social ladder.

This was true, for instance, of the Mendelssohn family. Its members saw greater possibilities after becoming Christians. In all probability, a Jewish background was perceived as a "deficiency," and it was felt necessary either to eliminate or at least to disguise it. There are numerous speculations about the younger son of Moses Mendelssohn, Abraham, who had his own children baptized (among them Felix and Fanny Mendelssohn Bartholdy) a whole year before he and his wife Lea converted. As a symbol of his conversion to Christianity he assumed the second name of Bartholdy, a step recommended by his brother-in-law Jakob Bartholdy. Jakob, who had converted in 1805, had not only led the way to the baptismal font, but he also suggested the name change as a way of distinguishing between the converted and the non-converted branches of the Mendelssohn family.

Abraham Mendelssohn was deeply occupied with his conversion and that of his family. In a letter to his daughter Fanny in 1820 upon the occasion of her confirmation, he wrote:

Does God exist? Is a part of us eternal, and does it live on after the other part is gone? And where [does it go]? And how? I don't know – and so I have never taught you anything about it. I only know that in me, and in you and all human beings, there is an eternal inclination toward everything Good, True and Just, and that there is a conscience to warn and guide us when we get too far away from these inclinations. I know it. I believe it. I live in this belief, and this is my religion.

Like many of his contemporaries who chose to cross over to Christianity, Abraham Mendelssohn was a supporter of a "rational religion." He saw himself as a man of the Enlightenment who followed in the footsteps of his father, and he thought – according to the scholar Felix Gilbert – in the simple but moral categories "of Either-Or and of the past and the present." Judaism, however, was not for him what it had been for his father: namely, "Revealed Law." Abraham was concerned with truth. He believed that there was a single One and that this One was eternal. But he considered the historic forms of religion to belong to the past. In the end, he thought it hardly mattered whether one chose Christianity or Judaism. The important thing was to acknowledge one's adherence to one religion, a religion that would answer to the demands of the present.

Schlesische privilegirte Zeitung

No. 34.   Sonnabends den 20. März 1813.

Se. Majestät der König haben mit Sr. Majestät dem Kaiser aller Reußen ein Off= und Defensiv=Bündniß abgeschlossen.

An Mein Volk.

So wenig für Mein treues Volk als für Deutsche, bedarf es einer Rechenschaft, über die Ursachen des Kriegs welcher jetzt beginnt. Klar liegen sie dem unverblendeten Europa vor Augen.

Wir erlagen unter der Uebermacht Frankreichs. Der Frieden, der die Hälfte Meiner Unterthanen Mir entriß, gab uns seine Segnungen nicht; denn er schlug uns tiefere Wunden, als selbst der Krieg. Das Mark des Landes ward ausgesogen, die Hauptfestungen blieben vom Feinde besetzt, der Ackerbau ward gelähmt so wie der sonst so hoch gebrachte Kunstfleiß unserer Städte. Die Freiheit des Handels ward gehemmt, und dadurch die Quelle des Erwerbs und des Wohlstands verstopft. Das Land ward ein Raub der Verarmung.

Durch die strengste Erfüllung eingegangener Verbindlichkeiten hoffte Ich Meinem Volke Erleichterung zu bereiten und den französischen Kaiser endlich zu überzeugen, daß es sein eigener Vortheil sey, Preußen seine Unabhängigkeit zu lassen. Aber Meine reinsten Absichten wurden durch Uebermuth und Treulosigkeit vereitelt, und nur zu deutlich sahen wir, daß des Kaisers Verträge mehr noch wie seine Kriege uns langsam verderben mußten. Jetzt ist der Augenblick gekommen, wo alle Täuschung über unsern Zustand aufhört.

Brandenburger, Preußen, Schlesier, Pommern, Litthauer! Ihr wißt was Ihr seit fast sieben Jahren erduldet habt, Ihr wißt was euer trauriges Loos ist, wenn wir den beginnenden Kampf nicht ehrenvoll enden. Erinnert Euch an die Vorzeit, an den großen Kurfürsten, den großen Friedrich. Bleibt eingedenk der Güter die unter

Above:
The Landwehr (East Prussian Defense Brigade) going off to combat in 1813 after a blessing in the Koenigsberg church. In the foreground, at right, a pair of Jewish parents bid their son farewell. Painting by Gustav Graef, 1860–61. Museum Ostdeutsche Galerie, Regensburg.

Below:
An appeal by Frederick Wilhelm III, to his "Brandenburgers, Prussians, Silesians, Pommeranians, Lithuanians!" to rise up against the occupation by Napoleon's forces, published March 20, 1813, in the Schlesische priviligirte Zeitung.

Above:
Moritz Daniel Oppenheim's
painting, The Return of the
Volunteer from the Wars
of Liberation to his Family,
According to Old Tradition.
A sabbath lamp hangs
above the table.
Leo Baeck Institute,
New York.

Below:
The Judenmajor
Meno Burg (1789–1853),
Royal Prussian Major of the
Artillery. The only Jewish
member of the Prussian
officer corps in the nineteenth
century. Burg was also a
member of the board of Berlin's
Jewish Community.

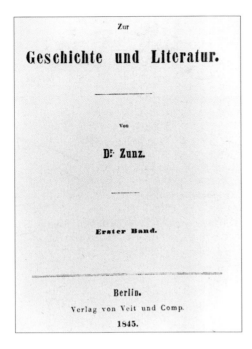

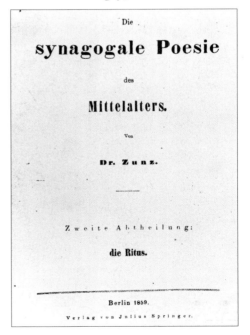

Leopold Zunz (1794–1886),
founder of the Science of Judaism.
Lithograph by Paul Rohbach after
a drawing by Julius Muhr.

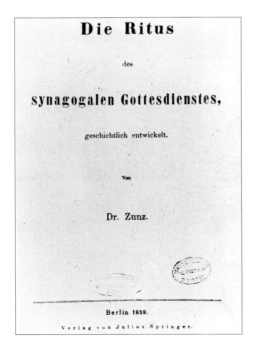

The poet Heinrich Heine
(1797–1856).

The law professor Eduard Gans,
(1798–1839).

Right:
Letter dated October 25, 1821,
to Eduard Gans and Leopold Zunz, in which the
Community Elders Veit, Gumpertz and Beer
greet the foundation of the
Verein der Wissenschaft des Judentums
(Association for the Science of Judaism).

Left page:
Title pages of some tracts by Zunz:
On History and Literature,
published in Berlin 1845,
The Rites of the Synagogue Service, *and*
The Synagogue Poetry of the Middle Ages,
both published in Berlin in 1859.

A soirée in Berlin ca. 1815,
as shown in a contemporary copper engraving.

Left: The composer Felix Mendelssohn Bartholdy (1809–47) in watercolor by James Warren Childe of 1829. Staatsbibliothek zu Berlin.
Above: Fanny Mendelssohn Bartholdy (1805–47), sister of the composer and wife of Wilhelm Hensel, who did this drawing of her. SMPK-Kupferstichkabinett.

The garden house of the home of Felix Mendelssohn Bartholdy at Leipziger Strasse 3 as shown in a watercolor by his brother-in-law Wilhelm Hensel, dated 1851. Staatsbibliothek zu Berlin.

Frederick Wilhelm IV's acclamation at Berlin's Lustgarten,
upon the occasion of his ascent to the Prussian throne, October 15, 1840.
Print after a painting by Franz Krueger.

The Limits to Adaptation

The distinct "turn" of Berlin's Jews toward *Deutschtum* (German culture) that took place between 1830 and 1847 extended to all areas of life and activity. Jews increasingly adapted the attire, language and habits of the Christian society surrounding them. The majority of Berlin's Jews no longer conceived of Judaism as a collective religious way of life but rather defined themselves as Prussians from Berlin. They wanted their Judaism to be understood as a personal commitment to a religion.

Berlin's new Jewish high-bourgeoisie of those years was not only prosperous. It was self-confident. It became a part of Berlin culture and society in general, and in doing so, developed a very special cachet. The Mendelssohn Bartholdy family, for example, "furnished" the musically talented brother and sister Felix and Fanny Mendelssohn Bartholdy. Noted scientists and writers issued from the family of Jacob and Amalia Beer. Wilhelm Beer became an important astronomer, his younger brother Michael a successful playwright.

But no matter how successful the process of adaptation or acculturation was for certain families, it remained a one-way street. Christian "society" continued to set the tone, and though it recognized the desire of Jews to improve their social and political positions, it was in no way prepared to accept Jews as

Woodcut detail of Franz Krueger's painting at left. On the spectators' platform are,
from right to left, the brothers Jakob and Wilhelm Grimm, Christian Rauch, Friedrich Wilhelm Schelling,
Ludwig Tieck, Alexander von Humboldt, Giacomo Meyerbeer.

equals. The Jews felt hurt by this attitude, and many complained that they were being slighted. No matter how successful they were, whether as merchants, scholars or artists, it was impossible to rise in certain circles or to join certain clubs or associations. Generally, the border of social acceptance was reached if someone openly acknowledged that he was Jewish – or if he was perceived as Jewish by others.

Between 1811 and 1849 the Jewish population in Berlin tripled. In the (elected) municipal boards and governing bodies, however, Jews were underrepresented. For the most part, people who corresponded to certain ideas of the Christian voters were elected. David Friedlaender was accepted, for exam-

ple, because he stood for adaptation. He served as syndic (a member of the city administration) between 1809 and 1814. But Friedlaender was an exception. Between 1815 and 1847 not a single Jew was to be found in the city administration. The banker Salomon Veit was a member of the city parliament from 1809 until 1822, but from then until 1837 no Jew was elected to the city parliament.

The exclusion of Jews from the municipal administration and elected bodies can be traced essentially to a reactionary mood that arose after the Wars of Liberation. A Christian-German state ideology and *voelkisch* thinking prevailed. An increasing number of anti-Jewish statements – such as Bruno

*A contemporary lithograph of revolutionaries fighting
on the barricades of Breite Strasse during the night of March 18–19, 1848.*

Bauer's comment "baptism alone does not make a Jew a German"– led disillusioned Jews to feel that the Edict of Emancipation of 1812 had, in fact, little or no meaning.

An example of this increasingly *vaterlaendische* climate was Achim von Arnim's founding of the Christlich-Deutsche Tischgesellschaft in 1810. Arnim's "Table Society" was considered an "anti-salon." It was not only against the Enlightenment but bore anti-Semitic overtones as well. The Society's rules mockingly (but nonetheless explicitly) excluded all "Jews, Frenchmen, philistines and women" from membership. Von Arnim's stream of anti-Jewish remarks led to his being challenged to a duel by the young Moritz Itzig. Von Arnim refused the challenge with the argument that a Jew would not be capable of "giving satisfaction." The remark so enraged Itzig that he thrashed von Arnim with his cane.

The law of July 23, 1847, *Gesetz ueber die Verhaeltnisse der Juden* (On the Relationships of the Jews) brought about a change in the way Jews saw themselves. Passed by the Vereinigte Landtage (United Provincial Parliaments) only with great reluctance, the law stipulated that the Jews had "the same rights and duties" as other citizens. In many ways, however, it proved a step backward from the 1812 Edict of Emancipation. The 1847 law legalized certain supplementary administrative practices that proved unfavorable to Jewish emancipation. It did have an important advantage over the 1812 law, however, in that it regulated the constitutions of the Jewish Communities. Prior to this, the Jewish Communities of Prussia – in contrast to the Protestant and Catholic Communities – had only been "tolerated." Now they were granted the same legal corporate status as their Christian equivalents. For the first time, Berlin's Jewish Community was granted autonomy in questions of worship, the possibility to establish its own schools, the right to levy taxes and entitlement to state and municipal subsidies.

The Revolution of 1848 and the Jews

For Berlin's Jews, the more vigorously they professed their allegiance to Prussia and *Deutschtum*, the more they relaxed their bonds to their collective Jewish past. The more they rejected the prevailing power structures, the harder they fought for a democratic organization of the state and society, for the elimination of national and social disadvantages. Many Jews therefore saw the events of March 1848 as a harbinger of progress – the dawn of a new age for Jews and non-Jews alike.

Internally, many Jews perceived the revolution in almost religious terms of salvation. The preacher and educator Leopold Zunz considered the events of March 1848 as tantamount to a "world court of judgement" before which the oppressors would be called and saw in the revolution the coming "Day of the Lord." Adelheid Zunz, who shared the expectations of her husband, wrote to a friend on June 28, 1848: "I believe that we think the same thing: that freedom, even if it takes a bloody path, is the final goal. It is the perfection of mankind."

The participation of Berlin Jews in the Revolution of 1848 was proportionally much greater than that of the general population. It is impossible to ascertain how many Jews died in the March revolt, since the names of the dead were not listed by religious affiliation. The only name that is certainly Jewish is that of the philosopher Levin Weiss. His death on the barricades did not go unnoticed in the newspapers. Nevertheless, neither the

Orient nor the *Allgemeine Zeitung des Judentums* listed the names of the Jewish dead.

Though many Jews certainly gave their lives for freedom in the March revolution in Berlin, it is completely untrue to state that it was instigated by Jewish intrigue. An anti-Jewish tone can be found in many contemporary accounts of the event, in for example the description of the many "Jewish faces" to be seen among the fighters on the barricades. Isolated anti-Jewish tumults occurred in Berlin on April 5, 1848. Such latent anti-Jewish sentiments were, however, balanced by sympathetic comments in the new, free press. In many cases, the papers made a direct connection between the Jews' struggle for emancipation and the general struggle for democracy. The *Spenersche Zeitung*, for instance, published a commentary about four Jewish freedom fighters who had died on the barricades (and whose bodies were lying in state alongside others in the Werdersche Church): "they are the best proof that, from now on, we will see no difference."

During the revolutionary year of 1848, Berlin Jews were not only at the barricades. They were also to be seen in the many assemblies and political rallies. They played an active role in democratic clubs and educational institutions. They participated, for instance, in the Volksverein (People's Association), founded by three Jewish brothers, Agathon,

The barricades on Alexanderplatz, as shown in a wood engraving (after a drawing by Kirchhoff), 1848.

Verzeichniß der an den Märztagen Gefallenen.

Gebhardt, Friedr., Müllergeselle, Wallstr. 11.
Borcharding, Carl, Tischlergef., Schillingsg. 32a.
Behm, Adelaide geb Neumann, Arbeitsfr. Gr. Frankfurterstr. 11.
Trost, Joh. Andr., Schuhmachermstr., Weymannstr. 18.
Müller, Carl Fr., Bäckergeselle.
Hinspeter, Jul., Buchbindergef., Kurstr. 48.
Hagenhausen, Fr. Ch., Maschinenbauer, Alexandrinenstr. 55.
Benzel, Auguste, unverehl., Klosterstr. 81.
Anders, Gottl., Arbeitsm., N. Königstr. 33.
Bartenfeld, Arbeitsm., Prenzlauerstr. 19.
Mengel, Buchbindergef., Gr. Hamburgerstr. 8
Hoffmann, Chr., Weber, Weberstr. 5.
Herrmann, Zimmergef.
Hahn, Tischlergef. aus Dresden.
Graf, Carl Heinr. Gust., Seidenwirkergef., Kl Frankfurterstr. 8.
Maton, Tischler, Niederwallstr.
Dill, Friedr., Arbeitsm., Kl. Frankfurterstr. 11.
Birn, Fr., Hausknecht, Friedrichstr. 115.
Schulz, Raschmacher, vor dem N. Königsthore.
Hartmann, Carl, Arbeitsm., Rosenq.-ergasse 14.
Dambach, Frl Charl., Ober-Steuerinsp.-Tochter, Jerusalemerstr. 20.
Kohn, Mor., Handlungsd., Spandauerstr. bei Bock
Bernstein, Magnus, Buchdrucker aus Ellrich.
Weiß, Levin, Student, aus Danzig.
von Holzendorff, Herrm., Stud jur., aus Jagow bei Prenzlau.
Franke, Ludwig Wilhelm, Buchhalter im Schickler'schen Handlungshause, Kochstraße 58.
Sabatier, Louis, Buchhalter.
Clauß, Carl, Schlossergeselle, Jüdenstraße.
Schötensack, Carl, Arbeitsmann, Weberstr. 35.
Moll, Malergehülfe, Kurstraße 43.
Heuscher, Maschinenmeister, Neue Friedrichstr. 24.
Leitzke, Albert, Knabe, taubstumm, Krausenstr. 3.
Bumke, Wilh., Schiffer, Wassergasse 22
Unterloff, Arbeitsmann, im Frankfurt.-thor-Bezirk.
Rudolph, Fr., Schlossergeselle, v. d. Oranienburgerthor.
Kumbold, Arbeitsmann.
Schlansky, Carl Dav., Seidenwirkergef., Büschingsstr. 13
Faß, Maschinenbauer, Linienstr. 116.
Mühlhoff, Carl, Schlossergeselle, Mauerstr. 12.
Fehrmann, Aug., Malerlehrling beim Maler Talmatey, Kochstraße.
Hohendorff, Hausdiener, Golnowstr. 24.
Allekopf, Arbeitsmann aus Charlottenburg.
Braun, Wilhelm, Eisenbahninspektor, Wilhelmstr.
Brüggemann, Tapezierer.
Erdmann, Friedr. Ed., Tischlergeselle, Schützenstraße 3
Freund, Tischlergeselle, aus Berlin.
Hoffmann, Schuhmacher, aus Leipzig.
Hinz, Benno, Schneider, aus Königsberg i. P
Heißler, M., Sattlergeselle, aus Berlin.
Koch, Schlosser.
Kleinfeld, Caroline, Oberwallstr. 12 u. 13 b. Friedheim
Körting, Schuhmachergeselle, aus Halberstadt
Kalinsky, Tischlergeselle, Köpnickerstr. 51.
Knideberg, Tischlergeselle, Stallschreiberstraße 9.
Klett, Speisewirth, Fischerstraße 23.
Kossez, Schneidergeselle Mehnerstraße.
Mailand, Carl Gottl. Hein., Schlosser, Schützenstr. 3.
Nizelsky, Schneider, Neue Königstr. 13.
Priebe, Schneidergeselle, aus Neu-Stettin
Pahmann, Carl, Schmierelehrling, Auguststraße 57
Riemer, Wilh., aus Tammsgarten bei Wollin
Richter, F. W. A., Lederwaarenfabrikant, Ritterstraße.
Rupprecht, Conditor, Werderstr. 3.
Schröder, Carl, Schuhmacher, Wollankstr 23.
Steinau, Tischlergeselle, aus Leipzig.
Specht, Tapezierer, Linkstr 18
Schulz, Louis, Riemerlehrl., Spandauerstr. Ecke r Königstr
Voigt, unbekannt.
Würdig, Daniel Fr., Kattundrucker aus Berlin.
Werlein, Tischlergeselle, aus Berlin.
Wegemann, Christine, aus Christianstadt.
Wegener, Tischlergeselle, Stralauerstr. 5.
Teichmann, Zimmergeselle, Linkstr. 23.
Hachar, Tischlergeselle, Blumenstr. 35
Hehnert, a. Berlin, Schneidergeselle, Jerusalemerstr. 53.
Werner, Carl, Kleidermacher, Charlottenstr. 32.
Lamprecht, Ferd., Maschinenbauer, Gr. Frankfurterstr. 74.

Matthes, Gust. Ad., Dresdnerstr. 87.
Wehrlein, Tischlergeselle.
Hesse, Heinr., Hausknecht, Jerusalemer- und Schützenstr.-Ecke, beim Kaufmann Eckert.
Lankford, Ad. Wilh., Kunstgießer, alte Jakobstr. 30.
Klein, Arbeitsmann, Friedrichsfelde.
Engel, Büchsenmachergef., Elisabethstr. 17.
Müller, Rur., Tischlergeselle.
Werpel, Maurergef., Kochstr. 34.
Pätzel, Casimir, Arbeiter bei Wöhlert, Brunnenstr. 19.
Freund, Tischlergef., Mauerstr. 2.
Gieseler, Franz, Maurergef., Elisabethstr. 11.
Frankenberg, Schlossergef. bei Borsig, Artilleriestr. 25.
Jungmann, Zeugschmied.
Tutsche, Christ. Fr. Wilh., Knecht in Wilmersdorf b. Schulzen Bliß.
Kemnitz, Zeugschmiedgef. b. Mstr. Wöhlert.
Seiffert, Seidenwirkergef.
Hering, Schneidergef.
Kuhn, Carl Ludw., Knabe, 12 Jahre alt, Linienstr. 27, beim Vater.
Thiemann, Ad., Schneidergef., Stralauer Mauer bei Puhlmann.
Eyrott, Casp., Tischlergef., Stallschreiberstr. 46.
Puls, unbekannt.
Junge, Arbeitsmann, Spittelmarktstr. b. Hennig.
Rudolph, Joh., Schlossergef., Gartenstr. 2.
Lemde, Karl Friedr. Herrm., Korbmacherlehrl., Ackerstr. 4.
von Stoczynsky, Florian, Kaufmann, aus Fraustadt im Großherzogth. Posen.
Benn, Jean, Buchbindergef., unbef.
Stahlberg, Friedr., Zimmergef.
Thämler, Joh. Friedr., Colorist, Lichtenberger Kietz.
Mauer, Seidenwirkergef.
Heintze, Carl Fr., Schuhmachergef., Golnowstr 40.
Schubach, George, Webergef., Roseng. 33a
Zinna, Ernst Fr. Rur., Schlosserlehrling, Jägerstr. 4. b Leining.
Baldschiedel, Friedr., Töpfergef., Augustfr 13.
Kirchner, Möbelpol., Roseng. 16.
Schmidt, Christ., Schlächtergef.
v. Lenski, Gust., Reg.-Ref.
Krüger, Joh. Kupferschmied.
Schulz, Frier., Tischlergef.
Dressler, Ernst, Bildhauer.
Reichstein, Schneidergef. aus Oblau, Krausen- u. Charlottenstr. Ecke.
Arnolt, männl. Leiche.
Siebert, männl. Leiche.
Häger, Tischlergeselle, Invalidenstr. 50.
Bauerfeld, Arbeitsmann, Gr. Hamburgerstr. 30.
Eben, Carl Wilh. Joh., Knabe, Gartenstr. 51.
Zimmermann, Schneider, unbekannt.
Bürfner, Ferd., Tischlergeselle, unbekannt.
Graubaum, Tischlergeselle, Wallstr. 17.
Bremer, Bergoldergehülfe, unbekannt.
Kloß, Wilh., Tischlergeselle, Mehnerstr. 1.
Dinze, Wilh., Tischlergeselle, Elisabethstr. 5—9
Behm, Buchbindergeselle aus Bromberg.
Behnert, Schneidergeselle, Splittgerbergasse 1.
Rosenfeld, Helene, geb Eichelmann, Arbeitsmannsfrau, Friedrichstr. 167.
Brünn, Leop., Kattundrucker, Stralauer Platz 24.
Riebe, Fried. Christian, Kattundrucker, Rosengasse 33.
Würdig, Wilh., Kattundrucker Mühlenstr. 65.
Blumenthal, Carl Wilh., Privat-Secretair, Große Hamburgerstr. 16.
Rand, Ludwig, Maurergeselle, Brunnenstraße.
Schmidt, Franz August Gottlieb, Tischlermeister, Brunnenstraße 41.
Gehrke, George, Schmiergeselle, Mohrenstr. 56.
Radmig, Maurerpolier u. Straßenaufseher bei der Straßen-Reinigungs-Anstalt unter den Frankfurter Linden.
Seiffert, Franz Isaac, Handlungsdiener, Kürassierstr. 15
Flügge, Tischlermeister, Alte Jakobstr. 102.
Tillad, Schlosser aus Sorau, Neue Königstr. 39.
Jungmann, Zeugschmied, Chausseestr. 7.
Behmer, Aug., pension. Grenz-Aufseher, Blumenstr. 30.
Fuchs, Seidenwirker, Große Frankfurterstraße
Anclam, Schuhmachergeselle, Friedrichsgracht.
Wentz, Tischlermeister, Markgrafenstr. 82.
Waschhagen, Vergolder, Jerusalemerstr. 45
Statir, Ludwig, Kattundrucker, Weberstr. 34.
Ohm, Tischlergeselle Anhalt. Komm. 13.

Die Namen der übrigen Gefallenen sind nicht zu ermitteln.

Verlag und Schnellpressendruck von G Lisiag. Aelrch. 6

A list of victims of the March fighting was posted in March 1848. The list is incomplete: "The names of the others who were killed could not be obtained." On the list can be found the names of Moritz Kohn, Magnus Bernstein and Levin Weiss.

Ceremonial funeral for the victims of March 1848.
From a woodcut of 1891.

Segens-Spruch

des

Rabbiner Dr. Michael Sachs

über

die Opfer des 18. und 19. März.

An ihren Särgen gesprochen den 22. März 1848.

———

Im Namen jenes uralten Bekenntnisses, das als lebendiger Zeuge der Weltgeschichte und Weltgeschicke seit Jahrtausenden dasteht, im Namen jener alten Gotteslehre, die der Menschheit ihren Gott gebracht, die sie gelehrt, in den Stürmen und Wogen der Ereignisse die leitende und waltende ewige Vorsehung zu schauen, die sie angeleitet, das Wehen des Gottesodems in dem Leben der Völker zu erkennen, die durch den begeisterten Mund ihrer Herolde, die Propheten, für Wahrheit und Recht das Wort genommen, im Namen jenes alten, ewigen Bundes, der den Gedanken der Brüderlichkeit, liebender Theilnahme des Menschen am Menschen in ihrem Kreise zuerst begründet und gepflanzt, nehme auch ich aus tiefbewegter Brust, aus ergriffener voller Seele das Wort in diesem erhabenen weihevollen Momente. Es war nicht der Tod, der sie Alle gleich gemacht, die hier ruhen, sondern die Kraft des Lebens, die Macht einer Idee, die Gluth der Begeisterung, die alle Dämme und Scheidewände niederriß, welche sonst den Menschen von sich selbst, den Menschen vom Menschen scheiden. Es war die Macht einer Ueberzeugung, eine Erhebung der edelsten Gefühle und Gedanken, die jene Hingeschiedenen, deren Gedächtniß hier in so ergreifender Weise

First page of the "Blessings" by Rabbi Michael Sachs "for the victims of March 18 and 19 [1848], spoken at their coffins."

Ferdinand and Heinrich Benary. In the left-liberal, later moderate-democratic Association for People's Rights, the baptized professor of mathematics Karl Gustav Jakob Jacobi played a central role. The Republican Club, politically on the far left, was organized by the publicist Heinrich Bernhard Oppenheim.

The period also witnessed the beginnings of a workers' movement, whose main figures, the young Stefan Born and Julius Brill, had great influence. Brill was reputed to be the only worker in the Prussian National Assembly. Almost without exception, the Jewish deputies to the Prussian parliament had leftward political leanings. One such deputy was the well-known doctor and writer Johann Jacoby. He was from Koenigsberg – even though he represented a Berlin election district – and is famous for having remarked to King Friedrich Wilhelm IV in November 1848: "It is the misfortune of kings that they refuse to hear the truth!"

The revolutionary mood in Berlin during 1848 was stirred up not only by the worsening economic and social conditions. A number of satirical political flyers written in a German-Jewish dialect could be seen all over the city. Though most of the authors wrote under a pseudonym, many of them were certainly Jews. Only Jews would have had such masterful command of the jargon used in the flyers. Furthermore, had the authors of the flyers not been Jews, their texts would probably have had anti-Semitic overtones.

The flyers of a certain "Isaac Moses Hersch" were received with great mirth. Equally amusing were the "appeals" of the "constitutional citissen Natan Satan" and the "speeches" of "Jacob Leibche Tulpenthal" (Jacob Littlebody Tulipvalley). Some of the flyers had rhymes in German-Jewish dialect: "Ess schteijt a ferd / Un macht ojf dr' erd" (There stands a horse / and drops a load on the earth). Or "Emancipation ho mir Jiden gekriegen / Ober wos nitzt, wenn de Geschaefte liegen? (Emancipation we Jews should have / But what's the use, when business is bad?). These were not merely caricatures of the revolutionary experience. At the same time, they declared that a necessary requirement for the realization of a democratic society involved the will of each individual to commit to the principle of freedom.

Equal Rights for Jews and Jewish Community Life

Even though the revolution of 1848 failed and much of the system it fought would survive for many more years, the situation of the Jews got better rather than worse. In the revised constitution of January 31, 1850 – in effect until November 9, 1918 – the Jews in Prussia were legally equal to non-Jews. Of course there was resistance, but this only slowed the process of equalization, rather than bringing it to a halt or reversing it. In 1856, an attempt by conservatives in the Prussian parliament was successfully opposed. They had sought to eliminate from Article 12 of the constitution the words "the exercise of the civil rights of citizens is independent of religious faith." Numerous Jewish Communities, among them Berlin's, appealed to the deputies that Jews not be robbed of their civil rights.

Despite the great resistance on the part of conservatives to the constitutional provisions for equal treatment, the Berlin Jewish Community was able to consolidate its relations. In keeping with the 1847 law "On the Relationships of the Jews," the Community formed its own official board of directors and a Representative Assembly. It passed a statute on May 23, 1861, aimed to preserve the Community's unity. Responsible members of the Community were intent on steering a cautious route between the proponents of Orthodox and religious reform and sought to stave off open conflict.

Title page of the translation of the Talmud by E. M. Pinner, published in 1849.

Above:
Sigismund Stern
(standing, in the middle),
founder of the
"German-Jewish Church,"
during a session of the board
of the Jewish Reform
Congregation in Berlin in
1855.

Below:
The Berlin Reform Temple,
which was built in 1854
and had an organ.

Above left:
Aaron Beer (1738–1821),
cantor of the
Jewish Community,
etching by B. H. Bendix,
1808.

Above right:
Aron Bernstein (1812–84),
who was beside
Sigismund Stern one of the
most important protagonists
of the Jewish
reform movement.

Below:
The synagogue of the
Reform congregation on
Johannisstrasse.
At right is the school and
administration building.
Photograph by
Abraham Pisarek ca. 1925.

On September 5, 1866, the liberal New Synagogue at Oranienburger Strasse 30 was opened. It was the Community's third synagogue after the one at Heidereutergasse 4 and the reform synagogue at Johannisstrasse 16. The dedication ceremony was attended by the important public figures of the day. Next to Otto von Bismarck sat the mayor of Berlin, and many representatives of the Prussian court were also present. The composer Louis Lewandowski – one of the reformers of the Jewish liturgy – conducted the choir through music that had been composed for the occasion.

The splendid New Synagogue immediately became one of the most famous Jewish religious buildings in Germany. Designed by Eduard Knoblauch, it had an intelligent lighting-system and a complicated vault construction. Friedrich August Stueler was responsible for construction. Contemporary reports celebrated it not only as a great architectural feat but also as a symbol of the self-confidence of the Berlin Jews.

The moderate policies of the Community's leaders encountered a block in 1866 regarding the successor to rabbi Michael Sachs, a rabbi who had been accepted by all the different religious congregations within the Community. Not only did the new rabbi, Joseph Aub, want to steer a liberal course, but he also wanted to deliver sermons – and to do so in German. His approach caused considerable dispute within the Community. Aub had seen to it that, at the dedication of the New Synagogue, decisive changes had been introduced into the liturgy. There was, for example, organ and choir music. Alterations had been made to the prayers. Many of these changes angered the Orthodox members of the Community.

The Community employed, in addition to Aub, another reform rabbi, Abraham Geiger. This, in addition to the liturgical changes mentioned above, led the proponents of strict Jewish law to secede from the Jewish Community. Their new congregation, called Adass Jisroel, was founded in 1869. The founding document stipulated that in order to maintain and exercise their religious duties, they felt it necessary to free themselves from the "tyranny of conscience brought about by certain co-religionists."

The fledgling Orthodox congregation elected Israel Hildesheimer as rabbi and remained a private religious association for the time being. It would fight for many years before it attained legal recognition from the state as a Community in its own right – legally equal to the larger Jewish Community of Berlin. (It should be noted, however, that not *all* Orthodox Jews joined Adass Jisroel. Many stayed in the Jewish Community of Berlin.)

Despite the success of Jews in attaining political and legal equality in Prussia between 1850 and 1870, it cannot be claimed that they attained the same social status as their Christian counterparts. In fact, it was quite the opposite. Social discrimination could be felt at all times and actually became stronger as the Jews were integrated into Prussia's political and legal systems. Jewish entry into the bureaucracy, the university and the military remained difficult, if not impossible. All manner of "unwritten laws" conspired to exclude Jews and prevent them from exercising legal, military or educational functions. This would remain the case throughout the Wilhelmine period and, indeed, until the German Reich came to an end in 1918.

Julius H. Schoeps

The Imperial Era
(1871–1918)

Compared to the dramatic events of 1933–45, the almost fifty years of German history between 1870 and 1914 seem in many ways idyllic and uneventful. For many who lived through the more recent past, the imperial period has been transfigured, transferred to the mythical realm of the "good old times." They see neither the many discontinuities nor the controversies, neither the battles nor the struggles, neither the successes nor the defeats that in fact marked the period.

With respect to the outside world, Germany enjoyed a period of general peace during this period. With respect to its internal affairs, however, the nation experienced an era of extraordinary intellectual development and economic advancement. Naturally, one should not overlook the fact that during these fifty years Germany was at the center of many international controversies and often teetered on the brink of war. Colonies were conquered and foreign cultures subjugated. Within the country, new lifestyles appeared and flourished. Germans attained hitherto unknown standards of living. Civil society developed as citizens learned to participate in government. Catholicism, resisted at first, was later courted. Workers began to form as a political force. And German Jews found their place in this country. They were not un-

The Kleine Judenhof, *not far from Alexanderplatz, ca. 1870.*

opposed, but they were there – so it seemed – for the duration.

How can we describe the period? How was society formed? How did the state function? Was the German Reich modeled along the lines of a bonapartist dictatorship or was it merely an authoritarian state? Was the state semi-constitutional, with party politics added on to it? Did the confederation of many states into a mighty empire, founded on Prussian military force, help the unified nation-state achieve unlimited rule?

In fact, all of these systems and values existed side by side. But it was also a period in which structures that promised positive developments became visible. This period saw the foundation of a legal system based on liberal principles. An institutional and legal framework was created, fostering an upswing of market-oriented industrial capitalism. An efficient educational system was developed. Culturally, the beginnings of modernism, which was marked by avant-gardist and individualist elements, can be traced to these years.

The German economy grew remarkably in these decades. Unfortunately, that growth was by no means consistent. The economic boom that followed the German victory in the Franco-Prussian War of 1870–71 was due at least partly to the immense indemnity France had to pay the victors. At the beginning of 1873, the economy was plunged into deep crisis, and it was not until the mid-1890s that it was entirely overcome. From then on, the German economy followed an upward curve. In 1913, the director of the Deutsche Bank, Karl Helfferich wrote (in a book celebrating Wilhelm II's twenty-fifth anniversary on the Imperial throne) that the German people enjoyed great prosperity. Tripling the nation's economic output in a mere twenty-five years was, without doubt, an accomplishment to be proud of.

"Illiberalism" as a System

By the turn of the century, the German Reich had become an economic, military and political power that many Germans were proud of – even if they were unsatisfied with the empire's structure and the personal conduct of the Kaiser. Jews participated in these developments in all areas, in both good times and bad. They participated in democratic structures. In as much as civic and social equality existed at all, German Jews were citizens on an equal footing with all others. Compared to the years preceding 1870, this was considered major progress. Germany, however, had not yet attained the status of a completely formed and functional democracy. Many strata of society were excluded from public life. This was not only true for the Jews, but they were one of the groups excluded from careers in the military and in the bureaucracy.

Legally, Jews were equal to all others. This is the result of the period in which the Reich was founded. As the historian Simon Dubnow noted correctly (if perhaps polemically) in his *History of the Jewish People*, German Jews saw it "as their responsibility to serve the new order. They strove, with hyper-patriotism and idolatry, to outshine the Germans in their praise and service to the idea of Germany as a great power."

The historian Fritz Stern has characterized the German Reich as "illiberal," stating that this quality permeated society throughout the entire period. German "illiberalism" contained the "old virtues of obedience and careful flattery of authority." It embodied the new faith in nationalism and in the overriding values of the nation-state. More than that, it signified a special form of civil immaturity. The economist Ludwig Bamberger is said by the historian Hans-Joachim Schoeps

The New Synagogue on Oranienburger Strasse, shown here in a photograph from about 1890, had seats for more than 3,000 people. It was dedicated on September 5, 1866. During the November pogrom of 1938 the Nazis tried to torch it, but it was only slightly damaged. In 1943, however, it was severely damaged by allied bombs. Parts of the building survived and were reconstructed between 1988 and 1995. It is now the Centrum Judaicum.

to have, in 1887, described the spirit of the German middle classes as "pompous servility."

The degree of illiberality could be gauged from many apparently insignificant things: small injustices and disadvantages, privileges and preferences, measures taken and measures omitted. During the imperial period, the nobility consistently enjoyed preferred treatment. These upper classes prevailed in four instances in particular: the *Kulturkampf* against the Catholic Church; the Law enacted against Socialism; the official toleration of the anti-Semitic movement; and the Prussian three-class voting system.

Fritz Stern has pointed to one of the central problems of the period: the secularization of modern Germany. As Nietzsche wrote,

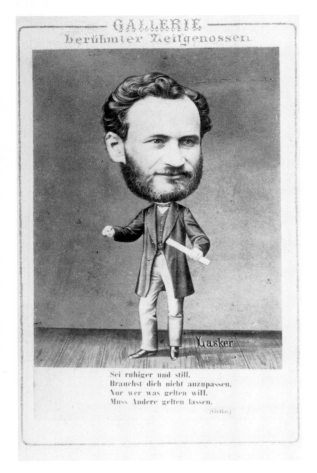

Left, above: Contemporary caricature of Eduard Lasker (1829–84), lawyer, politician and member of the Reichstag (1867–83).

Right, above: An invitation from Bismarck to Lasker, 1869.

Left, below: Lasker's identification as a deputy to the Prussian Legislature.

"God is dead. And we have killed him!" It was a cultural change of extraordinary importance. Real secularization was accompanied by the formal maintenance of a quasi-religious framework. Hypocrisy and an ever-growing sense of insecurity and anxiety were some of the side effects. The secular tendency expressed in Nietzsche's "God is dead. And we have killed him!" touched Jews as profoundly as it did Christians.

The imperial period can be subdivided into two phases, with a break occurring around 1890. This break began during the "year of the three Kaisers," 1888, in which first Wilhelm I, then his son Friedrich III died and Wilhelm II ascended the throne. His father, Friedrich, had been considered a liberal, but the brevity of his reign and his early death squelched the hopes of many for

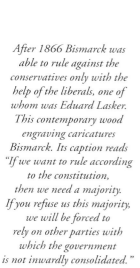

After 1866 Bismarck was able to rule against the conservatives only with the help of the liberals, one of whom was Eduard Lasker. This contemporary wood engraving caricatures Bismarck. Its caption reads "If we want to rule according to the constitution, then we need a majority. If you refuse us this majority, we will be forced to rely on other parties with which the government is not inwardly consolidated."

the advancement of liberalism, openness and commonality with the western nations, especially England and the United States. It is said that many Jews named their sons Friedrich in his memory. Two years later, in 1890, the new Kaiser Wilhelm II dismissed Otto von Bismarck, chancellor and founder of the German Reich, a statesman whose stewardship had been praised both at home and abroad.

The mid-1890s are said to have marked a "watershed between two epochs in the social history of capitalism." The period saw the development of technical improvements that had not been dreamt of in previous decades. After a long period of economic stagnation and a period of visible recession, the economy began a new phase of growth. A modern system of large industrial complexes evolved,

accompanied by advances in science and culture. The arts, too, gained momentum. In the fine arts, for example, the Berlin Secession emerged, bringing extraordinary effects in its wake. The entirely original works of Otto Brahm and Max Reinhardt graced the Berlin stage. German literature witnessed such young talents as Gerhart Hauptmann, Frank Wedekind and, later, Thomas and Heinrich Mann. The so-called "educated" classes had new subjects to discuss. They talked of religion, of Christendom and of Jewry. And they spoke of *Deutschtum* – a difficult term that may best be translated as "Germanness."

There was, however, a deep controversy about Jews and anti-Semitism, the effects of which would only be seen many years later. Of central importance was the question of whether Jews were a people unto themselves or whether they had a place in German culture and society. Did Germans and Jews make up a common nation, or did the latter remain a foreign body within the German *Volksgemeinschaft*? (This term designated a unity of ethnic Germans, the *Volk*.) Could one simultaneously be a Jew and a German, independent of the question of baptism? Anti-Semitism had always been present in Germany; sometimes it was strong; sometimes hidden. But now it left the lowly realm of the beer hall and became a suitable subject in "better" circles. It became a problem for society as a whole. Antagonism toward Jews, which had earlier been couched in religious terms, was now invoked in the name of a German nation-state. Christian anti-Semitism had mutated into an entirely racially motivated hatred of Jews.

Capital of the Empire

Berlin attracted ever-greater numbers of people throughout the nineteenth century. The city's actual appearance, however, didn't start to really change until the beginning of the 1860s. Thereafter, the city and its suburbs grew steadily. Most newcomers came from surrounding Brandenburg, and from such regions of eastern Prussia as Silesia. Among them there were many Jews. When, in 1871, Berlin became the capital of the new German Reich, the city grew in importance, territory and population. The old inner city had become the business district. Surrounding it were proletarian and residential districts. In the 1880s, the population had reached one million. By 1910 it was two million.

Around 1871, a little more than 36,000 Jews lived in Berlin, making up about 3.9 percent of the general population. This per-

centage was to remain until the Kaiser abdicated in 1918; the Jewish population grew proportionally to the general population. Jews tended, however, to settle in distinct city districts and a few particular suburbs. Early on, they favored homes in the old city center, in what was already known as Alt Berlin – where many of the institutions of the Jewish Community were located. In the 1880s the Jewish population started to move to the nearby Spandauer and Stralauer districts, to Luisenstadt and the Friedrichstadt. Toward the beginning of the twentieth century, many Jews moved to the newly built districts in the south and the west: Charlottenburg, Wilmersdorf and Schoeneberg. In 1916, 43,000 Jews lived in these districts, 16,000 of whom were obliged to pay taxes to the Jewish Community and were therefore voting members.

The capital city was economically attractive throughout this period. People were able to earn a good living. Wages, salaries and company profits were attractive. The tax base was strong. Nevertheless it had many of the problems of other large cities. Social problems such as inadequate housing, unemployment, among many others, beset the large city in growing numbers.

City administration at the time lay in the hands of a thin layer of local citizens. According to the Prussian three-class voting law, only high-income citizens could be elected to municipal office. This excluded the majority of the population: workers, middle- and low-level employees and women. It did not, however, exclude the Jews. They had, since 1809, been entitled to serve in the city government and city parliament, where they were for the most part, politically liberal.

Above:
Eduard Bernstein (1850–1932),
socialist writer and politician, member
of the Reichstag (with several large intermissions)
between 1902 and 1928.
The photograph was taken ca. 1895.

Below:
Social Democratic Reichstag deputies,
from left to right: Georg Schumacher,
Friedrich Harm, August Bebel, Heinrich Meister,
Carl Franz Frohme; standing, from the left:
Johann Dietz, Kuehn, Wilhelm Liebknecht,
Carl Grillenberg, Paul Singer.
Below a portrait of Fichte on the wall is
the quotation: "Even in war and through
common battle a people becomes a nation."
The photograph was taken by
Julius Braatz in 1889.

The Jews of Berlin

The Jewish population of Berlin grew three-fold in the three decades between 1871 and 1900: in 1871 there were about 36,000; in 1884, 54,000; in 1890, 80,000; and in 1900, there were 100,000. This growth placed an extraordinary burden on the Jewish Community and on religious services in particular. It strained the bonds that existed among individuals, congregations, and beliefs. The Jews who moved to Berlin in this period differed in many ways from those who stemmed from Berlin. The newcomers arrived largely from the then-Prussian province of Posen, where they were used to small congregations with family and religious ties. They were immediately confronted with a radically different way of life.

In 1895, according to the statistics on professions, the majority of Berlin's Jews were engaged in trade. The proportion of those employed in the "free professions" – such as law, medicine and architecture – was growing quickly, however. Since only a few of those Jews who had studied were welcomed into government service, it is not surprising that many of them became lawyers, doctors, engineers, journalists and teachers. The accessibility to these professions was one of the advantages of living in a large city, and especially of living in the capital of the Empire.

During the imperial period, Berlin's Jewish Community was in no way comparable in mission and work to the Jewish Community that has emerged since World War II. Of course they shared a concern with such religious matters relating to synagogues, cemeteries, care of the poor, religious schooling, ritual baths, dietary laws, and similar matters. But the Jewish Community of that time was not the political representative of Berlin's Jews, and its leaders did not act on their behalf as ombudsmen to city and state governments. The Jewish Community was for the most part concerned with its internal workings. Thus, Jewish Berliners would later have to create their own organizations, especially when it became necessary to combat growing anti-Semitism but also in order to influence lawmaking and government bureaucracy.

It is important to keep the narrower role of the Jewish Community in mind when one reads reports about the activities of individual Jews during these years. When Jews were active in social, cultural or even political affairs, it was not as members and representatives of the Jewish Community. This was the case when the banker Gerson von Bleichroeder stood close to Bismarck; when the industrialist and statesman Walther Rathenau traveled to the German colonies in Africa in 1907–08; when the textile merchant James Simon became a major donor to the Berlin museums; when Lina Morgenstern organized hot meals for the Berlin poor in many

Title page of the Volks-Zeitung, *founded in 1852 by A. Bernstein.*

*Title page of the
Berliner Volksblatt,
published by Paul Singer
from 1884 on.*

districts during the war winter of 1870–71. Such activities were personal and independent of the official Jewish Community, whose realm and activities were defined by laws. The Community's board members and leaders were restricted to operating within distinct limits.

Jews in Wilhelmine Berlin were not a marginal group. Nor were they what many might call a minority. They were, instead, an integral part of the city's citizenry. In 1905, the Jews of Berlin – though they numbered no more than four percent of the general population – paid over thirty percent of all municipal taxes. And in 1911, twelve of the twenty most prosperous Berliners were listed as Jews or of Jewish heritage. The list, which was headed by name of the Kaiser, contained the names of such Jewish entrepreneurs as Fritz von Friedlaender-Fuld, Rudolf Mosse, Sigmund Aschrott, Eduard Arnhold and James Simon. Their incomes and fortunes exceeded those of many bankers.

Jews were also proportionally overrepresented among journalists, lawyers and doctors, as well as in the sciences. In the case of the scholars, there was a restriction; professorial chairs in law and the *Geisteswissenschaften* (the humanities) were not open to Jews. They were able, however, to succeed in medicine and the natural sciences. The number of Nobel Prize winners among Jews is very impressive. Nor can one speak of the arts without reference to the Jewish contribution. As Gottfried Benn wrote: "The

splendor of the Empire, its inner and outer wealth, is owed essentially to the Jewish portion of the population." This dictum applied nowhere so much as to Berlin.

The Jewish Community of Berlin

All Jews in Berlin (exepting those belonging to Adass Jisroel, a smaller community) were part of the Jewish Community (Juedische Gemeinde). It did not differentiate among the various religious principles within Judaism. A majority of its members, however, held to liberal or reform Judaism. Indeed, the Berlin Community played a leading role in appointing liberal rabbis and providing places to train rabbis and teachers for coming generations.

The Hochschule fuer die Wissenschaft des Judentums (College for the Training in the Science of Judaism) was set up in 1872 to train liberal rabbis and teachers of religion. In 1885 its name was changed by a ministerial edict to a mere *Lehranstalt* (a teaching institute). It was independent of the Jewish Community and considered it its mission to connect traditional rabbinic wisdom to the science of Judaism, its philology and history. It was charged with raising the level of rabbinic teaching to university level. During its early, founding phase it owed much to the person and teachings of Abraham Geiger, one of the most important reformers of Jewish ritual and thought, appointed rabbi to the Jewish Community in 1870. Esriel Hildesheimer occupied the orthodox pole of the religious spectrum. Hildesheimer's seminary, founded in 1873, was devoted to training orthodox rabbis. Both institutions were located on Artilleriestrasse, now Tucholskystrasse.

At the outset of the Empire, in 1871, Berlin was graced with three synagogues: the Old Synagogue on Heidereutergasse (dedicated in 1714); the New Synagogue on Oranienburger Strasse (1866); and the synagogue on Kaiserstrasse (1869). On high holy days the services were, it is said, well attended – so well, it seems, that the congregation sometimes had to rent extra space. At any rate, the official statistics of 1867 show that the Jews made extensive use of their religious facilities. This was not to change in the following decades.

The number of synagogues grew rapidly. In the bulletin of Berlin's synagogue administration it was reported that in 1916 there were ten synagogues with a total of 33,467 seats. Together with private synagogues, of which there were many, the city had about 44,000 seats. The *Gemeindeblatt* (the Jewish Community newsletter) reported that in September 1914, during the high holy days all 42,441 seats were taken. That would mean that one-third of the Community members took part in the services. Compared to comparable attendance statistics for churches, especially of the Protestant churches, this was very high indeed.

Since the members of the Community who settled in the western sections of the city were mostly of liberal persuasion, several synagogues were built that contained organs. Two such synagogues were the synagogue on Lindenstrasse (built in 1891), not far from Berlin's press district and the synagogue on Luetzowstrasse (built in 1897–98), in the Tiergarten district. Both were designed to resemble north-German brick churches, and both were built at the back of other buildings and housed other synagogue functions. Another example is the synagogue on Rykestrasse (completed in 1904) in the district of Prenzlauer Berg.

The most important synagogue built after the New Synagogue on Oranienburger Strasse was the liberal synagogue on Fasanenstrasse in Charlottenburg. With its three cupolas and its imposing portal, it belonged to the most prominent buildings near Berlin's major shopping and entertainment boulevard, the Kurfuerstendamm. It opened on August 26, 1912. On October 31, the Kaiser, visiting the synagogue, expressed "his complete satisfaction with the building's architecture and appointments." Perhaps his royal pleasure was inspired by the fact that the synagogue's marriage hall was paved with tiles from the imperial factory.

The Community members of Charlottenburg were given the use of a synagogue on Pestalozzistrasse in 1915. In general there were still many private synagogues with different rituals and liturgies. The last great synagogue building to be built between 1913 and 1916 was the large synagogue on Kottbusser Ufer. It had a synagogue for weekdays and rooms for schoolchildren. With its so called "old" liturgy, it served as a meeting place for the Community members of the neighborhood who were Orthodox.

The Community as a Welfare Institution

Berlin's Jewish Community operated many institutions: cemeteries, hospitals, clinics, schools and much more. Especially after 1890 many associations were founded within its protective sphere to organize welfare action and activities in the Jewish vein. There was, for example, an organization to defend Jews against anti-Semitism, as well as a sporting association, a union of women, a youth club. By virtue of its place in the Wilhelmine capital, the Jewish Community was a stronghold for German Jewry nationwide. By 1910, about 24 percent of all German Jews were living in the capital (and a total of 35 percent of Prussia's registered Jews lived there).

A Jewish community is never solely religious in a narrow sense. Caring for the poor and needy has always been among its fundamental and defining tasks. Berlin's Jewish Community was there when its members needed help. There was always a box, the *kuppah*, in which contributions for the poor could be placed. The history of how Berlin's Jewish Community cared for its poor is exemplary of the way in which Jewish social work developed in general. Originating as an establishment that cared for migrants and mendicants, its modern welfare institutions evolved to encompass the care of children and the betterment of health and working conditions.

The leaders of the Community created special commissions to supervise the various welfare activities. After 1870 it operated two orphanages. One at Weinbergsweg, 13 (founded in 1872) was run by Sara and Moritz Reichenheim and funded with 250,000 talers. Another, at Berliner Strasse, 120–1 in the Pankow district, was begun in 1882 for "parentless children of Jews of Russian origin who had come to Berlin after the pogroms." It was founded through the initiative of the Berlin lawyer Hermann Makower, who served as speaker of the Community Representative Assembly from 1870 until 1892. The year 1912 saw the completion of a larger building with room for seventy boys, most of whom were trained in the handicrafts. The

synagogue there was equipped through donations by the Garbáty-Rosenthal family, which owned of a nearby tobacco factory. In general, the foundation and maintenance of various welfare institutions under the Community's umbrella owed much to private individuals, any many of them often filled important posts in the administration of the Community.

Perhaps the greatest Jewish philanthropists of the era were Moritz and Bertha Manheimer. Moritz Manheimer was a partner of the textile firm of Valentin Manheimer, which had introduced mass-produced clothing to Berlin in 1839. He served as a member of the Community's Representative Assembly for 38 years. To commemorate their twenty-fifth wedding anniversary, the Manheimers donated 300,000 marks for furnishings for the Community's second home for the aged. The home was in Prenzlauer Berg, at Schoenhauser Allee, 22, next to the Jewish cemetery (established in 1827). Other welfare projects to which the Manheimers gave their money were the hospital, the clinic and the home for apprentices in Pankow. In total, the couple contributed one million marks to various Community welfare institutions

Also erected through private donations was another home for the aged on Exerzierstrasse (now the Iranische Strasse) in the district of Wedding. Dedicated in 1902, it stood on property that the city had placed at the Community's disposal. In addition to managing its own institutions, the Community oversaw a number of private foundations and charitable institutions, such as the home for the blind and a home for the deaf and dumb.

In all the available statistics there is almost no mention of women, although they were an essential part of the Community's work. In addition to being the dominant force in their families, women were also decisive for

Kurz die Hose, lang der Rock,
Krumm die Nase und der Stock,
Augen schwarz und Seele grau,
Hut nach hinten, Miene schlau —

So ist Schmulchen Schievelbeiner.
(Schöner ist doch unsereiner!)

Schmulchen Schievelbeiner,
an anti-Semitic caricature by Wilhelm Busch
(1832–1908).

The historian and anti-Semite Heinrich von Treitschke (1834–96),
shown in this wood engraving by G. Koch of 1879 lecturing
at the Berlin university,.

Below, left:
Adolf Stoecker (1835–1909), protestant pastor and politician,
member of the Reichstag 1881–93 for the German Conservative Party.
He was known as the "Apostle of Intolerance" and a rabid anti-Semite.
Photograph by Hans Franke & Co, 1902.

Ein Wort
über
unser Judenthum
von
Heinrich von Treitschke.

Separatabdruck
aus dem 44. und 45. Bande der Preußischen Jahrbücher.

Dritte unveränderte Auflage.

Berlin.
Druck und Verlag von G. Reimer.
1880.

Below: right:
Title page of a scandalous
anti-Semitic tract:
A word about our Jewry,
by Heinrich von Treitschke,
third edition, Berlin 1880.

Title page of a list of the members of the
Central Association of German citizens of the Jewish faith
(Centralverein) founded in 1893 for the
"care of Jewish life as well as the spiritual, legal and economic
stewardship of Jews living in Germany."

The Jewish student association Maccabaea
in Berlin in a photograph taken ca. 1906.
In the middle, with cap and sash, is
Felix Rosenblueth (Pinhas Rosen), who became
Israel's first Minister of Justice.

the functioning of the many small and large businesses that Jews in Berlin had established over the years. It was only at the turn of the century that a Jewish women's movement was established, probably as a result of an international women's conference held in Berlin in 1904. That year Bertha Pappenheim took the initiative and founded the Juedische Frauenbund, or League of Jewish Women. Hundreds of individual organizations were combined under the League's umbrella. In general, it concerned itself with social and cultural themes: establishing homes for girls, providing help at railway stations as well as day rooms for working women, combatting prostitution, and much more.

Rapid social changes beginning in the second half of the nineteenth century affected the position of Jewish women both in their families and in the public activities of the Community. As traditional family obligations were being transferred to the public sphere, many social and pedagogical problems came to occupy the heart of the Community's work. These social concerns and the general wish for women's suffrage grew ever more important. It was not until later, however, that women were granted the right to vote. Only the Zionist movement had allowed women an equal role right from the beginning.

Between Reform and Orthodoxy

Although the New Synagogue on Oranienburger Strasse was completed in 1866, its importance for Berlin's Jews continued throughout the Wilhelmine period. The New Synagogue caused considerable tension within the Jewish Community even during its construction phase. As could be expected,

there was little agreement between the proponents of reform and Orthodox Judaism. The reformers – who were in the majority – accepted the building with great pride and self-confidence. Many who didn't approve of it seceded and formed an independent congregation of their own, the Orthodox Community of Adass Jisroel, which claimed greater fidelity to Jewish law.

It would be wrong, however, to understand Berlin's Jewish Community as a congregation with a single unified liturgy. This was the case neither before nor after the founding of Adass Jisroel. Since 1845 there had been, within the Community, an institution that was "unique in the Jewish cultural association": the Reformgemeinde (Reform Congregation). It had been established on May 8, 1845, at Sigismund Stern's initiative, as a mutual association for reform in Judaism. In 1854 the Reformgemeinde – already three hundred members strong – built a synagogue at Johannisstrasse 16. This first Reform synagogue was called a "temple." Its first rabbi, Samuel Holdheim, was regarded by his congregation as both a teacher and a preacher. Holdheim's services were remarkable in that they centered on a sermon rather than liturgy. Furthermore, he incorporated what he called "German song and German prayer" and authored his own prayer book. The traditional Hebrew liturgy disappeared almost completely from the service, and according to the scholar Ludwig Geiger, "all that referred to 'national rebirth' [that is, the return to Zion] was abandoned as well. Only the concept of the Messiah was retained for its purity."

It was into the Reformgemeinde that Wilhelm Klemperer, father of the historian Victor Klemperer, was summoned in 1891. According to his son, "the will to *Deutschtum*" had found here "one of its most radical expressions":

Constituirungs-Urkunde

der gesetzestreuen jüdischen Religionsgesellschaft

„ADASS JISROEL"

zu Berlin.

Die Repräsentantenwahlen der hiesigen jüdischen Gemeinde ergaben in den letzten Jahren wiederholt ein für die Interessen der Gesetzestreuen so ungünstiges Resultat, dass in Folge davon nunmehr die Leitung der Gemeinde in die Hände von Männern übergegangen ist, welche den alten conservativen Standpunkt des Judenthums verlassen haben und neologen Tendenzen huldigen. Die berechtigten Ansprüche zahlreicher Gemeindeangehöriger, dass an Stelle der dahingeschiedenen gesetzestreuen Mitglieder des Rabbinats-Collegiums Oettinger, Dr. Sachs und Rosenstein s. A. entsprechend gesinnungstüchtige und genügend gelehrte Rabbiner berufen würden, blieben unbefriedigt, und die an den Vorstand und die Repräsentanten ergangenen Petitionen wurden kaum beachtet. Unter diesen Verhältnissen halten wir Unterzeichnete es für unsere Pflicht, und sprechen es hiermit als unseren Entschluss aus, uns zu einer gesetzestreuen jüdischen Religionsgesellschaft zu constituiren, welche uns alle die von dem Religions-Gesetze gebotenen Institutionen, Einrichtungen und Anstalten einer jüdischen Gemeinde gewähren soll und als ihr ewig unveränderliches Gründungs-Statut und ihre feste unverrückbare Basis das überlieferte Gesetzbuch des Judenthums, den Schulchan Oruch, mit seinen gesetzlichen Commentaren anerkennt und festhält. Wir hegen mit dem Vertrauen zu unserer gerechten Sache die Hoffnung, dass eine hohe Regierung unseren aus der unverbrüchlichen Treue gegen unser heiliges Religionsgesetz stammenden Entschluss billigen und uns vor jedem Gewissenszwang schützen wird.

Wir berufen als unsern Rabbiner Herrn Dr. Israel Hildesheimer aus Eisenstadt, dem wir die endgültige Abfassung resp. Bestätigung unserer Statuten sowie die Wahl eines von uns anzustellenden unter seiner Leitung stehenden Dajanats überlassen.

Es sind Herrn Dr. I. Hildesheimer bereits die nothwendigsten Mittel zur Errichtung der confessionellen Lehranstalten durch Zeichnungen jährlicher Beiträge vorläufig auf drei Jahre garantirt und es haben bereits Hunderte der ehrenwerthesten Mitglieder der hiesigen jüdischen Gemeinde denselben durch ihre Namensunterschrift als ihren Rabbiner anerkannt und sich bereit erklärt, ihm mit Opferfreudigkeit zur Gründung und Erhaltung der religiösen Institutionen Mittel zu Gebote zu stellen.

So sprechen wir denn die frohe Hoffnung aus, dass wir durch die Constituirung der gesetzestreuen jüdischen Religionsgesellschaft den wahren Frieden und die Eintracht zwischen den hiesigen jüdischen Bekennern jüdischen Glaubens für alle Zukunft begründet und eine Garantie geschaffen haben, dass m. G. H. nun und nimmermehr den Gesetzestreuen die Wahrung und Ausübung unserer religiösen Pflichten durch Gewissenszwang von Seiten unserer eigenen Glaubensbrüder erschwert werde.

BERLIN, Thamus 5629 — im Juni 1869.

Folgen die Unterschriften:

Because many Orthodox members of the Berlin Jewish Community felt that the "legitimate right of many congregation members" to a "highly educated and correspondingly mindful rabbi" had not been accommodated, they seceded from the Community in 1869 and founded Adass Jisroel, a congregation "true to the law of Judaism."

The family of "Railroad King" Strousberg
painted by Ludwig Knaus in 1870. Stiftung Stadtmuseum Berlin.

From the Jewish cemetery on Schoenhauser Allee.

Here is where the religious kernel – and only the kernel – of Judaism is protected. The strict faithful (*Strengglaeubigen*) say that this is the place where Judaism is destroyed (*vernichtet).* The entire service is held – with the exception of a few words – in German; services take place on Sunday instead of on Saturday; all the prayers are said in German; the organ is played to the singing of a German choir; those who pray wear no head coverings; men sit together with the women. They do not deviate from German custom by one single inch.

Of course it should be said that this "radical reform movement" remained basically limited to Berlin's Reformgemeinde, whose membership, according to the scholar Max Joseph, was minute "in comparison to the growth of the rest of Berlin Jewry."

To the Jews of Berlin, the various theological positions and denominations – whether Orthodox or reform, whether part of Adass Jisroel or part of the Jewish Community of Berlin – had little or nothing to do with the question of nation. Both reform and tradi-

tional Jews considered themselves Germans, or German Jews. They wanted to be Germans – no more but certainly no less. In the same way that there were Germans who professed the Catholic faith and Germans of Evangelical faith, the Jews of Berlin saw themselves as Germans of Jewish faith.

The *Gruenderzeit* and Berlin's "Anti-Semitism Dispute"

Anti-Semitism took many different forms during the imperial period, but it was largely out in the open. The most visible episode, however, was known as the *Berliner Antisemitismusstreit,* (The Berlin Anti-Semitism Dispute) which started with the publication of a tract by the historian Heinrich von Treitschke, "The Jewish Question in Germany" on November 15, 1879. It was not so much the book's anti-Semitic content – much of what he wrote could be read earlier and elsewhere – as the fact that the author was a recognized historian, a scholar whose monumental *German History in the Nineteenth Century* was well known. His contemporary, the great historian Theodor Mommsen, wrote of Treitschke: "By writing certain things, he made it decent for others to say them. That was the explosive effect of this article, which we saw with our own eyes. All shame was removed from this 'profound and strong movement.' Now the waves were billowing and the froth was spewing." Treitschke's notorious sentence, "the Jews are our misfortune," was the groundswell of the wave of anti-Semitism in the Reich's first decades. Thus anti-Semitic agitation received the support of a recognized scholar.

This attack was appropriate to the times, known as the *Gruenderzeit* (Foundation Time). After the Franco-Prussian War, Germany – and especially Berlin – experienced a wave of founding new stock companies. Many rode the upsurge to prosperity and made their fortunes. They were gamblers, speculators, real-estate developers and builders. It was only a matter of time – 1873, to be precise – before their houses of cards tumbled down, bringing ruin to many who become so rich so quickly. To the question of whom, or what, was to be blamed, a remarkably quick answer appeared: "The Jews are our misfortune."

Only rarely is it possible to clearly trace an outbreak of anti-Semitism to a single source. Only rarely had so primitive and, for many, so convincing a wave of anti-Semitism established itself. The historian Fritz Stern generally considers the "scapegoat" theory of anti-Semitism to be unsatisfactory. In this instance, however, "it really looked as if the Jew was used to explain a muffled guilt of Christians. The upper classes were receptive to these charlatan phrases by demagogues, because anti-Semitism helped them regain their self-respect." Whoever was looking for simple answers found them here.

The spectacular bankruptcies and their causes were personified in the figure of "The Jew Strousberg": Bethel Henry Strousberg, railroad-king of the epoch and one of the century's greatest speculators. Bethel Henry Strousberg was born a Jew in the East Prussian town of Neidenburg in 1823. He was baptized at the age of twelve. After a stay in London, he arrived in Berlin in 1856 and purchased a concession for a railroad between Tilsit and Insterburg on behalf of an English consortium. At the time it was difficult to raise the necessary capital in Germany for such an operation; apparently it took too long for investors to see returns. Strousberg knew how get around the worries of his investors; he simply issued more shares than were covered by the investments. In this way,

stock prices fell, and the participating board members, directors, real-estate owners (from whom the land had to be bought) and railway industry manufacturers turned a handsome profit by selling their cheaply bought shares when the price was high. In 1862 the Tilsit-Insterburg line went into operation, and Strousberg was a "made" man.

Thereafter, people trusted Strousberg to finance large projects, and he was able to expand and refine his operations. He surrounded himself with a "court" of aristocrats, who helped him gain entry into the highest circles. Such connections were, in turn, important for getting permits. With this system Strousberg managed to build the East-Prussian Southern Railway, the Berlin-Goerlitz, Halle-Sorau, Hannover-Altenburg, and Maerkisch-Posener lines and the railroad along the right bank of the river Oder. In Hungary he created the Northeast Railroad, in Russia the line reaching from Brest to Grajewo. Later he built railway lines in Thuringia and initiated the construction of the major line between Paris and Narbonne on the Mediterranean coast.

To see Strousberg as a mere speculator – or a financial shark – is, in fact, false. His efforts brought many useful new buildings to Berlin. To relieve the city of the stench of the old slaughterhouse and fish market, he erected a large new slaughterhouse and a central market hall. To free his company from the tyrannical practices of certain manufacturers, he bought steelworks and the locomotive factory of Egestorff (later, Hanomag) in Hanover. He also contributed much aid to social projects in Berlin, feeding the poor, for instance, during the difficult winter of 1869–70.

Financial downfall came in 1872, however, with the failure of possibly his most ambitious project: the construction of a railway line in Romania. For the first time,

Above:
The publisher Rudolf Mosse (1843-1920) with his
brothers in 1891. Mosse founded the Berliner Tageblatt
in 1872 and published the Berliner Volkszeitung,
the 8-Uhr-Abendblatt *and the* Berliner Morgenzeitung
as well. Mosse served on the board of the Reform
congregation, he assumed control of the
Allgemeine Zeitung des Judentums, *which he later*
continued as C.V. Zeitung *(a paper for the Centralverein).*
The brothers Mosse, from left to right:
Albert, Salomon, Paul, Emil, Theodor,
Rudolf and Max.

Below: Edmund Edel's advertisement for the newspaper
B.Z. am Mittag, *which began in 1904.*

*Right: Leopold Ullstein (1826–1899),
publisher in a portrait by Carl Begas from the
mid-1880s. Ullstein founded his newspaper publishing
house in 1867 and expanded it considerably in the
following years to include the* Berliner Zeitung,
the Vossische Zeitung *and the founding of such
newspapers as the* Berliner Abendpost *and the*
Berliner Illustrierte Zeitung, *as well as a
book-publishing house. Ullstein's five sons worked
with him. All of them converted to Christianity and
withdrew from the Jewish Community.*

*Center:
Edmund Edel's design for a*
Berliner Morgenpost *advertisement.*

*Below:
Title of the* Berliner Morgenpost.

The Berlin stock exchange in 1889 in a wood engraving after a drawing by E. Thiel.
A man with a stereotypical Jewish profile is shown in the foreground.

Strousberg was not in a position to pay the investors their guaranteed interest; and by liquidating his investments in Romania, he lost most of his assets and investments in Germany. Bethel Henry Strousberg died a poor man in 1884 in Berlin. Although he had been baptized and did not consider himself a Jew, the downfall of "the Jew Strousberg" provided Berlin with a pretext for anti-Semitism.

The Battle Against Anti-Semitism

"In the youth of every German Jew there comes a painful moment which can never be forgotten: it is the first time he is conscious of the fact that he is a second-class citizen and that no talent or service will ever be able to free him from this situation." Walther Rathenau's dictum applied throughout the nineteenth century – and beyond. But never had such a frank, vulgar and universal form of anti-Semitism made itself so clear as it did in the last decades of the nineteenth century. It was the substance of baiting articles, of magazines for housewives, Catholic monthlies, and fraternity newspapers. There were anti-Semitic mass rallies and meetings among the "better" classes; at church functions and in election campaigns. And there were anti-Semitic petitions circulating for signatures.

In one respect, Treitschke was right: anti-Semitism was not merely for the rabble. Nor was it a "momentary agitation," or merely "brutal and spiteful, but a natural reaction of the feeling of German people to a foreign element." Anti-Semitism, in the form it took during the German Reich, was a social problem of the greatest magnitude. It encompassed all strata of society. It could be seen within the workers' movement, where Karl Marx himself posited the connection between capitalism and "rich Jews." It was also palpable within the bourgeoisie, which suddenly found itself embroiled in financial crisis; the economic optimism that had dominated previous decades was suddenly destroyed. And striking instances of anti-Semitism could be found among the better educated. The celebrated author Theodor Fontane wrote to Friedrich Paulsen on May 12, 1898, about the Jews:

> They are, in spite of all their talents, a terrible people. They are not an element that brings strength and freshness but a yeast in which ugly cultures of fermentation are virulent. From their beginnings they have borne something of the base. They and the Aryan world will not be able to stand each other much longer. They can be incorporated in body, but not in spirit.

The Jews themselves were taken by surprise by such instances of anti-Semitism. Many had been living under the illusion that in such an enlightened century such a sentiment was impossible. Had not the Jews helped bring about German unity? Had they not fought on the battlefields of the Franco-Prussian War, alongside other Germans? Berlin's Jewish Community lodged a formal protest with the Minister of the Interior against the anti-Semitic rants of Adolf Stoecker, the court preacher. It was only after reminding the minister four times of this complaint that the Community received a (hedged) answer: It would be more sucessful

– considering the court's structure – to use private intervention by respected individuals. Eventually, the influential Jewish banker Gerson von Bleichroeder was able to persuade the Kaiser to give the preacher a (lukewarm) dressing down.

The dispute continued well into the year 1881. Statements protesting the anti-Semitic agitation entered the fray, many of them authored by prominent citizens of Berlin, especially liberals. The "Revulsion of the Educated" found full expression in a declaration dated November 12, 1880, which was signed by 75 important people, among them members of the city government and citizens of Berlin and of other large cities. There was almost simultanesouly a great debate in the Prussian parliament (November 20–22, 1880) on "The Jewish Question."

It soon became clear that it would be insufficient to react at only these high levels. It would be necessary to utilize the legal system as well as the Jewish initiative. There was no lack of voices expressing anger over anti-Semitism during the heated controversy, but such voices were, as yet, isolated. They required unity. For some time, only one Jewish committee existed to fight anti-Semitic attacks; it was composed of influential citizens and worked largely behind the scenes. That the Jewish Community weighed, in 1893, the possibility of sending a delegation to the Kaiser "to beg him to give the Jews protection from the anti-Semites" was indicative of the way in which leading figures of the Community envisioned a solution to the problem.

The historian Arnold Paucker, long-time head of the Leo Baeck Institute in London, confirmed that the "Jewish attitude was characterized by a certain reticence to defend themselves in a militant manner." Action was taboo; leaders were concerned it might be interpreted as hostile to the state. Moreover, they considered it imprudent to draw attention to their Jewishness; to organize the public "defense" of Jews would only draw attention to the fact that integration and emancipation had not succeeded. It took two waves of anti-Semitism and 15 years of internal change before a general defense movement – despite the inadequate structure of the Community – would be organized. Finally, in the year 1893, the Centralverein (Central Association of German Citizens of the Jewish Faith) was founded.

There is no doubt that the Berlin anti-Semitism Dispute hastened a process that was urgently needed. It helped initiate a debate about Jewish identity, and a series of important questions were finally asked: Who are we? What do we want to be: German citizens of the Jewish faith? Jews in Germany? German Jews? Jewish Germans? Or Germans and Jews at the same time? Theodor Mommsen showed the way. In his last fundamental contribution to the discussion, the historian closed with an appeal to "the German Jews, too." He indicated that entrance into a great nation carried a price: "No Moses will lead the Jews back to the promised land; whether the Jews sell trousers or write books, it is their obligation to go as far as they can without disobeying their consciences, to stop being different and apart, to remove with all their energy the barriers that separate them from their German fellow citizens."

Jewry as an Independent Force

Many changes took place in Germany in the mid-1890s. They involved society as a whole, they affected many areas of public life, and they were felt in the Jewish Communities in Germany as well. Throughout Berlin, institutions, associations, clubs and

The merchant Hermann Tietz (1837–1907) based on a photograph of 1880. Tietz had learned modern business methods in New York and Paris and he used them successfully in Germany, after the founding of the German Empire in 1871. He opened department stores in many German cities, and had, until World War I, three branches in Berlin alone.

other organizations were founded during the decade that surrounded the turn of the century, including several important organizations founded by Jews for the exclusive use of Jews. Not only was this in keeping with the times, it was an internal necessity as well. Berlin's Jewish Community concentrated inward on itself, consolidating its internal relationships and structures. Synagogues had to be built and purchased. Religious schools, community centers and libraries were still being built. Jewish newcomers to Berlin thought, in particular, that religious teaching was inadequate, but nothing regarding education was really changed until the middle of the 1890s.

The Leipziger Strasse branch of the Tietz department store ca. 1900.

The *Religionsschule* (religious school) was a firmly established institution within Germany's Jewish communities. It had nothing in common with the faith-based schools of a later era, but was the place where all Jewish children (no matter where they attended school) learned about religion. The communities demanded that the Jewish religion be taught in the city's public schools – since that was the case with the Protestant and Catholic religions – but it was unable to accomplish this. According to the Berlin Community board's administration report for the period 1910–13, "attempts to achieve the teaching of the Jewish religion in public and private secular schools" were proceeding with success. Until the goal had been achieved, however, it would remain the Jewish Community's job to provide their own *Religionsschulen* for Jewish children. In 1913 Berlin had twelve such schools.

Religionsschule No. 12 embodied the first effort "to create a community school devoted entirely to the Hebrew disciplines." Gershom Scholem, however, found the teaching scandalous. As he wrote in memoirs of his youth, "before World War I, Berlin's large and prosperous Jewish Community stubbornly refused to allow a class that taught the *Mishna*, the Talmud or even Rashi's *Commentary* to the weekly section of the Torah – in a single *one* of its *Religionsschulen*."

During this period the Jewish Community in Berlin was weakened by three trends. For one thing, the Jewish birth rate was dropping quickly and continually. In 1876 it had been 46 births per thousand people. At the turn of the century it was down to 28, and in 1913 it was a mere 17 per thousand. Furthermore, a not-inconsiderable portion of former members had left the Community, and many of them had been big taxpayers. Finally, an increasing number of mixed marriages caused the Community great concern.

By the end of the Reich, such marriages were equal in number to marriages in which both partners were Jewish.

Felix Aaron Theilhaber's writings in 1914 made people aware of these problems. "Will the material and social ascent of the [Jewish] families be dangerous in respect to racial hygiene?" Theilhaber's statistics proved that "in Berlin only enough Jews are being born to replace two thirds of those who are no longer in the Community – a third will disappear after a single generation." His prize-winning book was entitled *The Damage to the Race Due to Social and Economic Ascent, Especially Among the Jews of Berlin*.

Anti-Semitism alone does not explain the fact that a number of important organizations for German Jews were started during this period, some of which were *not* under the umbrella of the Community. Of course, the Association for the Combat of Anti-Semitism (1890) and the aforementioned Centralverein (1893) had been expressly founded to fight it. But this was only peripherally true of such other organizations as the Jewish student fraternities, the Bar Kochba sports club (1898) and the League of Jewish Women (1903). Independent of the fact that many "German" student bodies rejected Jews, that the "German" sports associations were "Jew free" and wanted to stay that way, there was also the deep-seated wish on the part of Jews to be with other Jews. Rather than lament that they were unwelcome in "bourgeois" associations – or that they would only be accepted with difficulty – they sought a place where they could meet as Jews.

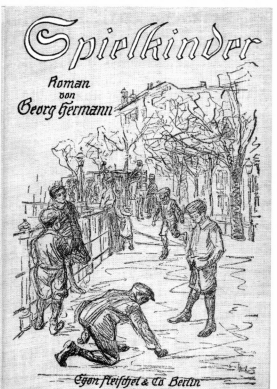

Above, left: The author Georg Hermann (1871–1943)
in a portrait by Erich Buettner ca. 1918. He was murdered by
the National Socialists. Neue Nationalgalerie Berlin.
Above, right: Samuel Fischer (1859–1934), publisher and
founder in 1886 of the S. Fischer publishing house in a
1915 portrait by Max Liebermann. Schiller National-
Museum/Deutsches Literaturarchiv, Marbach.

Below, left: Title page of Georg Hermann's novel
Children at Play, *the first edition of which appeared in 1892.*
Below, right: Poster for Gerhart Hauptmann's play
The Weavers, *which S. Fischer first published in 1892.*
This 1897 design is by Emil Orlik.

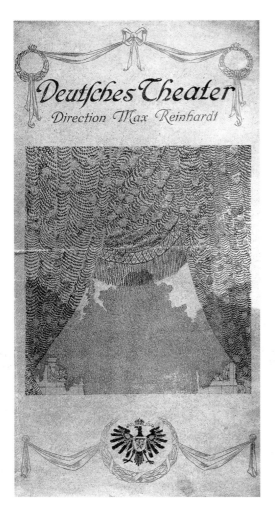

The Jews and
the Modern City

In the course of a few decades, much had changed for the Jews. As the historian Shulamit Volkov has pointed out, most of "traditional Jewry" had disappeared. There was only a small contingent of Orthodox Jews left in the city. "Instead a new and modern Jewish society grew to maturity. It had in almost every aspect new demographic parameters – social, professional, and regarding their socio-cultural identity – and it was not in a traditional, but, rather in a new sense." The Jews in Berlin lived near each other; they sought almost only the friendship of other Jews. There occurred what has been described as a "crystallization of a specific Jewish character, in many cases unbeknownst to the subject." This was evinced in an individual's choice of profession, neighborhood, and in the intimate culture of family life – for instance, in the number of children and their education. If it follows that the German Jews had formed their own intimate culture

within modern German society, it should not be overlooked that almost all other social groups went through a similar process within large cities at the time: immigrants from Silesia or Pomerania, for instance; proletarians or small businessmen; Catholics or Jews; men and women alike. In the melting pot, one became somebody special; one became a "Berliner."

On the whole, Berlin's Jews were much less concerned with religious practice and much more with the position of Jews within the German state. How were German Jews part of the larger *Staatsvolk* – the nation's people? For that purpose it formed organizations that would articulate ideas and problems using all available legal means. In many parts of Germany, the civil rights of Jews existed more on paper than they did in reality. In Prussia there were 'unwritten laws' that still made it impossible for a Jew to become a military officer or to receive a tenured professorship at a university. Even in the elementary schools Jewish teachers were restricted to mathematics and the natural sciences. History and German, in particular, were subjects deemed too important "for the cultivation of political spirit" among German youth to entrust to Jewish teachers.

Within this context, the *Interpellation* (parliamentary question) of February 1901 in the Prussian lower house was significant. The Prussian Minister of Justice, Karl Heinrich Schoenstedt, was asked why he barred Jews from becoming judges and refused to confirm "even the most worthy Jewish candidates" as public notaries. His answer: "I cannot deny the excellent qualities of Jewish notaries – their honesty, their devotion to duty, their conscientiousness. But I cannot leave unconsidered the fact that a great portion of the Christian population is greatly mistrustful of the Jews." Several Prussian Jewish communities protested this unconstitutional statement, but their protests remained unanswered by the Prussian government.

Martin Philippson, chairman of the Deutsch-Israelitische Gemeindebund (The German-Israelite Union of Congregations), described this situation in an appeal to the German Jews of 1901:

> We tried to avoid everything that made us appear as Jews to the world. We tried hard not to 'look' Jewish, not to be conspicuous. We tried hard not to remind others of our independent existence. Everybody knows what we accomplished. The anti-Semites aimed all their hate, all their invectives, all their barbarism at precisely those who were cowardly, who hid behind every available bush.

Things had to change. Philippson demanded that a *Judentag* (an Assembly of Jews) be convened to permit Jews effective political representation. This *Judentag* was to be the political body that would put into practice the promise of the equal treatment and existence of the Jews. It was never convened. In 1904, however, a private society, the Verband der Deutschen Juden (Association of German Jews) was founded to establish a representation of the Jews vis-à-vis established political institutions.

In addition to Martin Philippson and Bernhard Breslauer, both leaders of the Centralverein, the founding members were Eugen Fuchs and Maximilian Horowitz. The main, or "noblest" aim of the Verband der Deutschen Juden was to attain for the Jewish Community the same rights that were already enjoyed by the Christian churches. Their efforts were not without success. For instance, the Verband represented Germany's Jewish Communities and their employees during German parliamentary sessions between 1908 and 1913 in regard to budget deliberations and legislation on elementary school maintenance. It was through the Verband's diligent work that the parliament shelved legislation that would have prohibited kosher ritual slaughtering, and laws "enforcing the Sunday peace" (i.e., blue laws) were made less severe. Although the Verband did not, in fact, represent all Jews in a formal sense, it largely filled the goals it set for itself.

The Question of Identity

In the second half of the Wilhelmine period (roughly 1895–1918), the work of Berlin's Jewish Community was exceptionally successful. A growing number of synagogues, hospitals, old-age homes, and other institutions enhanced the reputation of Berlin's Jews, not only in Germany but, indeed, worldwide. No other city could compare in the stature of its Jews with the capital of the German Reich. Berlin had become the undisputed center of German Jewry. All the important Jewish organizations in the country had their headquarters in the capital.

Above: The Berlin Secession, founded in 1893 by Max Liebermann, had its second exhibition in the summer of 1900. The design for this poster is by Schulz.

Right: Portrait of Paul Cassirer (1871–1926), publisher and art dealer, by Leopold von Kalckreuth.

Invitation to Paul Cassirer's salon in 1902. Cassirer, who introduced the French impressionists to Germany, was also the honorary chairman of the Berliner Secession, which contributed to the success of his salon.

Only Jewish Orthodoxy, which concentrated its forces in Frankfurt-am-Main and Halberstadt, was an exception.

Within Berlin's Jewish Community, however, considerable tensions still existed, perhaps with less intensity than earlier, but nonetheless with equal constancy. In 1898 the radical Reformfreunde (Friends of Reform) started agitating for the transfer of the public Sabbath services from Saturday to Sunday, so that those working on Saturdays could also participate. This was opposed not only by Orthodox Jews but also by moderate liberals. The rabbis and a majority in the Community's Representative Assembly vehemently opposed such a "mongrel Sabbath."

A decade later another attempt was made to introduce religious liberalism. The founding in 1908 of the Association for Liberal Judaism in Germany set up a commission of rabbis and educated laymen to draw up religious guidelines. The resulting draft postulated three unalterable articles of the Jewish faith: the dogma of a single God of pure spirituality, justice and love; the similarity of man to God as the bearer of striving to attain eternal perfection; and the dogma of the unity of mankind as all the children of God, leading toward the realization of the messianic ideal of peace and justice on earth. "Regarding the rules of ritual, the draft left untouched only those laws relating to circumcision and the observance of the Sabbath and holy days. Whereas for prayer it would be possible to have simultaneous services in Hebrew and German." Perceived as a portent of potential religious schism, the draft was rejected in 1912.

In the years leading up to World War I, the Jewish Community faced a range of new demands, some of which proved challenging. Demographically, there was the problem of Ostjuden (eastern European Jews) who came from Galicia, Russia, Poland, Romania and Hungary and either traveled through Berlin or were living there permanently. Culturally, the movement known as the "Jewish Renaissance" arose, questioning the assimilationist tendencies of the liberal German Jewish "Establishment." And politically, Zionists were proclaiming that Jews constituted a nation and were calling for a Jewish state.

The majority of Berlin's Jews believed that it was possible to lead a dual existence as both Jews and Germans. Moritz Heimann, chief editor of the S. Fischer publishing house, formulated it thus: "It is not unnatural for a body to have an orbit with two centers. Several comets do it, and so do many planets." Several younger Jews, however, argued vigorously about this point. The Bar Kochba sports club, founded October 22, 1898, furnishes a good example of this. All 48 founding members were agreed that they had founded an independent club for sports and gymnastics for Jews. The quarrel began when they started to talk about the club's "tendency." Some wanted a "Zionist" club, others a "neutral" sports club for Jews. The members finally decided to make the "care of the national Jewish idea" a fundamental tenet of their club. Apparently they were united in thinking that Jewry was based on a common heritage and history, but not exclusively on the basis of a common religion, "although it has its peculiar character of spirit and soul and has maintained its feeling of togetherness up to the present day."

Ostjuden in Berlin

For the "proud, Germanized Jews of the West" it was easy to see who was an Ostjude (a Jew from eastern Europe) and who was not. Georg Klemperer, himself a convert to Christianity, wrote: "Posen is not a place one

Various Jewish newspapers,
January to March 1903.

goes, only a place from which one comes!" The Jews arriving in Berlin from eastern Europe only served to remind the German Jews of their origins. According to the historian Shulamit Volkov, the *Ostjuden* were blamed by their German counterparts for keeping alive "the negative image of Jews." They represented "everything that the assimilated Jews did not want to be, which deepened and hastened their alienation from Judaism." It was felt that eastern Jews threatened the survival of the social and cultural identity of those Jews who had been living in Germany for some time already, and various German Jewish organizations tried to limit the influx of Jews from eastern Europe.

Statistics for Berlin in 1910 show where particular groups of *Ostjuden* lived. Of the 12,955 *Ostjuden* living in Berlin and in five important suburbs (the future Greater Berlin), some 6,098 were from Galicia, 3,606 from Russia and 550 from Romania; Charlottenburg (not yet part of Greater Berlin) had only 265 Galician Jews and 154 Romanian Jews but over 1,000 Russian Jews. In Wilmersdorf (another city not yet incorporated into Greater Berlin), the situation was similar: 186 from Galicia, 35 from Romania and 446 from Russia.

Professionally, too, the means with which these Jews earned a living was related to their country and region of origin. The 1910 statistics provided on the 6,153 *Ostjuden* employed in the main fields of trade, industry and the "free professions" showed that 45 percent of those in trade were Galicians, while only 35 percent were Russians. In industry, 50 percent were Russians and 57 percent were Galicians. In the free professions (such as law, journalism, and medicine) the percentages were very small for both groups:

Darwinistisches.

Wie sich der Chanukaleuchler des Ziegenfellhändlers **Cohn** in Pinne zum Christbaum des Kommerzienrats **Conrad** in der Tiergartenstraße (Berlin W.) entwickelte.

Zionist caricature from Schlemiel, *January 1904 protesting the assimilation of German Jews. It shows the evolution of a menorah owned by the goatskin dealer Cohn into the Christmas tree of Big-Businessman Conrad.*

A self-portrait of the graphic artist Ephraim Mose Lilien (1874–1925), one of the founders of the Juedischer Verlag.

The founders of the Juedischer Verlag *ca. 1902. The writer Berthold Feiwel (born 1875) sitting in front of Ephraim Mose Lilien. Chaim Weizmann (1874–1952), biochemist and later first President of Israel; Martin Buber (1878–1965), philosopher of religion; and Leo Motzkin (1867–1933), later a leading Zionist activist.*

JVEDISCHER
ALMANACH

JVEDISCHER VERLAG BERLIN

Left: Cover of the Jewish Almanac, *published in 1904.*

Right: Title page of the Zionist tract "Auto-Emancipation," by Juda Loeb Pinsker (1821–1892), published in Berlin in 1882.

„Autoemancipation!"

Mahnruf an seine Stammesgenossen

von

einem russischen Juden.

Berlin SW.
Commissions-Verlag von W. Issleib (G. Schuhr).
1882.

2 percent Galicians and 12 percent Russians. In his study of *Ostjuden* in Germany, Shalom Adler-Rudel points to the fact that the influx of Jews from eastern Europe essentially changed the demographic-professional tilt of the statistics. The proportion of Jews employed in the handicrafts grew, while the percentage of those engaged in trade and commerce declined. *Ostjuden* also contributed to an increase in the number of rabbis, teachers, kosher butchers, cantors, Torah scribes and typesetters of Hebrew.

Socially, however, the Jews of eastern Europe had very little contact with the majority of German Jews. Apart from their common legal obligation to belong to the Jewish Community and thus pay the appropriate taxes, the mostly liberal German Jews took little notice of the foreign Jews in their midst. Of course the Orthodox German Jews were more closely connected to their Galician counterparts; both shared a traditional understanding of the faith; the arrival of more religious Jews from the east served, in part, to reinforce the conservative minority within the Jewish Community.

The other – albeit relatively insignificant – group within German Jewry to occasionally speak up for *Ostjuden* were the members of the Zionist movement. They had a more friendly and positive attitude, but aside from that had no strong personal ties. Until the beginning of World War I, not a single non-German Jew belonged to the leadership of the Zionist movement in Germany. The historian Adler-Rudel concludes that "the role of foreign [that is, non-German speaking] Jews within Zionism seems to have consisted of filling seats at Zionist rallies and providing an audience for young Zionist speakers to address."

Thus it was that the majority of foreign Jews – small tradesmen, shoemakers, tailors, watchmakers, cigar makers, beggars, etc. –

could fall back on nobody but themselves. They made and consumed their own produce and culture and carried on in the traditions of the villages and towns from which they had come. Even then, there were differences among them that prevented their forming a homogenous group. The Galician merchants had, for example, little in common with Russian cigar makers, and Russian tailors had little in common with Romanian peddlers.

Berlin's so-called *Scheunenviertel* (or "barn quarter") in the Mitte district had something of a special character. It was a place for the poor, a neighborhood of the down-and-out, and had, furthermore, a reputation for petty crime and prostitution. Jews from Russia and Austria-Hungary began to move to this quarter in the 1880s. Although the *Ostjuden* gave the quarter a special flavor, the *Scheunenviertel* never took on the character of a ghetto. The eastern Jews were able to live their lives and maintain their habits as they wished, regardless of what their non-Jewish neighbors thought of them.

As difficult as it was for the "establishment" within the Jewish Community to deal with *Ostjuden*, many younger members were attracted to them. They created a kind of cult that encompassed everything related to eastern European Jewry. Martin Buber's books on Chassidism were widely read. His *Tales of Rabbi Nachman* and *Legend of Baal-schem* made Buber famous. "In each Jew we met from Russia, Poland, Galicia," recalled Gershom Scholem in his memoirs, "we saw something like an incarnation of Baal-schem; [we saw] in any case, the essence of an unaltered and fascinating Jewishness."

The Search for Origins

For many decades there had been an interest in tracing the sources, or origins, of Judaism. This was the main goal of the Hochschule der Wissenschaft vom Judentum (College for the Training in the Science of Judaism), and it remained an important part of the work there. Nevertheless, it was for a long time uncertain what this search entailed. The orientalist and bibliographer Moritz Steinschneider, one of the Hochschule's major proponents, is reported (by Gershom Scholem) to have declared: "We have nothing left to do but give the remains of Judaism a decent burial." Now it became the task to revive the sources, to return the Jews to the culture of their past and to rescue it from oblivion. Three enterprises deserve special mention in this regard: The publishing house Der Juedische Verlag, the magazine *Der Jude* and the illustrated monthly for modern Judaism *Ost und West*. It was here that Martin Buber published his thesis on the "Jewish Renaissance" and his appeals for a national Jewish art. In the first year, 1901, there were essays on "The Jewish gymnastics movement," "Traces of Jews in the Alps," poems by Else Lasker-Schueler and an essay by the artist Lesser Ury entitled "Thoughts on Jewish Art."

This interest in beginnings, this search for origins and sources, was by no means exclusively Jewish. The notion of *Volk* – and with it, the *Voelkische* – were generally quite popular, particularly among the Germans for whom such terms as "Germanness" had become fashionable. It was, therefore, as part of the general spirit of the times that the Jews were hoping for and looking for a cultural renaissance. At the Fifth Zionist Congress in Basel in 1901, Martin Buber gave voice to these longings. With the artist Ephraim

Above: head of the Zionist newspaper Die Welt.
*Below: Members of the Zionist sports club
Bar Kochba, in Berlin, ca. 1904.*

Mose Lilien, he had organized an exhibition of works by Jewish artists. The exhibition was successful, but especially memorable was Buber's opening speech. The speech was to signal the cultural rebirth of the Jewish people.

Buber appealed to the Jews to "accept the past in the interest of a dreamt future." He demanded that they make themselves familiar with the Jewish creations of the past in order to recognize them as "partial representation of a great process of renaissance." In its "aestheticism, its reception of Nietzsche, and its high respect for the Jews of eastern Europe," Buber's "Jewish movement" was self-confidently setting itself against the establishment of German Jewry. It sought a Jewish *Gemeinschaft* (the community as a whole, itself distinct from the the legal entity of Community). It sought a Jewish answer to the question of how it would be possible "to live as a Jew" in the modern world.

Even if this movement found only a faint echo among the Jews of Germany – more precisely, of Berlin – it nevertheless had some surprising effects on the art of the twentieth century. It led to more than just the understanding that it is rewarding and sensible to preserve certain aspects of the past – for instance in the way of building synagogues, in the way of arranging and decorating the prayer rooms and in the music for choir and organ. Several of the debate's most popular concepts were quickly forgotten. The effects of others, however, would be visible throughout the century. Among them were: Race, *Volk,* Blood, Origin, and Earth. These concepts were not very precise, but for Jews and Gentiles alike, they were often emotionally freighted.

Buber's aim was to bring about the revival of everything Jewish that had seemed lost for centuries. His search for origins encompassed the Kabbala, Jewish mysticism, old myths and legends, Chassidic stories. Moreover, he explored the Jewish present, especially the work of Jewish artists. In conjunction with the Zionist congress, he edited the book *Jewish Artists,* in which six writers addressed the "specific Jewishness" of six artists: Fritz Stahl wrote about Jozef Israel; Alfred Gold about Ephraim Mose Lilien; Georg Hermann about Max Liebermann; S. L. Bensusan about Solomon J. Solomon; Franz Servaes about Jehudo Epstein; and Buber himself wrote about Lesser Ury. Two of these six artists (Ury and Liebermann) were from Berlin. Buber wrote with committment and empathy about Ury's paintings. Still, the specific "Jewishness" of the art remained difficult to grasp. Buber described a "longing struggle for unlimitedness" and a "feeling of the limitless unity of the world." These, he wrote, "have for all time been the fundamental powers of the Jewish people." Buber saw Ury as a stormy prophet of "restless unendingness."

The answer to the Jewish Renaissance would come much later from a man who had devoted his life to delving into the history of the Jews, and the history of its mystics in particular. Gershom Scholem, as his biographer David Biale has shown, sought a third way between the rationalism of the "Science of Judaism" and Martin Buber's irrationalism. Scholem's "third way" was aimed at avoiding what Nietzsche had called "monumental historiography," namely, "to create historic myths to strengthen the chauvinist goals of the contemporary nation."

Zionism in Berlin

Topics relating to the Jewish Renaissance were often grouped under the heading "cultural Zionism," which was not difficult to understand at the time, inasmuch as Zionism had not yet received an exclusively politically definition. At any rate, an intense new debate broke out over whether or not Jews were Germans and whether or not they did or did not belong to German culture.

As has already been mentioned, Berlin's Jews had long made their importance felt in many areas. In the free professions – especially in medicine and law – they were proportionally dominant, and they were internationally acclaimed for their achievements in the sciences. Many outstanding writers, journalists, and publishers were Jewish, more so in Berlin than anywhere else. This cultural dominance enabled a Jewish scholar of German literature named Moritz Goldstein to maintain polemically: "We Jews are administering the spiritual property of a nation that denies our right and our ability to do so." According to Goldstein, German Jews were fighting a war on two fronts. On one side, they fought against the "envious German-Christian-Germanic idiots." On the other, they faced "even worse enemies": namely, those assimilationist Jews "who notice nothing, who continually produce German culture, who play make-believe and try to make themselves unrecognizable . . . Such [assimilated Jews] should be removed from their posts, wherever they are. They are falsely representing Jewry."

Goldstein was a Zionist, and he opposed German Jewry whenever and wherever he could. He continually asked himself and other Jews in Germany the question: "Where do we go from here?" His own answer: "I would follow my instincts and leave. I would no longer like to be hated. I would give all my talents to those who are ready to use them and bring them where the people are ready to use them. If I only knew where that was!" Goldstein's writings make it clear that, in these years, the answers that Zionism provided found only slight resonance among most Jews. Zionism, as reinforced at the end of the nineteenth century by Theodor Herzl, had only a small following among the Jewish notables of Berlin. While it is true that many Berlin Jews had followed the Dreyfus Affair in France with alarm, most felt that they could trust the German legal system.

Thus, Zionism – at least in its early phase – did not take hold in Berlin. Herzl himself had great difficulties spreading the Zionist mission in Germany. In Berlin, even his small number of supporters was splintered by rivalries and often seemed incapable of harmony. One thing is quite certain, however. Berlin's Zionists were not interested in what they called "political Zionism." They had no desire, at least at this time, to orient themselves toward Palestine. They saw themselves first and foremost as "cultural Zionists," a concept introduced by Buber but felt to mean different things to different people. In 1912, Walter Benjamin wrote of a "Zionism of the spirit," in conscious opposition to political and cultural Zionism, in his letters to Ludwig Strauss.

Although concrete figures for Berlin in the following years are lacking, it is possible to see that both the quantity and quality of the Zionist movement grew. In 1903, there were 4,500 members in the German Reich, in 1911, 7,800, and in 1912–13, there were 8,900. Berlin sent 290 members to the Third Zionist Congress in 1899. It did not escape the notice of some of the older members that the younger generation frequently voiced both questions of Jewish identity and concerns about the future's uncertainty.

Identity crisis was characteristic of society as a whole during this period. So were clashes between generations, dissatisfaction with the present and fear of the future. Jews were no different from the general population in this respect. To the "establishment" within the Jewish Community, Zionism proved unsettling. Not only did it question the Germanness of German Jews, it rejected their Germanness entirely. In that respect, Zionists were seen by many to be on equal footing with the anti-Semites.

In the years between 1900 and 1910 the Jewish Community of Berlin and the leadership of the major Jewish organizations were relatively indifferent to the Zionist movement – at least at the outset. Later they showed concern. This was the background for the suspension, in 1907, of a young rabbi named Emil Bernhard Cohn by the Community's board of directors; the board based its decision on the claim that Cohn had not kept a promise that he would not openly embrace Zionism. The "Cohn Affair" was for many months the major theme of the Jewish press, both in Germany and abroad. But neither campaigns in the Zionist press nor protest rallies were able to reverse the board's decision. The strict methods of the Berlin board and, more importantly, the suggestion by Rabbi Heinemann Vogelstein to boycott Zionist rabbis and teachers in general, prove that the Cohn Affair was not a locally limited conflict. This incident brought to light even more tensions, and the increasing pressure of the Zionist movement would become more visible in the years ahead.

The headquarters of the World Zionist Organization were relocated to Berlin in 1911, and Otto Warburg was elected its president. The botanist from Berlin (with a specialty in tropical plants) was a figure of international reputation. Early on he had proven his interest in Jewish settlements in Palestine. Many support programs could be traced to his initiative: the Olive Tree Contribution of the Jewish National Fund (1904); the arts-and-crafts school of Bezalel in Jerusalem (1905); and the agricultural experiment station in Atlit (1911).

In the last years before World War I, Zionism was able to gain respect and supporters. In 1912 the Zionist Union for Germany at its congress in Posen forced the Jews of Berlin to take a position. The Union decided that all its members had to embrace the personal program of "emigration and settlement in Palestine." This was more than the Berlin Jews could stand. In 1913, the Berlin-based Centralverein issued the following statement: "We cannot, however, claim unity with the Zionist, who denies his German national feeling, who considers himself to be a guest among a foreign host people (*Wirtsvolk*) and whose national sentiment is exclusively Jewish."

War and Patriotism

On August 1, 1914, the Association of German Jews, together with the Centralverein, printed a proclamation on the first page of the *Gemeindeblatt der Juedische Gemeinde* (The newsletter of Berlin's Jewish Community): "In this hour of destiny, our fatherland calls its sons to arms. It goes without saying that every German Jew is prepared to sacrifice his life and property as duty demands. Fellow Jews! We summon you to dedicate your energy beyond duty to the fatherland. Run quickly to enlist. All of you – men and women – must do what you personally can and help with money and property and service to the fatherland." Jews who considered themselves German and Zionists alike answered the appeal.

Rabbi Leo Baeck compiled a Jewish prayer book for Jewish soldiers fighting on the front. For the war, a special passage was inserted into the traditional prayer for leaders, a prayer for the Kaiser: "Bless the brave sons of our people who have gone to the front to fight for Germany's right and honor! Let them fulfil loyally and with joyful obedience their sacred duty to defend their fatherland with firm confidence in Your support, and may they return victorious to their homes one day!" Louis Sachs, the leader of Berlin's Jewish Community, declared in the Asssembly of Representatives: "May hostile threats and trickery break upon the mighty rock of German loyalty and German bravery!" His remark received much applause.

The first war issue of the *Gemeindeblatt* reported that one of the employees of the

Abonnements

auf die wöchentlich am Freitag erscheinende „Jüdische Rundschau" kosten bei der Expedition und bei allen Postanstalten vierteljährlich 1,50 M., außerhalb Deutschlands und Oesterreich-Ungarns 2,— M.; für Mitglieder jüdischer Vereine im Sammelbezug durch den Verein 1,— M.

Jüdische Rundschau, G. m. b. H. BERLIN W. 15, Sächsische Straße 8. Telephon: Amt Uhland 845, 846, 868 Postscheckkonto: Berlin Nr. 17392.

JUEDISCHE RUNDSCHAU
ALLGEMEINE JUEDISCHE ZEITUNG

Anzeigen

kosten für die sechsgespaltene Petitzeile oder deren Raum 40 Pf.; Stellen-Angebote und -Gesuche sowie Vereins-Mitteilungen und „Kleine Anzeigen" o o o o nur 30 Pfennig. o o o o Manuskripte werden, wenn Porto beiliegt, stets zurückgesandt. Redaktionsschluß: Mittwoch vormittags.

Redaktion Jüdische Rundschau BERLIN W. 15, Sächsische Straße 8. Telephon: Amt Uhland 845, 846, 868. Postscheckkonto: Berlin Nr. 17392.

Nummer 32 — Berlin, den 7. August 1914 — 15. Ab 5674 — XIX. Jahrgang.

„Der Zionismus erstrebt für das jüdische Volk die Schaffung einer öffentlich-rechtlich gesicherten Heimstätte in Palästina." Baseler Programm

Deutsche Juden!

In dieser Stunde gilt es für uns aufs neue zu zeigen, dass wir stammesstolzen Juden zu den besten Söhnen des Vaterlandes gehören. Der Adel unserer vieltausendjährigen Geschichte verpflichtet.

Wir erwarten, daß unsere Jugend freudigen Herzens freiwillig zu den Fahnen eilt.

Deutsche Juden!

Wir rufen Euch auf, im Sinne des alten jüdischen Pflichtgebots mit ganzem Herzen, ganzer Seele und ganzem Vermögen Euch dem Dienste des Vaterlandes hinzugeben.

Der Reichsverein der Deutschen Juden   **Zionistische Vereinigung für Deutschland**

*

*   *

Wir schließen uns dem Aufruf des Reichsvereins der Deutschen Juden und der Zionistischen Vereinigung für Deutschland an.

Wir vertrauen, daß unsere Jugend, durch die Pflege jüdischen Bewußtseins und körperliche Ausbildung in idealer Gesinnung und Mannesmut erstarkt, sich in allen kriegerischen Tugenden auszeichnen wird.

Das Präsidium des Kartells Jüdischer Verbindungen
Der Ausschuß der Jüdischen Turnerschaft

Title, headline and clipping from newspaper Juedische Rundschau *from August 7, 1914, with the appeal by Jewish organizers to Jewish men to volunteer for military service.*

Community, Adolf Schrauer, had already died "the hero's death for his fatherland" on September 16, 1914. It was also proudly reported that the Community teacher Gottfried Sender and the pallbearer Adolf Kantorowicz had been awarded the Iron Cross. A draft of a resolution was circulated within the Assembly of Representatives that Berlin's synagogues be flagged whenever victory bulletins were received. Leo Baeck's reports of his work as a rabbi on the front could be read in the *Gemeindeblatt.*

The majority of German Jews reacted to the news of the war as all the other Germans did: the young rushed to enlist, and the older citizens waited eagerly for victory bulletins.

Left:
The Berlin lawyer
Hermann Jalowicz (1877–1941)
as a soldier in World War I.

Right page:
Berliners cheering Wilhelm II
after the declaration of war
on August 1, 1914.

rected his statement to the Jews specifically, it [nonetheless] inspired enthusiastic jubilation among them."

On August 4, 1914, the Kaiser concluded his speech with a request: "As proof of those who are firmly committed to stand together without regard to their party affiliations, their status or religion, for better or worse, through death and want, I expect their leaders to step forward and solemnly extend their hands to me." Whereupon the representative of Berlin's Jewish Community, Max Rothmann, swore loyalty to the Kaiser on behalf of his Jewish brethren. One of his sons had earlier tried gain entrance into the Prussian corps of cadets – in vain, it turned out, since the schools were officially considered "institutions for teaching Christian values." Rothmann's oldest son was killed in October 1914, "one of the first volunteers of his regiment."

The truce applied to the Community as well. Elections were held by consensus: "In the period of the great World War all differences and causes of irritation among the various factions within the Community should disappear." And, indeed, they all held to this dictum. On February 3, 1915, the *Juedische Rundschau*, the German Zionist newspaper, declared: "We entered the war not because we were Jews, but because we were Zionists." Many Jews also felt that the truce was observed with respect to outbreaks of anti-Semitism. Outwardly everything appeared to

Gershom Scholem recalled that "there was a definite line of division in the attitudes toward the war," but also that there was hardly any opposition. Berlin's Jews were no less patriotic than the Germans around them. They, too, were caught up in the general mood and honored the Kaiser's proclamation of a *Burgfrieden* (truce) among all factions within political parties, associations, clubs and religious faiths. This "truce" gave more buoyancy to the Jews than any other event since the proclamation of equality in 1869. The historian Peter Pulzer writes: "The words of the Kaiser – 'I no longer recognize political parties, I only recognize Germans' – were an offer of reconciliation. Though he had not di-

be going well. The earlier and onerous restrictions on Jews in the military were suspended: Jews could now become officers. From the very beginning of the war the "traditional" discriminations were gone. Many Jews saw it as a meaningful sign that the Ministry of War had selected a Jew, Walther Rathenau, to head the Department of Military Raw Materials. For German Jews, the war was the venue for them to demonstrate their patriotism and their love of the Reich. The general enthusiasm for the war and for the common interest that gripped the entire country also gripped the Jews.

War and the Welfare of Eastern European Jews

Aside from its contribution to the war effort the Jewish Community as an institution had to deal with many other questions. It was an economic entity of great importance and simultaneously an organization with many employees. It had to administer hospitals and clinics, homes for orphans and the aged, cemeteries and places for the poor. Held together by a broad network of volunteers, thirty commissions participated in decisions that covered all aspects of welfare. During the war everything was concentrated on the measures designed to fight and win. For that reason, it was hardly possible to work on internal reforms. As long as the war went on, the Community's priority was to secure the funding necessary "for our brave soldiers and their dependents." Extra expenditures for the war and the decline in taxes placed a heavy burden on its budget. The heads of the Community nevertheless "held it to be their honorable duty to prove their patriotism on all fronts."

The war caused major problems for the eastern European Jews living in Berlin. Galician Jews were citizens of Austria-Hungary and therefore had to do their military service there. Many had to give up what they had worked so hard for in Berlin. Russian Jews had a worse fate; they were interned in camps as "enemy aliens." In contrast to the German government's measures toward Russian Jews was its attempt to win over the sympathy of Jews living in Poland. An appeal by the general commands of the United Armies of Germany and Austria in September 1914 was widely distributed in Yiddish and in Hebrew. It read, in part: "We come to you as friends and saviors. Our flags will bring you freedom and the rule of law."

Not only the German High Command but also large numbers of German Jews discovered their "love of *Ostjuden*" at this time. The German Committee for the Liberation of Russian Jews, initiated by Max Bodenheimer and Franz Oppenheimer, was founded in Berlin at the end of August 1914. Many Jewish groups thought that the composition of the committee was not evenly balanced and negotiations were conducted to enlarge and reorganize it. The result was the founding of a Committee for the East in January 1915, whose aim was to mediate between the Central European Powers and the Jews of eastern Europe as well as the neutral nations.

At the same time that hundreds of thousands of Jews in the occupied countries were

jobless and threatened by hunger, there was a general labor shortage in Germany. This prompted the German authorities to recruit workers in the east. The conduct of this recruitment was placed in the hands of the semi-official Deutsche Arbeiterzentrale (German Labor Agency), an organization that had, before the war, organized seasonal harvest workers for German farms. During the war, nobody – not even the unions – felt concern about the working conditions of these foreign workers. Thus it came about that about 15,000 Jewish laborers, who had come to Germany from the east and – because they spoke Yiddish – had been able to integrate themselves fairly easily, were loosely organized in Germany into a "black labor market," especially in Berlin. It was not until December 1916 that the German government took measures to make their conditions somewhat more tolerable. In 1917 a Jewish section of the German Labor Agency was organized in Warsaw. Its task was to make sure that eastern European Jews were protected "in a reasonable way."

As the war went on, people started talking about the "specter of an eastern European Jewish danger," more precisely about the danger that masses of *Ostjuden* would flood Germany once the war was over. Recruiting them was regarded by many to be the beginning of a mass migration, and for that reason many demanded that the borders be closed to them. This, of course, prompted a hue and cry within Jewish circles. The philosopher and politician Gustav Landauer took these policies to task in a widely distributed article "East European Jews and the German Empire" for the periodical *Der Jude*. The protests, however, were of little avail. On April 23, 1918, the Prussian government closed the borders to Polish-Jewish laborers, thereby completely prohibiting the recruitment of Jewish laborers for Germany. The pretext for this anti-Semitic law against foreigners was preposterous: that the Jews would bring spotted fever into Germany.

With a wave of Jewish immigrants from Poland, the Jewish Community of Berlin was faced with new problems, and it was only with great difficulty that some of them could be solved. The group formed to care for mendicants was especially hard-pressed, since it had to address the cares and problems of Jews who came to Berlin as "guest-workers" as well.

In the third year of the war, on September 9, 1917, the Central Welfare Committee for the German Jews was founded to solve the problems caused by the influx of eastern European Jews. It combined the German-Israelite Union of Congregations with the Grand Lodge of Bne Briss and the Jewish Women's Union. Bertha Pappenheim was its initiator, chairwoman, and *spiritus rector*. It was her idea to combine the Jewish welfare institutions in order to provide help more effectively.

The *Judenzaehlung* (Counting the Jews)

As soon as the war enthusiasm flagged, a new awareness arose based on the experiences of the war itself. The beginning had brought nothing but news of German victories; soon the armies were bogged down in the trenches. The "spirit of 1914" quickly vanished and gave way to the old prejudices. The search for a scapegoat began. Ugly prejudices and anti-Semitic clichés reappeared. They found expression in the attitude toward the labor potential of *Ostjuden*; in the hate-tirades against giving Jews "good jobs;" in the reproach that Jews were "goldbrickers"; and in an episode that came to be known as the

Judenzaehlung (the Counting of the Jews). In the opinion of historian Golo Mann, anti-Semitism at the end of the Wilhelmine era (1918–19) was stronger and more fanatic than it was at the time the National Socialists took power in 1933.

The *Judenzaehlung* amounted to a hypocritical question of whether the Jews were shouldering their share of the war burden. A survey was ordered to investigate "how many Jews, and in what positions, were serving on the front?" The question itself was an act of anti-Semitism and was perceived as such. Ernst Simon recorded the mood of the Jews when they were informed of the survey: "Everybody thought that we were foreign, that we alone had to stand aside, to be singled-out and counted, registered and treated. Our dream of commonality was gone. With one terrible blow we realized that there was once again a deep gulf between us and the Germans, a gulf that we had considered long gone."

The administrators of the *Judenzaehlung* selected the date of November 1, 1916, as the point of reference. The count was made among the soldiers at the front, at the rear, those in the occupying forces and those in training. The result, however, was never officially made public. The reasons for this are not really known, but it cannot be dismissed that the statistics would have allowed varying interpretations, inasmuch as all the numbers relating to non-Jewish soldiers were lacking. Results or no, the psychological effects of the count were devastating. For years, anti-Semites maintained that Jews had shied away from military service in general and service on the front in particular.

To date there has been no serious attempt to study the Berlin Jews during World War I. There are, however, statistics for Germany as a whole. When the war began in 1914, 50,000 Jews were eligible for military service,

Kriegsbriefe
gefallener Deutscher Juden

Herausgegeben vom
Reichsbund Jüdischer Frontsoldaten E.V.

Mit einer Zeichnung von Max Liebermann

RjF

1 9 3 5

Vortrupp Verlag / Berlin SW 29

Above:
The title page of
Letters of German Jews Killed During the War,
published by the Reichs Union
of Jewish Front Soldiers two years
after the Nazis had assumed power. The book was
published by the Vortrupp Verlag in 1935
and featured a drawing by
Max Liebermann.

Below:
Flyer of the Reichs Union of Jewish Front Soldiers.
It announces that 12,000 Jews were killed
in World War I and appeals
to German mothers to not allow that
"Jewish mothers are scorned in their pain."

AN DIE DEUTSCHEN MÜTTER!

72 000 jüdische Soldaten sind für das Vaterland auf dem Felde der Ehre gefallen

Christliche und jüdische Helden haben gemeinsam gekämpft und ruhen gemeinsam in fremder Erde.

12 000 Juden fielen im Kampf !

Blindwütiger Parteihass macht vor den Gräbern der Toten nicht Halt.

Deutsche Frauen,

duldet nicht, dass die jüdische Mutter in ihrem Schmerz verhöhnt wird.

Reichsbund jüdischer Frontsoldaten E.V.

and it is fair to assume that a similar number may be added to that for each of the four years that followed. That would mean that 17 percent of all German Jews served in the German Army during the war. Around 4,000 of them were promoted to the rank of officer. It is known that 1,500 Jews received the Iron Cross, First Class, and that tens of thousands of Jews were awarded the Iron Cross, Second Class. During World War I more than 12,000 Jews were killed in action of whom 1,917 were from Berlin.

The *Judenzaehlung* produced a deep impression on German Jews. It was a sign that the "truce" would not last much longer. The next Minister of War was obliged to withdraw the order for the count, admitting that "the conduct of Jewish soldiers and citizens during the war gave my predecessor no cause to demand the survey." This declaration so impressed the Verband der deutschen Juden (Association of German Jews) that it immediately sent a patriotic telegram to the Kaiser claiming that without Germany's glory and greatness a "true German Jew" could not "live, or even breathe."

The change in consciousness that took place during the war was, in fact, general, but it had varying results. For most Berlin Jews the war brought, perhaps, new knowledge, but it did not bring about a consciousness that their lives would change. Only few Jews realized that they would be more directly confronted with anti-Semitism than in the past. Others were deeply affected by their first contacts with Jews from eastern Europe. There were many personal and objective reasons for German Jews – even those who, in normal times, had placed little value in their belonging to Judaism – to take a decidedly Jewish position.

The newly awakened interest in Judaism, in Jewish religion and science, in the linguistic connections between Yiddish and German, in the political, social and economic problems of the *Ostjuden,* went far beyond Jewish circles and encompassed many non-Jewish Germans as well. Parallel to the public treatment of the question of the *Ostjuden,* a private transformation, barely noticeable in public, was taking place: the return of a large number of younger Jews to Judaism. Before the war, many of them had belonged to Zionist student associations. Others had had hardly any relationship to their Jewishness before they encountered *Ostjuden* for the first time on the front. Many were put off. Repelled by a picture of dirt and poverty that had been worsened by war, they rejected anything to do with the eastern Jews. Others, however, were deeply affected by what Martin Buber called the "strength and *Innerlichkeit* (inwardness), the faith in God and the idealism to be found, beneath a crust of need and poverty, in this throng [of people]."

For Martin Buber, the war and their common war experiences helped Jews forge a "community of destiny." The war had given the "disoriented Jews of the West" a new form of self-confidence. Buber named his new periodical *Der Jude*:

> We have given to our magazine the same name [as our people], but we do not mean the individual Jew, but the Jew as carrier of Judaism (*Volkstum*) and of its mission. We do not demand freedom of conscience on behalf of the members of a faith, but freedom to live and work for a community of people long held down, treated today like a powerless object of circumstances: that they be free subjects of their destiny and of their works. . . . To struggle for this freedom, that is the motto of *our* war.

Toward the end of the war, the writer Georg Hermann drew his own conclusions for German Jewry from the war experience and omnipresent anti-Semitism:

And slowly, in the course of five years, with each new disappointment . . . the scales of *Deutschtum* rose and those of *Judentum* fell ever faster. . . . We were greatly disappointed by the Germans, and our disappointment grows by the hour. Allow me a frank and perhaps harsh word – why be silent? Why keep it secret? The Germans have shown themselves to be bad keepers of the seal of humanity.

Martin Buber. Georg Hermann. Ernst Simon. These are sonorous names in the Jewish world of the twentieth century. Their opinions and their lives affected many young Jews of their time. They did not, however, represent the majority of German Jews. Even their supporters within the Jewish Community of Berlin formed a minority. But they articulated an awareness that was more and more felt, especially by the young Gershom Scholem:

> It is only fair to say that we were a very, very tiny group, which – in its spiritual attitude and with increasing knowledge of Judaism – was driven into a very sharp and perhaps even extreme criticism of German Jewry, as we saw and felt it. . . . We all had the common conviction that the overwhelming majority of our Jewish environment lived in a vacuum and – even more difficult and, for us, more exciting – in a state of self-delusion, in which they held fast to their illusions and thought they saw a harmony between Jews and Germans that did not in fact exist.

The End of Empire

Marcus Melchior, who would later become chief rabbi of Denmark, reported the events of November 9, 1918, the day of Kaiser Wilhelm II's abdication. Many Jews had assembled in the synagogue of Adass Jisroel. Apparently all the other rabbis had agreed to expunge the words "prayer for Kaiser and fatherland" from the daily liturgy. Rabbi Esra Munk of the Adass Jisroel congregation opposed the idea. He was a "patriot down to his fingertips," and for him "love of the fatherland was identical to love of a hereditary kingdom and Kaiser." Rabbi Munk cited 1 Samuel. 15, which recounts how the Prophet Samuel, in God's rage, rejected King Saul as the King of Israel in order to give Israel a new king, namely David. Saul begged the prophet: "I have sinned: yet honor me now, I pray thee, before the elders of my people, and before Israel, and turn again with me, that I may worship the LORD thy God." The prophet fulfilled Saul's wish that the people of Israel not learn of his humiliation. Rabbi Munk concluded the story with the words: "In this sense let us now say a prayer for the Kaiser and his family."

A few days after power changed hands, Julius Stern, then leader of the Jewish Community in Berlin, declared to the Assembly of Representatives that "it would be arrogant to predict the future for our people and our fatherland. . . . It should be clear by now that the status of our Community and the status of Jews in Germany will undergo some fundamental changes." For the Jews of Berlin, who had been so successful for so long, the political and social conditions changed fundamentally. During the war, the entire nation had fallen from great prosperity and to an economic and a social low. The social system was breaking down. This affected the Jews as it affected all others. The social fabric of the Wilhelmine era was falling apart. An integral component of this fabric, the Jews would be hit especially hard by Germany's breakdown.

Chana C. Schütz

THE WEIMAR YEARS
(1919–1932)

On Unter den Linden they trot and gallop,
By foot, on horse, in pairs,
With a watch on the arm and a hat on
*   the head,*
And none has time to spare!

This song, entitled "Heimat Berlin" (Berlin as home) was presented in Max Reinhardt's famous cabaret "Schall und Rauch" (Sound and Smoke). It reflected the life and rhythm in the Prussian metropolis during the not-always-Golden Twenties. The show was entitled *Berlin Tempo*, but the name was soon translated into "Jewish haste" by those in the audience who had glanced at the program. Walter Mehring wrote the text; Friedrich Hollaender composed the music; Paul Graetz starred on stage. Indeed, Berlin's cabaret and revue scene was strongly identified with Jewish names, so strongly that the cabaret artist Werner Finck – himself certainly free of anti-Semitic sentiments – jokingly gave this reason for naming his cabaret "The Catacombs": "Two thousand years ago they were the place of refuge for the first Christians. Today they serve the same purpose for the last Christians."

One could say that Berlin's "Golden Twenties" might not have been so golden without the Jews. This is what Artur Landsberger argued in his "tragic satire" of 1925, *Berlin without Jews*. Imagine Berlin without the newspapers published by Mosse or Ull-

stein. Imagine *not* shopping at Tietz and Wertheim. Imagine Berlin without the stage productions by Max Reinhardt and Leopold Jessner; without the performances of Elisabeth Bergner and Fritz Kortner; without the music of Arnold Schoenberg and Kurt Weill; without the paintings of Max Liebermann and Lesser Ury; without Alfred Doeblin's *Berlin Alexanderplatz* or Vicki Baum's *Grand Hotel*; without Kurt Tucholsky's stinging satires or Georg Hermann's literary portraits; without Emil Ludwig's well-written popular biographies. Even if it is a mistake to equate Berlin's "Golden Twenties" with Jews or a "uniformly Jewish contribution," it is probably correct to assume that those years will always be connected with a particular spirit. It was, in many ways, the same spirit that Theodor Fontane – writing years before the end of the nineteenth century – had described as one of "negation, criticism, practical jokes and sometimes humor."

Just as it is impossible to reduce the cultural life of Berlin to the contribution of its Jews, it is impossible to equate Jewish life in this period with a particular "Berlin-Jewish-spirit." The history of the Jews in Berlin between 1918 and 1933 was both more and less. There was, on one hand, a quick growth of the official Jewish Community (the *Juedische Gemeinde*) as it expanded into the arenas of politics, and social and cultural affairs. Simultaneously, but often in spheres quite

Left page:
During the street fighting of January and February 1919 the Mosse building at the corner of Schuetzenstrasse and Jerusalemer Strasse was damaged. The pock-marks of bullets are clearly visible in the façade in this contemporary photograph.

Right:
Barricades in the newspaper district were made of newsprint

separate from those of the Community, a renaissance of Jewish culture was taking place. Periodicals, publishers, concerts and art exhibitions flourished. But there were also signs of impending crisis. Non-Jewish Berliners were questioning social integration, and violent anti-Semitic activity saw its beginnings.

The period between 1918 and 1933 bears the name of Weimar, since it was in Weimar that the framers of a new German Constitution met to conduct their proceedings. The framers preferred the bucolic somnolence of the home of Goethe and Schiller to Berlin's noisy and precarious streets. But the Weimar Republic was in fact a Berlin Republic. Berlin was still the capital of Prussia and still the capital of the Republic-cum-Empire. In Berlin stood the government. In Berlin stood the parliament. Berlin remained the cultural capital of Germany. Before 1918 the kings of Bavaria and Saxony as well as the smaller princes of Germany's provincial capitals had seen to it that German culture was "particu-

lar," even parochial. Now, in a centralized Germany, culture came alive and thrived. Berlin was magnetic and was able to rival – sometimes even overtake – Paris, London, New York and Chicago.

The city's prominence had a major effect on the position of the Jews all over Germany. At the beginning of the Empire in 1871, only 7 percent of German Jews lived in Berlin. By 1910 the number was over 23 percent. Jews continued to move to Berlin into the 1920s, so that by the end of the Weimar Republic, every third Jew living in Germany was in Berlin. The highpoint was reached in 1925, when the Jewish population of Berlin reached 173,000, making up 4.3 percent of the city's population. Almost 80 percent of these Jews lived in the historic center (the Mitte district) or the neighboring districts of Charlottenburg, and Wilmersdorf, around the Schoeneberg district's Bayerischer Platz and in parts of Prenzlauer Berg district. The Jewish Community resembled a large city administration and had similar tasks to ful-

Die **Verfaſſung des Deutſchen Reichs.**
Vom 11. August 1919.

Das Deutſche Volk, einig in ſeinen Stämmen und von dem Willen beſeelt, ſein Reich in Freiheit und Gerechtigkeit zu erneuen und zu feſtigen, dem inneren und dem äußeren Frieden zu dienen und den geſellſchaft= lichen Fortſchritt zu fördern, hat ſich dieſe Verfaſſung gegeben.

Erſter Hauptteil.

Aufbau und Aufgaben des Reichs.

Erſter Abſchnitt.

Reich und Länder.

Artifel 1.

Das Deutſche Reich iſt eine Republik.
Die Staatsgewalt geht vom Volfe aus.

Artifel 2.

Das Reichsgebiet beſteht aus den Gebieten der deutſchen Länder. Andere Gebiete können durch Reichs= geſetz in das Reich aufgenommen werden, wenn es ihre Bevölferung fraft des Selbſtbeſtimmungsrechts begehrt.

Artifel 3.

Die Reichsfarben ſind ſchwarz=rot=gold. Die Handels= flagge iſt ſchwarz=weiß=rot mit den Reichsfarben in der oberen inneren Ecke.

Artifel 4.

Die allgemein anerfannten Regeln des Völferrechts gelten als bindende Beſtandteile des deutſchen Reichsrechts.

Artifel 5.

Die Staatsgewalt wird in Reichsangelegenheiten durch die Organe des Reichs auf Grund der Reichsver= faſſung, in Landesangelegenheiten durch die Organe der Länder auf Grund der Landesverfaſſungen ausgeübt.

Artifel 6.

Das Reich hat die ausſchließliche Geſetzgebung über:
1. die Beziehungen zum Ausland;
2. das Kolonialweſen;

The first page of the Weimar Constitution (August 11, 1919),
drafted by Hugo Preuss.

Above: The SPD-Reichstag deputy Eduard Bernstein on his way to the Reichstag in 1920

Below, from the left: Paul Hirsch (1868–1940), Governor of Prussia 1918–20, shown here ca. 1918; Rosa Luxemburg (1870–1919), co-founder of the Spartacus-Union, murdered by right-wing extremists in Berlin 1919, in a photograph of 1912. Hugo Preuss, scholar of state law and Reichs Minister of the Interior from February to June 1919.

fill. The Community employed 1,500 in its various departments and offices: the welfare department, the employment office, the statistical department, the Community library, its art collection and, of course, its many religious institutions. Toward the end of the 1920s, the Community's annual budget was more than ten million Reichsmarks.

Of course, the importance of the Jews in Berlin may be demonstrated by means other than statistics. Many Jewish intellectuals came to Berlin on the eve of World War I. Arnold Zweig and Lion Feuchtwanger came from Bavaria; Arnold Schoenberg and Joseph Roth from Vienna; Franz Kafka visited from Prague. Berlin attracted Jewish intellectuals and artists from eastern Europe. It was home, at least temporarily, to the Russian avant-garde artists Marc Chagall and El Lissitzky and to such figures of modern Hebrew literature as S. Y. Agnon and Chajim Nachman Bialik. The Hebrew and Yiddish publishing houses and periodicals they founded in Berlin were valuable cultural contributions to the city. Together with several German-Jewish institutions the eastern European intellectuals brought about a remarkable renaissance in Jewish culture.

It is possible to categorize Jewish life during the Weimar Republic as unfolding in three different realms, or on three different stages. The first, and central realm was that of the Jewish Community itself and the numerous institutions, organizations and associations it supervised. Many particular interests made themselves felt in Community leadership elections. The Jewish Community dealt with a major influx of Jewish immigrants from eastern Europe and, because of economic crisis, an influx of many impoverished middle-class Jews as well. The second "realm" involved the great Jewish Renaissance, a renewed interest in Jewish culture forged by both new and old arrivals. This renaissance was in many ways independent of the Jewish Community's institutions. Finally, in the face of the hackneyed concept of "Berlin's Jewish-Spirit," one must address a third realm. This involved troubling questions of Jewish integration and alienation as well as the growing threat of anti-Semitic agitation.

Religious or Ethnic Community?

Unlike practicing Jews in most other European countries, as well as the United States, Jews in Germany were not organized in private associations. Instead they belonged to *Gemeinden* (Communities) governed by public law. Citizens were obliged to belong to a particular religious *Gemeinde* and pay taxes to it. Prussian law of 1876 made it possible for a congregation to secede from the Community. It was also possible to establish new Communities. Weimar-era Berlin, for example, actually had two Jewish *Gemeinden*: the large Jewish Community of Berlin – to which most Jews belonged, regardless of the particular liturgy they adhered to – and the proportionally tiny Community of Adass Jisroel, whose members were exclusively Orthodox. Even after 1919, when it became legally possible not to register with a Community and still maintain one's Jewishness, only a few of Berlin's Jews took advantage of this option. Conversion to Christianity, which had been a mass phenomenon during the nineteenth century, had largely disappeared. The overwhelming majority of the Berlin Jews remained members of the Jewish Community and paid their taxes to it. Because of Adass Jisroel's tiny size, it is possible to speak of Berlin's Community as a unified entity – an *Einheitsgemeinde* – as in other German cities.

Above: A view of Grenadierstrasse,
where many Jewish immigrants from Eastern Europe lived.
This photograph by Walter Gircke is from 1928.

Title page of a 1920 tract published by the Workers'
Welfare Agency of the Jewish Organizations.

Grenadierstrasse photographed
by Friedrich Seidenstuecker in 1932.

This unity did not entail a rejection of religious and ideological diversity. Liberal and Orthodox synagogues existed under the umbrella of the Jewish Community's *Einheitsgemeinde*, and diverse Jewish parties conducted vehement campaigns for the leadership positions within it. During the nineteenth century, religious questions – such as whether organ music could be introduced into services or which prayer books should be used – had dominated the election campaigns. With the rise of Zionism as a political movement at the turn of the century, and with Theodor Herzl's appeal to "conquer the Communities," the struggles took on an increasingly political character. During the 1920s the election campaigns concentrated ever more strongly on two contrasting ideas of the Jewish Community. Was it to remain the "religious community" that it had become during the nineteenth century? Or was it to become a *Volksgemeinde* (ethnic community) and encompass the pre-emancipatory structures of the *Kehillah* (the traditional Jewish community)?

The two strongest parties within the Jewish Community campaigned on opposite sides of these questions. On one side there were the liberals, who had been the dominating force in the Community since the middle of the nineteenth century. By World War I, being "liberal" had political as well as religious implications. Politically it meant supporting liberal political parties made up for the most part of bourgeois, German-speaking Jews. From the point of view of religion, being liberal meant being open to the reform of religious rituals and liturgy in synagogues and cemeteries. Tellingly, these Jews referred to themselves as "German citizens of the Jewish faith."

Opposing the liberals from 1919 onward was the Juedische Volkspartei (The Jewish People's Party, JVP), which was made up of Zionists, eastern European Jewish organizations and other forces of Jewish nationalism. The JVP considered the religious institutions an integral component of the Jewish Community but considered social and secular institutions to be just as important. Behind the idea of the *Volksgemeinde* stood another idea of Jewish Community – defined more by ethnicity and culture than by religion.

Hans Goslar, a high official in the provincial Prussian government, was a supporter of religious Zionism and a representative of the JVP. He compared the party to the traditional *Kehillah* of pre-emancipation times:

> It should . . . be said here in all clarity that the JVP and the Zionist and non-Zionist groups which have associated themselves with it to form the Jewish *Volksgemeinde* consider themselves to be the organic continuation of the traditional *Kehillah*. . . . A Kehillah or a *Volksgemeinde* is a community that concerns itself not *only* with the synagogues, liturgy, and religious teaching . . . but concerns itself with *all* manifestations of the life of Jews in a city.

In practice this meant that the JVP wanted to found more Jewish schools, including schools in which it was possible to learn Hebrew. The liberals, on the other hand, had worked hard and – in many instances successfully – to create non-denominational schools, especially in the large cities. But the JVP went much further than demanding a revival of Jewish schools. It sought to completely revolutionize all Jewish teaching in the schools – henceforth it was to be not a school based on faith, but a school for Jewish nationalism. The Jewish Communities were to become the bearers of a widespread social network. During the campaign of 1920 for the Jewish Assembly of Representatives, the JVP demanded the establishment of Jewish savings banks, cooperatives, employment

The head of an eastern European Jew,
etching by Hermann Struck (1876–1944).

associations, soup kitchens, homes for transients and a welfare agency. The Community would become a "city within the city." The local organization of the "People's Community" was the smallest link in the overall organization of German Jews. Above them would be associations on a provincial and on a national level. These aims were popularized by the presence of some prominent Jews on JVP rolls. Among them were the painter Lesser Ury, the writer Arnold Zweig, and Simon Dubnow, the father of Jewish autonomism in eastern Europe, who had been living in Berlin since 1922.

Between the liberals and the JVP stood the conservatives and the Orthodox Jews. During the nineteenth century, they were the natural adversaries of the liberals. By the Twenties, however, they had lost much of their importance. In many instances, however, they were able to tip the balance one way or the other, thereby maintaining some influence. Nevertheless, they could not halt the trend toward increased secularization. The

*Hermann Struck's depiction
of the painter Lesser Ury (1861–1931), 1921.
Tel Aviv Museum.*

secularizing tendency can be seen in the founding of many smaller parties within the Community that had no specific religious programs – from the Deutsche Liste to the Social Democratic Poalei Zion.

Compared to the Wilhelmine period, the most important political change in the Weimar Republic was the democratization of election laws, first through the abolition of the outdated imperial three-tiered voting system, and after 1925, with the introduction of suffrage for women and "non-German" citizens. The elections held every four years within Germany's Jewish communities mirrored those of general elections. Rallies, meetings, speeches and assemblies involving more than one thousand people were not rare. Each party printed posters, sent letters to Jewish households, invited prominent speakers to their rallies. In order to get as many people to vote as possible, the parties organized *Schlepperarbeit* "dragging services," which consisted of bringing voters from their homes to and from polling stations. In the 1930 "Instructions for the District Election Heads for the Work on Election Day" in Berlin, one could read this rule for *Schlepperarbeit*: "It should be made clear to the schleppers that they should take the people to the polling place and that they should be sure to announce whether there are aged, infirm or weak persons who will need to be picked up by auto and cared for."

Democratizing election laws resulted in a large increase in the number of Berlin's Jewish voters. Whereas in 1910, 9,500 persons voted, by 1926 they numbered 48,000, and by 1930, were as many as 75,000. In terms of percentages, this was a considerable rise – from 10 percent to 60 percent of the city's adult Jewish population.

The strongest party within the Jewish Community elections remained that of the Liberals during the Weimar Republic. But on occasion they sustained losses and could only maintain their supremacy by joining forces with the Orthodox parties – by forging, in other words, previously unthinkable coalitions. From time to time they became the opposition to a majority of Orthodox and JVP. In Berlin this was the case in 1926, when the Liberals won a mere 10 of the 21 seats on the Community Council. Community leadership was taken over by a coalition consisting of JVP and Orthodox party members, plus the one-man faction of Poalei Zion led by Oskar Cohn (a former Reichstag deputy). Perhaps it would be better to say that the coalition, rather than leading the Community, fought it for two years in court – the Liberals had taken their claims that the election was rigged to everybody, including the prefect of police.

Even after the police department confirmed that the election had, in fact, not been rigged, the vigorous fights in Berlin between the Liberals and the JVP continued unabated. The Liberals, in their "Jewish Liberal Newspaper" even went so far as to threaten that they would not cooperate with the administration of the Jewish Community. The high – or rather low – point was reached when the Zionist Georg Kareski was named head of the Jewish Community in 1929. Kareski was one of the most colorful figures in Berlin Jewish Community politics. He had begun his career addressing mass rallies in Posen; he was a member of the board of the Reich Association of German Industry; he became a candidate for the Prussian Lower House (his name was on the list of the Catholic Center Party); he was a director of the Iwria-Bank and treasurer of the Prussian State Association of Jewish Communities; finally, he would later be indicted for collaborating with the Gestapo. These were some of the stations in the checkered career of the Berlin Jewish Community's only Zionist

*A newspaper vendor in 1915,
by Hermann Struck.*

chairman. When he took up his post in 1929, the Liberals were distraught. Kareski had been one of their most active party political rivals.

At the next elections to the Community Council, in November 1930, the Liberals won the election, and it was the turn of the Orthodox parties to suffer. In 1926 they had gained (with the Religious Middle Party) 17 percent of the vote. Now, with only 4 percent, they were an almost meaningless minority. Most of their members had switched to the JVP, which was able to improve its vote from 16,000 to 26,000. The clear winners were, however, the Liberals, who had understood how to mobilize masses of new voters. They won more than 40,000 votes (54 percent) and thus had a considerable majority. All in all, ten different Jewish parties campaigned during the election. But the Liberals and the JVP together constituted 90 percent of the votes.

Below left: title page of the evening edition of the Social Democrat newspaper Vorwaerts *with the headline about the assassination of Rathenau.*

Below right: Title page of Rathenau's book The New Economy, *published in Berlin in 1918 by S. Fischer Verlag.*

*Left page above:
After Rathenau's
assassination in 1922,
republican-minded
youth demonstrated
in front of the
Berlin City Castle
(Berliner Stadtschloss).*

*Walther Rathenau
(1867–1922),
politician and industrialist,
son and successor to Emil
Rathenau, the founder of
AEG, in a portrait of 1907
by Edvard Munch.
He was named Minister of
Foreign Affairs on
January 21, 1922.
He was murdered in Berlin
on June 24, 1922
by anti-Semitic right-wing
extremists.
Stiftung Stadtmuseum
Berlin.*

Leading representatives of Jewry, especially Rabbi Leo Baeck, had appealed that all party disputes be avoided. Why not, he suggested, create a single list of candidates instead of conducting self-defeating campaigns? The appeal was a response to outside events. The National Socialists had won 107 seats in the Reichstag elections of September 1930 – an alarming victory. Alas, Baeck's and other appeals to end inner friction fell on deaf ears. It was the Liberals who demanded that they get a majority. One of their representatives, the vice-president of the Berlin police, Bernhard Weiss, said in a rally: "Whether or not the brown shirts send 107 of their own into the Reichstag . . . need not worry us Jews. There isn't the slightest occasion in which a Jew should be forced to conduct himself in response to the deeds of Jewish opponents."

Even after the 1930 elections and the ever-increasing successes of the National Socialists, the members of the Berlin Jewish Community didn't see the need to end their internal friction. After the success of the Liberals, it was the JVP's turn to cast doubt on the election's legality. There had, they claimed, been a secret agreement between the Liberals and the JVP, which the liberals broke. The JVP representatives in the Assembly of Representatives left the meeting en masse. It took two months before another meeting could be called. It was only in July 1932 that a "truce" within the Community was proclaimed. By then Hitler stood *ante portas* and the period of the Weimar Republic was drawing to an end.

During the last years of the Weimar Republic the frictions between the JVP and the Liberals revolved more around different theoretical ideas of Judaism and the Jewish Community than around practical differences in the Community's daily work. Concerning religion, the JVP was frequently in-

clined toward making compromises. During the period in which Kareski headed the Community, the first synagogue with mixed-seating was opened, despite hefty opposition by the Orthodox Jews within the Community. This meant that families could now sit together during services. Moreover the synagogue's modern round interior enabled contacts among those assembled in prayer. The synagogue opened two days after the elections in September 1930. One could already notice the concern for Germany's political future: "At present it is unfortunately not possible to stay proud and joyful," the Community head addressed those assembled. "We do not yet know how our life and our position will develop after these decisions." What is certain is that none of those assembled had the slightest idea that this would be the last synagogue to be built in Berlin before the Nazis began a systematic destruction of Jews and their institutions. It and most of Berlin's other synagogues would be in ruins only a few years later.

As the 1930s got under way, the synagogue on Prinzregentenstrasse had seats for 2,300 visitors. It decisively helped accommodate the growing Berlin Jewish Community, which now had fourteen synagogues. Between 1926 and 1930 the total number of synagogue seats rose from 19,000 to 23,000. In addition to these, several dozen small private synagogues and prayer rooms continued to exist. Special significance can be attached to the Liberal Synagogue North on Schoenhauser Allee, which was founded in 1923. Its services involved the active participation of all present, and the combination of prayers in German and in Hebrew was highly innovative. That same year in the west part of Berlin, a conservative synagogue was founded and was transferred in 1929 to Franzensbader Strasse. It became important because of its conservative rabbi, the writer Emil

Bernhard Cohn. This was the same Rabbi Cohn who had been suspended by the Jewish Community for his Zionist views and activities in the so-called "Cohn Affair" of 1907.

In his 1930 budget speech as head of the Community, Kareski maintained, "for the first time in many years we have to admit to a certain shortage of seats in the synagogues and prayer rooms." For many that seemed like a signal for religious renewal. During the High Holy Days of 1930 more than half of Berlin's Jews attended a service, some of them even in spaces rented from the city, such as the Philharmonic.

In 1927 the exclusively Orthodox Community of Adass Jisroel had 350 regular and 2,500 "non-regular" members. The lines between both Adass Jisroel and the Jewish Community of Berlin were very clearly drawn. Relations between the "main" and the "secessionist" communities however were more harmonious than they were in Frankfurt-am-Main, where the Orthodox secession had started. Adass Jisroel had in its rabbi Esra Munk not only a prominent and erudite scholar but also a leader who knew how to keep the varying interests in tow. His best-known accomplishment is the organization of the school system that, in 1931, had a total of 789 pupils in lower, middle and other schools. Politically, Munk was like Kareski in supporting the Catholic Center party for the Reichstag elections of 1932.

The Weimar period saw an interesting shift in the way the budget of Berlin's Jewish Community was used. Despite the flowering of Jewish religious activity in the city, the percentage of expenses for religious purposes was lowered while the portion spent on welfare increased.

This was a direct result of the economic crises that plagued the Weimar Republic. In 1930 the Community's welfare expenses reached 40 percent of its budget – twice the amount spent on cultural activities. Three years later, the number of welfare recipients was almost as high as that of taxpayers. While welfare expenses skyrocketed, the number of those who were able to pay taxes plummeted. It is possible to compare figures from 1912 with those of 1924. In 1912, 9 percent of the taxpayers had a taxable high income of 25,000 Reichsmarks, while 46 percent belonged to the low-income groups (with incomes below 3,600 Reichsmarks). Twelve years later, only 3.6 percent belonged to the upper bracket, while the lower bracket was filled with a figure of 51.5 percent.

It is true that during the Weimar years almost half of all Jewish breadwinners were independently employed. But the figure declined by 23 percent between 1925 and 1933. More and more, German Jews were drifting toward a certain proletarianization, especially in the large cities. Whereas a Jewish factory worker was something of an exception, countless small family businesses teetered on the brink of insolvency, bankruptcy, receivership and liquidation. Unemployment was a big problem – it was the bane of Jews and non-Jews alike. Because the great number of self-employed was not registered, the available statistics are somewhat inconclusive. In July 1929, some 3,605 Jews registered for unemployment benefits. The employment office could only offer jobs to 467 of them. In March 1930 the number of unemployed had risen to 6,912. Of this group, 3,137 were women, and only 404 jobs could be found for them.

The suicide rate during this period was quite high among Berlin's Jews. A double explanation may be offered for this: economic crises and ever-increasing anti-Semitism. The *Juedische Rundschau* in October 1927 reported that 117 of 100,000 Berlin Jews had taken their lives in 1925, and that this was double the figure from 1922. The ratios for non-Jewish Berliners were considerably smaller: for Protestants, 45:100,000 and for Catholics, 32:100,000.

The extremely unfavorable economic situation was not only the result of a general recession but was also due to the considerable number of *Ostjuden* (east European Jews) who had emigrated to Germany after World War I. In 1925 one-quarter of all Jews in Berlin (that is, 43,838 of them) were foreign citizens – practically identical with east European origins. There were, of course, many *Ostjuden* who had actually been born in Berlin – the term meant different things to different people. Among them there was a high percentage from the lower classes. They were occupied in street markets and as street peddlers and were also many workers in industry.

Compared to Paris or London, where the *Ostjuden* stuck to their quarters – in the Parisian *Pletzl* or London's Whitechapel in the East End – there was not single zone in Berlin where east European Jews concentrated. A relatively large number of them could be found in the proletarian *Scheunenviertel* (long known as the "barn quarter") near Alexanderplatz. Here one could order a *Tscholent* at a kosher restaurant or find bookshops that sold books printed in Yiddish. Here also were small private prayer rooms. Also, as Joseph Roth wrote in 1927, it was a place for petty crime: "There are east European Jewish criminals in Berlin – pickpockets, marriage swindlers, tricksters, forgers, speculators – but [there are] almost no burglars, murderers, or robber-murderers." Most of the *Scheunenviertel*'s Jews earned an honest though meager living as peddlers, dealers, craftsmen and workers.

No homogenous attitude toward the immigrants from eastern Europe existed among the other Jews of Berlin. The small number of German-Nationalist Jews surrounding

The physicist Albert Einstein (1879–1955) directed Berlin's Kaiser-Wilhelm-Institute for Physics between 1913 and 1933, after which he emigrated to the USA. This 1917 drawing is by Erich Buettner.

Max Naumann kept clear of them and refused to be mentioned in the same breath with them. In the Jewish Community elections of 1930 his party, the Deutsche Liste, branded *Ostjuden* as a danger for the established German Jews. Their posters proclaimed a battle of *Volk gegen Volk* (literally "people against people" but here the implication was of "Germans against foreigners").

The Deutsche Liste received a mere 1.8 percent of the vote in the 1930 elections – too little to send even one representative to the Community assembly. Most of the Jews found such attempts at alienation distasteful. They saw the *Ostjuden* as their brethren in faith and felt strongly about defending them against anti-Semitic attacks. The liberal position was that it was more important to integrate them than to alienate them. Few had forgotten that they too, or their parents, had

The Einstein Tower, near Potsdam, by architect Erich Mendelsohn (1887-1953), photograph ca. 1930.
Left: Mendelsohn's sketches. Kunstbibliothek der Staatlichen Museen zu Berlin.

The Berlin Committee for Psychoanalysis. From left to right, standing: Otto Rank, Karl Abraham, Max Eitingon,
Ernest Jones; seated: Sigmund Freud, Sandor Ferenczi, Hanns Sachs. Photograph 1922.

moved to Berlin from Posen or West Prussia in the not-so-distant past. There was, moreover, a small but growing group of German Jews who showed great enthusiasm for the "authentic" Jewishness of the *Ostjuden*.

The Jewish Renaissance

Acculturated German Jews had met *Ostjuden* in Berlin's *Scheunenviertel* or had come across them on the eastern front during World War I. To many, they represented "real" Jewish folk traditions and customs that many believed had been long lost. In his mid-1920s travels in Poland, Alfred Doeblin noted, "I . . . believed that those busy people I had seen in Germany – those businessmen who bathed in their sense of family and were slowly getting fat, those agile intellectuals, those uncounted, unsure, unhappy "fine" people – were the Jews. Now I see: They are but scattered remnants, far from the core of the people living and thriving here." The *Ostjuden* were the real Jews. In the interval, they had moved to the *Scheunenviertel*. Later they would appear in the opening chapter of Doeblin's famous novel *Berlin Alexanderplatz*, published in 1929. When the novel's protagonist Franz Biberkopf leaves the Tegel prison and wanders the streets around Rosenthaler Strasse (near Alexanderplatz), he meets a Jew with a "full red beard, a small man in a great-coat, black felt hat, carrying a cane." It is from this "red" man – a caricature of the typical *Scheunenviertel Ostjude* – that Biberkopf, fresh out of prison, hears the first stories of the area, albeit in a poor imitation of Yiddish.

It was possible to hear better Yiddish if one went to the theater, to Maxim Sakaschansky's small establishment, for example. His cabaret belonged to the small number of Jewish theaters in the Berlin scene. It was here that in the fall of 1930 Hugo Doeblin (the author's brother) heaved onstage carrying a huge sack marked with the number "107" on his back – hinting at the immense burden the 107 National Socialist deputies in the Reichstag represented for Weimar democracy.

It was also possible to hear Yiddish in a performance on Piscator's theater at Nollendorfplatz in September 1929. The premiere of Walter Mehring's drama *The Merchant of Berlin* was accompanied by scandal. The play told about the quick rise and fall of one Simon Chajim Kaftan, an *Ostjude* who had moved from the *Scheunenviertel* to aristocratic Potsdam. For the play Mehring had studied Yiddish. Piscator brought the renowned Yiddish actor Paul Baratoff all the way from New York City to play the main role. The play was attacked from all sides. German nationalists saw in the caricature an insult to German soldiers. Meanwhile the liberal Centralverein (Central Association of German Citizens of the Jewish Faith) saw the honor of German Jews sullied. Mehring had, in fact, done nothing but attack the reigning attitude toward *Ostjuden*.

The same German Jews who flinched when they heard Yiddish spoken on the German stage waxed enthusiastic when ensembles were imported to Berlin from eastern Europe to act in Yiddish and Hebrew. Though these Jews had little sympathy for the popular theater of the *Scheunenviertel*, they supported it when they thought it represented avant-garde ideas. Such was the case of the "Wilnaer Truppe," an ensemble from Vilnius in Lithuania. The Moscow Jewish State Theater and of the Hebrew language Habimah Theater had similar success. Doeblin commented favorably when the group from Vilnius supplanted the well-established Berlin Yiddish theater of the

Herrnfeld brothers: "Now we have real Jewish theater. Undignified self-prostitution and vulgar speech now belong to the past. Here we see and hear spontaneous accomplishments of a thriving branch of the Jewish people. . . . There are now in Berlin only two unassailably good and serious ensembles: the Russian theater and the Jewish Theater from Vilnius."

It would be a mistake, however, to think that Hebrew and Yiddish culture could be found only in the theaters. A look at the row of hallowed graves at the Jewish cemetery in Weissensee gives even today a good impression of the presence of Hebrew authors in Berlin at the beginning of the 1920s. In the space of only a few months, Micha Josef Berdiczewsky (Bin Gorion), David Frischmann and Saul Israel (Shai Ish) Hurwitz were buried there. They had, shortly before the beginning of World War I, been together with such intellectuals as Salman Schneur, Saul Tchernichowsky, Jacob Kahan and Simon Bernfeld at the center of the Hebrew-speaking colony in Berlin whose regular meeting place was the Café Monopol.

Many more joined them during and after the war: S. Y. Agnon, Chajim Nachman Bialik, Uri Zvi Greenberg, Moshe Kleinmann, Chajim Tchernovitz, Shmuel Abba Horodetzky, Jacob Klatzkin, Benzion Katz, Jakob Fichmann, Benzion Dinaburg and Simon Rawidowicz. Many Hebrew-language publishing houses and periodicals had their headquarters or offices in Berlin during this time, among them the official organ of the Zionist World Organization *Haolam* (The World). There were also many Russian-Jewish students in Berlin. Their 1924 congress was opened by Albert Einstein. Among them were several who became famous in philosophy and Bible-science, such as Abraham Joschua Heschel and Jecheskel Kaufmann.

In January 1923 the Berlin Philharmonic was the scene of an unusual event. It was the fiftieth birthday of the great author Chajim Nachman Bialik. In the lobby and on the stage one could hear not only German and Yiddish but also Hebrew, a language that had only recently been revived for daily use. Here were some of the most illustrious names from Hebrew letters from all over the world, and the celebration and ceremonies were noted also by the non-Jewish public. In a story in the *Berliner Tageblatt*, Bialik was placed on the same level as the Russian Maxim Gorky and the great Indian poet Rabindranath Tagore. Bialik, who had come from Russia only one year earlier, was heartily welcomed into Berlin's colony of Hebrew writers. He was so impressed by the Hebrew culture he found in Berlin that he stressed shortly after his arrival that in all the countries he had visited so far he had always felt a barrier between the native and the Hebrew cultures. In Berlin, however, he felt that the barrier did not exist.

Berlin might have been the undisputed center of Hebrew culture in Europe, but it still took a back seat compared to the Yiddish literature scenes in Paris, Warsaw and New York. Berlin was, however, home to one of the most beautiful Yiddish art magazines that ever appeared. This was called *Milgrojim*, and it was also available to those who spoke Hebrew under the title *Rimon*. Contributors, among others, were Marc Chagall and El Lissitzky, and Mark Wishnitzer was the leading figure. Another magazine, *Albatros*, was an avant-garde art periodical edited by Uri Zvi Greenberg (and also occasionally named *Berlin* after its place of publication).

The most important accomplishments of Berlin's Yiddish speakers took place in the scholarly arena. The Jewish Scientific Institute – the YIVO – was conceived of and founded in Berlin. Only later did it move to Vilnius. Among the founders were the historians Simon Dubnow, Elias Tcherikower and Nachum Shtif, the sociologist Jacob Lestschinsky, and Lenin's former Minister of Justice, Isaac Nachman Steinberg. They were all living in exile in Berlin. In 1921 the group formed around Tcherikower and started an east European Jewish historical archive, the main aim of which was to collect and process information about the pogroms that occurred in the Ukraine between 1917 and 1921. In 1924 a meeting was held in Steinberg's home and a commission founded to plan a Yiddish-language research institute. After only one year the YIVO was able to open its doors to researchers and scholars. When Shtif and Tcherikower emigrated to Vilnius, most of the institute's staff went with them, but two important commissions remained behind in Berlin.

The Berlin office of YIVO actively advertised and promoted its activities among German Jewish circles and especially among Jewish scholars. It published in German the *Mitteilungen der Auslandszentrale des Jiddischen Wissenschaftlichen Instituts* (Bulletin of the Foreign Headquarters of the Yiddish Scientific Institute) and organized weekly lectures and seminars in German about east European Jewry. Among German Jewish scholars, however, there was not much resonance. After several lectures in which none of them appeared, a representative of the YIVO stated resignedly: "Either the scholars of Jewish Studies know what we want and do not want it, or they don't even want to know about it. In any case, we are not placing our hopes in them."

While the Yiddish-speaking YIVO remained somewhat marginalized in Berlin's Jewish life – it is well-known for its work in Vilnius – German-speaking Jewish scholars and their institutions played a central role in Berlin's intellectual life. Among the most important institutions were two rivals: the liberal Hochschule fuer die Wissenschaft des Judentums (Institute for the Science of Judaism) and the Orthodox Rabbinical Seminary. There were also post-World-War-I foundations such as the Academy for the Science of Judaism and the Adult Education School. The Hochschule had been founded in 1872 to train liberal rabbis and as a research center for the science of Judaism, though it had been forcibly renamed a *Lehranstalt* (Teaching Institute) in 1883. It reassumed its old name after World War I, only to be renamed again by the Nazis in 1934.

More important than the name was the change in the character of the student body within the school during the 1920s. Fewer students were interested in studying to become rabbis. Now they pursued their studies simply in order to become more knowledgeable about Jewish lore and to get information they could not acquire in their families and schools. One of those who attended lectures was Franz Kafka. Toward the end of 1923 he confided to his friend Robert Klopstock that he considered the Hochschule a "place of peace in otherwise wild Berlin and in the wild recesses of my inner self. . . . [It has] a whole house full of beautiful auditoriums and classrooms, a large library, peace, well-heated, few students – and all for free."

Only a few blocks away, also on Artilleriestrasse, the Seminary for Orthodox Rabbis, founded in 1873 by Esriel Hildesheimer could be found. Their proximity, however, was purely geographical. Ideologically, the institutions were miles apart. One taught the Bible and how to criticize it, while the other promoted research in learning based on the Torah. The promotion of religious reforms in one was juxtaposed by unassailable obedience to the Jewish laws in the other. The Rabbinical Seminary was open only to men. In contrast, in 1932, the Hochschule had among its 155 registered

Above left:
Magnus Hirschfeld (1868–1935), physician and sexologist
who lived in Berlin after 1896, was a major force
behind the academic-humanitarian committee
to combat criminal prosecution of homosexuals.
Hirschfeld died in exile in Nice.

Above:
Poster designed by Josef Fenneker in 1919 for a
"social hygienic film" about prostitution supported
by Hirschfeld.

No. 7   4. bis 10. Tausend

Alkohol und ⚮ Geschlechtsleben

Ein Vortrag
von Dr. Magnus Hirschfeld, Arzt

nebst einem Anhang über Animier-Kneipen

Verlag: Deutscher Arbeiter-
Abstinenten-Bund (J. Michaelis)
Berlin O. 17, Lange Straße 11

Below, left:
Title page of a lecture by Hirschfeld
about alcohol and sex, with an appendix
on "animation-bars," undated.

students 27 women. One of its students, Regina Jonas, became in 1935 the first ordained woman rabbi. She called herself "Fraeulein Rabbinerin Jonas" (Miss Rabbi Jonas). She had already preached on Sabbath holy days in Berlin synagogues during the Weimar years. Both institutions, the Seminary and the Hochschule, attracted prestigious teachers. The historian Ismar Elbogen, the philosopher Julius Guttmann and the most highly regarded rabbi in Berlin, Leo Baeck taught at the Hochschule. The great Talmudist Jechiel Jakob Weinberg taught at the rabbinical Seminary, and David Hoffmann was rector there until he died in 1921.

The Academy of the Science of Judaism on Luetzowstrasse was founded in 1919. It had been originally conceived – according to an open letter by Franz Rosenzweig to Hermann Cohen – as a place to teach Jewish teachers of religion. Its first director, the scholar of ancient history Eugen Taeubler conceived it to be a pure research institute, however. Taeubler stressed that the new academy should not neglect a single area of science: "The field is unlimited . . . it encompasses philosophy, law, linguistics, natural sciences, astronomy, learning Psalms, novellas, tragic verse and naive folk tales." As many as 25 scholars were connected with the academy and many made important contributions and published rare source materials. Among them was Hermann Cohen who began in the 1920s to edit the complete writings of Moses Mendelssohn.

The Adult Education School opened its doors the same year as the Academy. This institution concerned itself with teaching adults only – it was in its concept closer to Franz Rosenzweig's idea and affiliated with Frankfurt's Free Jewish Teaching House, which was founded a few months later. Its courses covered everything from Bible science to modern Hebrew language, and there

were as many as 2,000 registered students. It was the special achievement of the Adult Education School to introduce courses in Jewish sociology, Jewish art and Jewish music. Several courses concerned themselves with the position of women and with the migration of Jews. The School was not a place for scholarly research, but it made the fruits of Jewish scholarly research accessible to a much broader audience.

Not only was there a renaissance of works written in Hebrew and Yiddish. The Jewish renaissance begun by Martin Buber at the turn of the century, continued to flourish with works written and published in German. It was only after the war that the audience spread out to a broader audience beyond the Zionist camp. There were also many successful attempts in art and music to combine modern artistic forms of expression with Jewish themes.

The two best-known Jewish expressionist painters, Ludwig Meidner and Jakob Steinhardt – known before the war as part of a group called the *Patheten* – concerned themselves more openly after the war with their Jewish heritage. Steinhardt presented scenes of east European Jewish life. Meidner portrayed himself in a *tallis*, a Jewish prayer shawl. Steinhardt's Passover Haggadah and his illustrations of the *Book of Jesus ben Sira* are among the most remarkable examples of modern Jewish book art. Jewish book art became so popular that a Jewish bibliophile association was formed, the Soncino Society for the Friends of the Jewish Book. It managed to publish 82 works of Jewish literature before the Third Reich closed it down.

The Jewish renaissance was not only in the visual arts. It could be seen and heard in the field of music. Composers and interpreters sought to find specifically Jewish forms of musical expression, and frequently they revived to "authentic" forms of Jewish

Left: Gershom Scholem (1897–1982), researcher on the Kabbala and friend of Walter Benjamin, emigrated to Palestine in 1923 and taught from 1933 to 1965 at the University of Jerusalem.

Right: The writer and cultural scholar Walter Benjamin (1892–1940) emigrated in 1933. In 1940 he committed suicide at the border between France and Spain, fearing he would fall into the hands of the Gestapo.

music – mostly east European Jewish songs and Yemenite melodies. This could already be easily heard in the music written for the Jewish liturgy during the nineteenth century's period of secularization. If synagogues were often empty on Saturday mornings, concert halls offering Jewish music programs were generally well attended on Sunday mornings.

One must, however, make a distinction – as in the visual arts – between the small circles of community activists who sought to introduce Jewish themes into their art and the most prominent representatives of contemporary music. The composer Arnold Schoenberg, for example, had converted to Protestantism in 1898. He moved from Vienna to Berlin in 1925 and started to look for a way back to Judaism during the 1920s. His renewed interest in Judaism can be found in his unpublished drama *The Biblical Path*, as well as in his great opera *Moses and Aaron*. He finally reconverted to Judaism in Paris in 1933.

The Weimar Republic was a productive and innovative time for synagogue music.

Most important in this respect was the work of the writer, painter and composer Arno Nadel. Before the war he had, as a critic, recognized the achievements of Arnold Schoenberg. Between 1916 and 1938 he directed the choir at the Synagogue on Kottbuser Ufer, and through that he exercised a major influence in Jewish musical life during the 1920s. So did his Berlin colleague Leo Kopf. Both composed modern compositions for the Sabbath services. Nadel was also one of the first to recognize the possibilities that the radio offered for bringing Jewish music to wider audiences. After long negotiations he was able, in 1929, to organize an introductory radio program about Jewish liturgy. It was performed by the cantor Leo Gollanin and the choir of the Luetzowstrasse synagogue.

Another technical medium which found more and more application, even in the synagogue, was the gramophone. The Berlin Jewish Reform Congregation began in the early 1930s to play records at prayer services – and the critics were enthusiastic when they heard, in such services, not only classics of Jewish

The image on the right contains the following text:

Sonntag den 23. November zur Mittelpartei

Religiöse Mittelpartei für Frieden
und Einheit in der Gemeinde

Ehren-Vorsitzender: Rabbiner Dr. S. Weisse
Vorsitzender: Kommerzienrat Gerson Simon
Stellv. Vorsitzender: Prof. Dr. M. Sobernheim

ZWEI KUNDGEBUNGEN

IM WESTEN

Sonntag, 23. November
vorm. 11 Uhr im

Logenhaus
Joachimsthaler Straße 13
dicht am Bf. Zoolog. Garten

Leitung: Prof. Dr. M. Sobernheim

Es sprechen:
Prof. Georg Bernhard
Ernestine Eschelbacher
Syndikus
Dr. Alfred Wiener

Musikalische Umrahmung:
Gemischter Chor
(Doppelquartett)   Chor-
dirigent: Max Wachsmann

25. Psalm: „Ewiger zu
Dir erheb ich meine Seele"
Lewandowski

Violinsolo über ein hebrä-
isches Motiv, arr. und vorge-
tragen von Max Wachsmann

100. Psalm:
„Jauchzet dem Herrn alle
Welt!"   .   Mendelssohn

IM ZENTRUM

Sonntag, 23. November
vorm. 11 Uhr im

**Festsaal
des Hackeschen Hofes**
Rosenthaler Straße 40-41
dicht am Bahnhof Börse

Leitung: Obermagistratsrat
Dr. Neumann

Es sprechen:
Rechtsanwalt
Dr. G. Hollander
Margarete Fried
Rabbiner Dr. Berger
Frl. Rechtsanwalt
Dr. Hanna Katz

Musikalische Umrahmung:
Händel, Arioso (Gesang)
Dr. W. Rosenthal
Schubert, Allmacht
Brahms,
Aus ernsten Gesängen
Frau Dr. Toni Davidsohn
Beethoven,
„Ehre Gottes in der Natur"
(Gesang) Dr. W. Rosenthal

Wer Frieden, Ausgleich, Unparteilichkeit
in der Gemeinde wünscht, wähli nur   **LISTE 3**

The lower image contains the text:

Preußischer Landesverband
jüd. Gemeinden – Verbandstag 1932

liturgy, but also music by Bach, Bruckner and even Richard Wagner. Among the cantors, who in most cases sang music by Louis Lewandowski in German, was the famous tenor Joseph Schmidt. These introductions should be seen against the background of a general enthusiasm for modern technology and the so-called *Neue Sachlichkeit*, or new rationalism. Once in a while articles could be read exhorting people to forgo concerts for records. Parents were occasionally even encouraged to take their children "off" piano lessons and to have them practice with records instead.

Musical life in Jewish Berlin (these technical enthusiasms notwithstanding) was in most ways quite conventional. In the newspaper *Juedische Rundschau* one could regularly read reviews by the music critic Alice Jacob-Loewenson. In her round-up of the musical winter of 1928–29 she reported on such musical events as concerts by the Berlin synagogue choirs, concerts of young Jewish composers from the US, evenings of Yiddish and Hebrew Lieder, programs about New Jewish Music and Yiddish theater music performed at the Free Jewish Adult Education School and in the school of Jewish youth. A visible change had taken place during the Weimar Republic; Jewish music went from religious music to concert music.

It is quite justified in this context to speak of a tendency toward "museum culture" – something many critics writing in the 1920s were already beginning to do. Quotidian Jewish life continued to cede to secularization in the 1920s, at the same time that there was growing interest in Jewish literature, art and music as a cultural phenomenon – as a "moment" that did not require a major religious intervention in already secularized lifestyles. It was only logical, therefore that the idea of founding a Jewish museum

in Berlin, as in other large cities, gained in popularity.

The first Jewish museums had been founded around the turn of the century in Hamburg and Vienna. Berlin was, in a sense, a latecomer. It was only in 1917 that the art collection of the Jewish Community was opened to the general public. Even then it led a rather prosaic existence until the art historian Karl Schwarz took charge. "When I began my work," Schwarz wrote, the entire collection was in a terrible state of disorder." Not only did he order the collection, he expanded it considerably. Within five years he was able to increase the number of paintings from 20 to 80 and of ceremonial objects from 227 to 348. It became obvious that there was no space for these objects to be either stored or exhibited. It was only when the Jewish home for the aged next door moved in 1932 to Oranienburger Strasse that it became possible for Schwarz and his staff to find adequately large quarters.

On January 24, 1933, the museum opened. By then, the ailing Weimar Republic was already in its death throes. The congratulations of the Weimar minister Trendelenburg, who headed a delegation there on March 2, 1933, sounded to many like an obituary. Only a few blocks away lay the ravages of the Reichstag fire, which had occurred on February 27, 1933. And only three days later, on March 5, 1933, Hitler emerged victorious in the general elections. The painter Max Liebermann, who served as honorary president of the Museum Association, decided the time had come for him to resign as honorary president of the Prussian Academy of Arts.

*The composer Kurt Weill (1900–50)
in 1929.*

Jews enjoyed a short-lived prominence in Berlin's local politics during the heady days of the revolution of 1918–19. There was Hugo Heimann of the Social Democrats (SPD) serving at the head of the City Council as well as in the Government of the Peoples' Representatives. Two other Jewish lawyers, Hugo Haase and Otto Landsberg, were also in this government. A Jewish governor, Paul Hirsch, stood at the head of the Prussian government. Hugo Preuss was rector of the Berlin Commercial Academy, state secretary in the Reich Ministry of the Interior and

Integration and Alienation

That a Jew, Max Liebermann, had become president of the Prussian Academy of Arts would only have been possible during the Weimar Republic. During the Wilhelmine period Jews had de jure the same rights as others, but without baptism it was impossible to become an officer or minister of state or to hold any other important or influential office. That was also true in many cases, before 1918, of professorships at any German institution of higher learning. Being of the "wrong" religion could make life very difficult. And even though many things had changed since 1918, Jews were still exposed to remarkably antagonistic feelings in society. The statesman and industrialist Walther Rathenau paid for his exceptional rise to the position of Minister of Foreign Affairs with his life. On June 24, 1922, he was assassinated in the Koenigsallee near his villa in Grunewald by members of an anti-Semitic, extreme right-wing organization.

*Arnold Schoenberg (1874–1951),
modernist composer and founder of twelve-tone music,
around 1930.*

co-founder of the German Democratic Party (DDP). Preuss is considered the principle framer of the Weimar Constitution. Finally there was Rosa Luxemburg, a radical from the left and the most famous woman of her time in German politics. (Haase and Luxemburg were both assassinated).

Only very few of these leaders considered themselves to be Jews in the religious sense, and while several maintained their formal membership in the Jewish Community, others turned their backs on the religion of their fathers. The Jewish Community considered most of the politicians of Jewish origin more a burden than a blessing. On December 19, 1918, the *Deutsche Israelitische Zeitung* complained in a leading article with the title "Too many Jews at the Top," that "this sudden *embarras de richesses* of Jewish politicians in high and responsible places in the new government is certainly no blessing for Jewry as a whole."

Nor did this visible significance of politicians of Jewish descent last very long. All in all, the number of Jewish ministers during the Weimar Republic remained quite small and, during the late 1920s, most political parties (with the exception of those on the left) hesitated to place Jewish candidates at the top of their lists. Many Jewish politicians continued to work on a local level or even within the Jewish Community. After his short period as Governor of Prussia (1918–20), Paul Hirsch was instrumental in the Prussian Constitutional Convention in bringing about the incorporation of Greater Berlin (April 1920). He then became deputy mayor of Berlin's Charlottenburg district.

Another member of the Prussian Constitutional Convention, Oskar Cohn, was a high official in the Reich Ministry of Justice and a major figure in the social democratic list Poalei Zion within the Jewish Community's Assembly of Representatives. Bernhard

Weiss was one of the favorite targets of anti-Semitic propaganda. In 1918 he became a high-ranking official in the Prussian Ministry of the Interior and in 1927 vice-president of the Berlin police. Among the Jewish deputies who sat in the Reichstag during the Weimar Republic was the physician Julius Moses. He would later be murdered in the concentration camp of Theresienstadt. Werner Scholem, brother of Gershom Scholem, represented the Communist Party of Germany in the Reichstag. He was later killed in Buchenwald.

One should of course avoid speculating about the political leanings of the all Jews based on the leanings of the above-named representatives. All the polls and samplings conducted during the period point to the fact that most Jews cast their votes for bourgeois parties, in particular for the liberal DDP (German Democratic Party). It was only in 1930, after the party's demise, that many Jews cast their votes for the Social Democrats. Even then many influential Jews looked for bourgeois alternatives.

Most spectacular was the conduct of Georg Kareski – the Zionist and head of the Berlin Jewish Community. He campaigned at the beginning of the1930s for a seat for the Catholic Center Party and even founded a committee for Jewish voters within the Center Party, also supported by other Zionists and Orthodox. From the very beginning, this campaign was futile.

It was in the field of political journalism that many Jews made their mark. Beginning as early as the middle of the nineteenth century, this phenomenon existed well into the Weimar period. Friedrich Stampfer was editor-in-chief of the SPD newspaper *Vorwaerts* (Forward), and Rudolf Hilferding of USPD's paper *Freiheit* (Freedom). (USPD was a left-wing splinter party of the Social Democrats that emerged after the vote for war credits in

Mascha Kaléko

Kleines Lesebuch

für Große

Left:
The art dealer Alfred Flechtheim (1878–1937)
ca. 1928.

Below:
Book cover for Alfred Doeblin's
Im Buch – zu Haus – Auf der Strasse,
presented by Alfred Doeblin and Oskar Loerke,
published 1928 by S. Fischer. Left, a photomontage
with the tower of the Berlin City Hall.

Left page, above:
Actors in Max Reinhardt's famous
Schall und Rauch cabaret
photographed in 1920.
From left to right:
Martin Zickel, Friedrich Kayssler,
Max Reinhardt.

Left page, below left:
The poet Hans Davidsohn, a.k.a.
Jacob van Hoddis (1887–1942)
in a drawing by Ludwig Meidner,
1913. He was murdered by the
National Socialists.

Left page, below middle: The poet
Else Lasker-Schueler (1869–1945)
in a "self-portrait in a coat of stars"
ca. 1913. She emigrated via
Switzerland to Palestine in 1933.

Left page, below right:
Book cover for the
1934 Small Reader for Adults,
by Mascha Kaléko (1912–74).
The poet emigrated to the US in 1938.

1914.) If one heard anti-Semites speak of the "Jewish press," however, it was because of the preponderance of Jews in the large daily newspapers. Among these papers were *Vossische Zeitung* and *B.Z. am Mittag* published by the house of Ullstein, and the *Berliner Tageblatt* and *Berliner Volks-Zeitung* published by the Mosse house.

These newspaper publishers all began their work in the days of the Reich, but Ullstein expanded his operations during the Weimar Republic very rapidly. In 1924 he published the monthly *Querschnitt*, founded by the art dealer Alfred Flechtheim, as well as *Uhu* (eagle owl); in 1925 a magazine was added for nature and science, *Koralle* (coral); a few years later the weekend newspaper *Die gruene Post* and the evening newspaper *Tempo* appeared.

The fact that the newspaper publishers and some of their most famous editors – Theodor Wolff of the *Berliner Tageblatt*, for instance – were Jewish did not, of course, make them "Jewish" newspapers. Nor were specifically Jewish themes easily to be found inside. If one wanted to learn of the goings-on in the Jewish Community one had to read specifically Jewish newspapers, such as the *Juedische Gemeindeblatt* or the *Juedische Rundschau* or the *Centralverein-Zeitung*. In Berlin in 1930 there were about fifty Jewish periodicals, among them the liberal *Morgen*, the Orthodox *Jeschurun*, *Der Nationaldeutsche Jude* and the *Juedische Frau*.

The decided absence of a "Jewish" voice was characteristic of the newspapers published by Ullstein and Mosse. What irked the anti-Semites most was that these papers held to a liberal democratic position. They represented "home" to liberal opinion leaders and the "enemy camp" to opponents.

There was, however, a third press empire, which was not owned by a Jewish family. It belonged to the German nationalist Alfred Hugenberg. Not only did he fight a press war with the liberal newspapers, he fought the Weimar Republic itself. An editorial in the *Vossische Zeitung* from November 9, 1931, was quick to predict that that "Hugenberg's goal would be reached in a wagon hitched to the Hitler party."

Hugenberg's activities and his newspapers clearly show how the newspapers of Ullstein and Mosse served as watchdogs for democracy and liberalism. But it would be wrong to think of these two publishing houses as being on the left. Especially in the last years of the Weimar Republic, the Mosse newspapers started to aim at right-wing conservative readers in order to maintain circulation.

One paper that did situate itself politically on the left was *Die Weltbuehne*, founded as the *Schaubuehne* in 1905 by Siegfried Jacobsohn. Jacobsohn himself was considered "assimilated," but he sought in no way to conceal his Jewishness. In a 1919 review of the play *Jaákobs Traum* (Jacob's Dream) by Richard Beer-Hofmann, Jacobsohn wrote, "I am Jew enough to feel that *Jaákobs Traum* is a national epic poem." For Jacobsohn, as for many secular Jews, the Bible had lost its religious meaning. He called the play a "substitute for the Bible."

The best known of the *Weltbuehne*'s contributors was Kurt Tucholsky. Gershom Scholem once characterized Tucholsky (unjustly it would seem) as "one of the most talented and repulsive Jewish authors, whose goal in life seemed to be to achieve at a very high level what anti-Semites could not." It does not seem right, in retrospect, to reproach Tucholsky with "Jewish self-hatred." Tucholsky tried, and in many ways succeeded, to unmask with "pitiless bare photographs" the foibles of Berlin's Jewish bourgeoisie. But in fact Tucholsky did not take aim at Jews in general so much as at those

Jews who denied their Jewishness. (For example, he wrote favorable articles about Yiddish theater.) This might seem ironic for a writer who had converted to Protestantism on the eve of World War I, but it is obviously attached to self-criticism.

In the character of Mr. Wendriner, Tucholsky created and played out this role to satirical perfection. Under the pseudonym of Kaspar Hauser, Tucholsky published between 1922 and 1930 some 16 "Wendriner essays" in the *Weltbuehne*. There, in long monologues and using a Berlin dialect spiked with Yiddish expressions, Wendriner pleads for authoritarian education, relates how he cheats on his wife and wishes aloud for a "strong" government. In the last and perhaps most biting of these essays (1930) Tucholsky's Wendriner aligns himself with the National Socialists, who have just assumed power. He is pleased to get his "yellow card," which identifies him as a "protected citizen." "Well," he declares, "at any rate order reigns. Therefore: order reigns, at any rate."

Of course Tucholsky could not imagine that the National Socialists would really gain power less than three years later and that there would soon be no such thing as Jewish "protected citizens." And his warnings about German nationalism, written under the pseudonyms of Peter Panter, Theobald Tiger and Ignaz Wrobel, proved to be even more accurate than his idea of National Socialist policies about Jews. In 1929 he published his grand polemical book *Deutschland, Deutschland ueber alles*, with illustrations by the artist John Heartfield (pseudonym of Helmut Herzfelde). Tucholsky sharply attacked the German justice system, the military, fraternity students and major industrialists. From 1924 on, Tucholsky lived mostly in Parisian exile, much as another German-Jewish-converted satirist, Heinrich Heine, had done in the nineteenth century. And much

like Heine, Tucholsky knew in his heart that it was really impossible to just "step out of" being a Jew.

In 1925 Tucholsky envisioned his burial at the Jewish cemetery in Weissensee, the largest in Europe:

There, where I have often been
to mourn
thither you will come, thither I will come,
when everything is over.
You love. You travel. You delight, you –
Field U –
Waiting in absentia
Field A.
The clock is ticking. Your grave can wait,
three meters long, one meter wide.
You'll see perhaps three, four foreign cities
Perhaps a nude Greta,
and also snow, perhaps twenty or thirty times
and then:
Field P – in Weissensee –
in Weissensee.

Although the Weissensee cemetery contains the grave of his father and a place for his mother, Kurt Tucholsky is not to be found there. His remains lie far from Berlin, in southern Sweden, where he committed suicide in 1935.

Tucholsky, seen from France and Sweden, might have been the incarnation of the "Berlin-Jewish spirit." There was another critic who, until 1933 was physically bound up with Berlin. The most powerful theater critic of his time, Alfred Kerr was both celebrated and feared. His columns appeared in the *Berliner Tageblatt* between 1919 and 1933. To Max Hermann-Neisse, Kerr's contributions were "not miserly, office-narrow, aesthetisizing or preachy but direct, brand-new, honestly subjective, full of progressive attitudes, and [marked with] a lust for the attack." Instead of poking fun or being sopho-

Rainy Day, Unter den Linden, *1926, by Lesser Ury (1862–1931).*
Private collection.

moric, self-important, ponderous and bull-ish, Hermann-Neisse saw the pieces as epito-mizing "lightness, grace and wit."

Most of the Jewish actors in Berlin – and there were a great many of them – did not perform in Yiddish, although many of the greatest stars had had to teach themselves German. Two of the greatest, Alexander Granach and Elisabeth Bergner, came from Galicia. Fritz Kortner came from Vienna, Ernst Deutsch from Prague.

Among the great directors, Max Rein-hardt's name stands out above all others. During the 1920s, however, he moved his major work from Berlin to Salzburg and Vienna. Reinhardt's great period had been the decade before World War I. In the 1920s his name had even come to be used pejora-tively in connection with "establishment" theater and apolitical aestheticism: people would say "enough of Reinhardt!" Never-theless it is impossible to underestimate Reinhardt's sustained influence on popular theater and cabaret.

Another great director was Leopold Jess-ner, who served as head of the Berlin State Theater beginning in 1919. Jessner was a representative of the "New Theater." His expressionist staging of *Wilhelm Tell* on December 12, 1919, was a clear political metaphor of the new Republic and against the tyranny of the old regime. The old was personified in the character of General Gessler, more a caricature than a convincing figure. During the premiere the audience broke into a tumult and could only be calmed down after the intervention of the ac-tors Fritz Kortner and Albert Bassermann.

There were other theaters in which Jews had the position of *intendant*. Viktor Barnowsky was at the Lessing Theater, the Hebbel Theater and the Lustspielhaus. There was Ferdinand Bruckner (i.e. Theodor Tag-ger), the founder of the Renaissance Theater.

Ernst Josef Aufricht founded the Theater am Schiffbauerdamm, which in August 1928 opened with the *Threepenny Opera* by Bertolt Brecht and Kurt Weill. Nor should one for-get the light theater, revue and cabaret – with such major figures as Erik Charell and Friedrich Hollaender.

Prominent Jewish names could be found in all aspects of Berlin's cultural life. One need only think of the conductors Otto Klemperer at the Kroll Opera House and Bruno Walter at the Philharmonic; the archi-tects Erich Mendelsohn and Oskar Kauf-mann; the playwrights Ernst Toller and Paul Kornfeld; the critics Walter Benjamin and Julius Bab. Jewish scientists and scholars were established at the most distinguished German-language universities: the chemist Richard Willstaetter in Munich and later in Zurich; the physicist Max Born in Goettin-gen; the historian Alfred Kantorowicz in Heidelberg; and the philosopher Ernst Cas-sirer in Hamburg. Berlin was home during the 1920s to Albert Einstein, and although Freud remained in Vienna, two of his disci-ples – Karl Abraham and Max Eitingon – founded the first institute for the academic training of psychoanalysts in Berlin-Witte-nau. As with the founders, most of the stu-dents were of Jewish origin. One of the ini-tiators of the institute, Ernst Simmel, was the President of the Berlin Psychoanalytical Soci-ety between 1925 and 1930.

When in 1919 the Institute for Sexual Science opened its doors in Berlin, Magnus Hirschfeld was its first director. Among his colleagues was Felix Theilhaber, who also made a name for himself as a Zionist author. The titles of his books reflect the depressed mood of the time in certain circles (*The Demise of German Jews*, and *Sterile Berlin*, among them). Less well known is his chilias-tic novel *Thy Kingdom Come!* in which he draws a portrait of the world during the time of the seventeenth-century false messiah Sabbatai Zvi.

It is thus impossible to overlook the cultural and scholarly Jewish contribution to the "Golden Twenties." But one should not fall prey to the illusion that only Jews mattered in Berlin's cultural life. Aside from the painters Max Liebermann and Lesser Ury – already somewhat out of fashion – almost no other major Berlin artist of the period was Jewish. And with the exception of Schoenberg, most of the important modern composers were not Jewish. Berlin theater boasted the names of Bertolt Brecht and Erwin Piscator, both of whom were not Jews, and in addition to the actors Elisabeth Bergner and Fritz Kortner who were Jewish there were Emil Jannings and Heinrich George who were not. More important is the question of whether the achievements of the Jewish artists and intellectuals differed in any way from those of their non-Jewish colleagues. Is it indeed possible to speak of a decidedly *Jewish* contribution? The historian Peter Gay has written that the legend of a "Berlin-Jewish Spirit" is just that: a legend and an absurdity.

Would someone attending Leopold Jessner's Expressionist production of Schiller's *Wilhelm Tell* or Max Reinhardt's extravagant production of Shakespeare's *A Midsummer Night's Dream*; watching Elisabeth Bergner do *Maria Stuart* or Fritz Kortner do *Hamlet*; listening to Bruno Walter's interpretation of Beethoven's Ninth Symphony or Paul Dessau's interpretation of his own compositions; hearing Fritz Kreisler play the violin or Artur Schnabel play the piano; reading Siegfried Trebitsch's translations of Shaw or Alfred Wolfenstein's translations of Shelley, suspect in any way that these artists and writers were Jewish? Was that influential left-wing journal, *Die Weltbuehne*, more "Jewish" under its first editor, Siegfried Jacobsohn, than it became under its second editor, Carl von Ossietzky? Was Brecht-Weill's phenomenally successful *Dreigroschenoper* Jewish in its music but not in its libretto? Just as there was no Jewish way to cut furs, there was no Jewish way to paint portraits, play Beethoven, produce Ibsen or fence in the Olympics.

And the audiences? What of the public? There was, of course, a great number of Jews who attended concerts and plays in Weimar Berlin, but again it is impossible to single out a group and call them "a Jewish audience." Only a few weeks before the Nazis seized power, in an official and somewhat "establishment" performance presented by the government at the State Theater, the diplomat and writer Count Harry Kessler jotted down the following picture in ·his diary:

I had a seat in the second row of the orchestra behind the Einsteins, the painter Konrad von Kardorff and Heinrich Mann. Next to me sat the banker and erstwhile USPD Minister of Finance Hugo Simon. In the row behind us sat Saxony's Minister of State, Alfred von Nostitz. On my other side sat the comedy writer Ludwig Fulda and Lieutenant General Hans von Seeckt.

Did such a mixed seating order signal the successful social integration of the Jews? In a certain sense this integration was much further along in the Twenties in Berlin than in other places in Germany and at other times in the history of the Jews in Germany. Gershom Scholem remarked that, despite his parents' numerous memberships in many

Wohlfahrts- und Jugendamt der Jüdischen Gemeinde

Rosenstraße 2—4. Fernsprecher: Norden 5710

Vorsitzender: Eugen Caspary   Syndikus: R.-A. Dr. Lamm
Hauptsekretariat: Marg. Loewenthal   Zentralauskunftstelle: Doris Goldmann

Bezirkssekretariat I: Hanna Schall

Mitte A (Alte Synagoge)	Arnold Ascher, Max Seefeld, Rabb. Dr. Freyer. Sprechstunde: Rosenstr. 2-4, Donnerstag 5-7	**Friedrichshain I** (Synagoge Lippmann Tauß)	Dr. A. Steinert, Gustav Lewandowsky. Sprechstunde: Gollnowstraße 12, Donnerstag 6-7	**Linden-straße**	Henry Feilchenfeld, Erich Burin, Adolf Wittkowsky, Rabb. Dr. Warschauer. Sprecht.: Synagoge Lindenstraße, Dienstag 6-7
		Kreuzberg	San.-Rat Dr. Caspari, Frau Bianca Rosenberg, Rabb. Dr. Silberberg. Sprecht. bei Rinkel, Hornstraße 19, Montag 10-11 vorm., Donnerstag 5-6 nachm.		

Bezirkssekretariat II: Gertrud Brzezinski

Mitte C (Synagoge Kaiserstraße)	Max Moschytz, Paul Pintus, Rabb. Dr. Loewenthal. Sprechstunden: Kaiserstraße 3, Mittwoch 7 nachm., Sonntag 9½ vorm.	**Mitte D** (Invalidenstr.)	Dr. Ludwig Mendelsohn, H. Michelsohn, A. Bilewski, Rabb. Nobel. Sprechstunde: Zehdenicker Str. 16, Sonntag vorm. 10 Uhr, Donnerstag nachm. 6 Uhr	**Friedrichshain II** (Frankfurter Allee)	Frau Clara Birnbaum, San.-Rat Dr. Rosenthal, Rabb. Dr. Rosenthal. Sprechstunde: Frankfurter Allee 67 (½8-½9 vorm.)

Bezirkssekretariat III: Dora Silbermann

Prenzlauer Berg (Synagoge Rykestr.)	Gustav Loeffer, Dr. Chaskel, S. Rocheljohn, Rabb. Dr. Weyl. Sprechstunde: Schönhauser Allee 25, Mittwoch 4-5	**NW** (Synagoge Levetzowstr.)	Gustav Zamory, Frau Betty Struck, Rabb. Dr. Lewkowitz. Sprechstunde: Claudiusstr. 7, Mittwoch 5-6	**Wedding**	Ernst Rosenbach, Frau Mathilde Bock, Rabb. Dr. Alexander. Sprechstunde: Exerzierstr. 11a, Mittwoch 7-8 abends
		Pankow-Niederschönhausen	Felix Heimann, Direktor Israel, Frau Justizrat Goldberg, Rabb. Dr. Pick. Sprechstunde: Parkstraße 8a, Montag bis Donnerstag 5-6	**Charlottenburg III** (Synagoge Fasanenstr.) mit Halensee u. Grunewald	Felix Meyerhof, Frau Julie Casparius, Rabb. Dr. Bergmann. Sprechstunde: Synagoge Fasanenstraße, Mittwoch 4-5

Bezirkssekretariat IV: Paula Schwersenz

Süden (Synagoge Kottbuser Ufer)	Theodor Herzog, Moritz Rosenstein, Rabb. Dr. Bleichrode. Sprechstunde: Synagoge Kottbuser Ufer, Mittwoch und Sonntag 8-9 vorm.	**Wilmersdorf**	R.-A. Dr. Georg Baum, Dr. Leo Caro, Rabb. Dr. Zelski. Sprechstunde: Synagoge Fasanenstraße, Montag 4½-5½	**Westen** (Synagoge Lützowstraße)	Max Klein, Frau Frieda Lehr, Rabb. Dr. Wiener. Sprechstunde: Synagoge Lützowstraße, Mittwoch von 5-6
Steglitz-Friedenau	Frau Dr. Laserstein, Frau Mannheim, Rabb. Dr. Winter. Sprechstunden: Handjerystraße 60-62, Dienstag und Freitag ½11-½12	**Charlottenburg** (Synagoge Pestalozzistr.)	Hermann Aron, Arnold Wasser, Frau Prof. Dessau, Rabb. Dr. Emil Levy. Sprechstunden: Pestalozzistr. 14, Montag und Donnerstag 9-10	**Charlottenburg II** (Synagoge Passauer Str.)	Frau Hermine Lesser, Rabbiner Dr. H. Carlebach. Sprechstunde: Marburger Straße 11, Montag und Donnerstag 3-4

Bezirkssekretariat V: Dr. Adelheid Levy

Schöneberg (Synagoge Münchener Str.)	Martin Buchholz, Rabb. Dr. Arthur Levy. Sprechstunde: Münchener Str. 37, Montag und Donnerstag 11-12	**Lichtenberg**	Otto J. Kraft, Frau Selma Littauer, Rabb. Dr. Rosenthal. Sprechstunde: Finowstraße 30, Donnerstag 6-7	**Neukölln**	Hermann Müller, Heinrich Roß, Rabb. Dr. Kantorowsky. Sprechstunde: Jarstraße 8, Donnerstag 3-5
Cöpenick:	Frau Prediger Frank, Frau R.-A. Zippert, Prediger Frank. Sprechstunde: täglich Borgmannstraße 6	**Karlshorst**	Rechtsanwalt Hamburger, Theodor Baron, Prediger Frank. Sprechstunde: Stolzenfelsstr. 2, Sonntag 10 Uhr	**Mitte B** (Neue Synagoge)	Dr. Rosenzweig, H. Rubenjohn, Rabb. Dr. Blumenthal. Sprechstunde: Oranienburger Straße 29, Montag und Donnerstag 5-6

Organizational plan for the Jewish welfare organizations during the 1920s
More than one thousand volunteers were working.
The organization was led by Eugen Caspary (1863–1931), who did much to
modernize Jewish welfare operations. From the Juedisches Gemeindeblatt
(the newsletter of the Jewish Community) in 1927.

Above:
The Fasanenstrasse
synagogue after services
photographed by
Hans G. Casparius
in 1929.

Below:
Rear view of the
Levetzowstrasse synagogue
drawn in 1932
by the pupil
Ingeborg Hufenbach.

non-Jewish societies and clubs and despite the feeling that the family was completely assimilated, his parents never had non-Jewish guests in their home. Nor were they ever invited to the homes of non-Jews. This held more for the period leading up to World War I than for the Weimar Republic. As the years rolled on, social bonds became stronger, and as a result the number of mixed marriages increased as well. During the 1920s and at the beginning of the 1930s, more than 20 percent of all Jews chose a non-Jew as partner in marriage. The memoirs of this period often tell stories of the social contacts inside and outside the family home.

It was nevertheless a period of growing anti-Semitism, which ran counter to all these experiences. This was most easily seen among the younger generation. In the last years of the Reich, those responsible within the Jewish Community had closed Jewish schools and clubs in order to promote social integration. Now they were forced by the increasingly unfriendly climate of Germany's youth movements, fraternities, and student organizations to re-establish Jewish institutions.

The Jewish Youth Movement with its romantic emphasis on hiking and country-side-excursions was in great demand among young Jewish Berliners. All ethical and religious tendencies had such clubs. Clubs ranged from those for Zionists (Blue-White), liberals (Comrades); German nationalist Jews (Little Black Flag); to the Orthodox (Esra). Indded, all the branches of Jewish thought were represented.

Jewish sports clubs were also being founded or were already flourishing. All branches of Jewish thought and life were represented. Bar Kochba, the first sports club, had been founded at the turn of the century to answer the call by the Zionist Max Nordau for what he called "muscled

Jewry." Before World War I these clubs and associations were generally strictly limited to Zionists, and for that reason were not recognized by the liberal Community figures. This resulted in Bar Kochba not being able to use a gym owned and operated by the Jewish Community.

During the 1920s, however, the liberal Jews also started to organize separate Jewish sports clubs. But they did not bring national fame (as the champion soccer team Hakoach Wien had done in Austria). The *Reichsbund Juedischer Frontsoldaten* (The Reich Association of Jewish Frontline Soldiers) founded the Schild-Vereine (Shield-Clubs). The club would win a master title in Jiu-Jitsu, a Japanese form of self-defense – an irony that was probably lost on most people.

Most significant for the formation of a reinforced Jewish social milieu among the youth was the founding of new Jewish schools. Between 1919 and 1933 five new Jewish schools were established, partially as private foundations, partially under the supervision of the Jewish Community. The number of pupils in Berlin's Jewish schools rose from 1,170 in 1913 to almost 3,000 on the eve of the Nazi seizure of power. Though the general population of Jewish school-age children itself diminished, in the few years between 1927 and 1931 more Jews attended Jewish schools than ever before. In the boys' school, attendance rose from 203 to 296. That of the girls' school rose from 108 to 171. The majority of pupils in Jewish schools were from either Orthodox or east European Jewish families, but there was a growing tendency for a small minority from liberal homes to attend as well.

Initially, the supporters of liberal Judaism had been friendly toward these interfaith "simultaneous schools" in theory, but in practice preferred to keep their distance. They sent their children to Christian-oriented schools, which kept Christian holidays and expected pupils to show up on Saturday mornings. Moreover, most of these "simultaneous schools" were located in workers' districts and, since the majority of the pupils were workers' children, most bourgeois parents stayed away.

This changed, however, as parents became increasingly anxious about the rising anti-Semitism to be found in most non-Jewish schools. They turned to Jewish schools. "The Jewish Popular School is no longer the poor step-child of respectable Jewish circles," stated an observer in 1930. "It has managed to succeed . . . All strata of the Jewish population, in their social, religious and Jewish-political nuances, now send their children to the Jewish Popular school."

As a reaction to the new Jewish high schools (*gymnasiums* and *lyceums*) in other large cities of Germany, the Jewish Community of Berlin produced plans in 1930 to establish such a school in Berlin. This and another school also conceived of at this time (for the study of the Talmud) could not be realized during the Weimar Republic. In 1919, however, the diploma (*Abitur*) issued by the Jewish *Gymnasium* operated by the Community of Adass Jisroel was recognized by the state as being acceptable for entry into a state-operated university.

In contrast to other states in the German Reich, 80 percent of Berlin's Jewish children attended interfaith schools by this time. The same was true of membership in sports' clubs. It is impossible to overlook the trend of closing ranks and turning inward in the face of the external threat. When, at the beginning of the 1930s, anti-Semitic incidents began to become more frequent and violent – and many German youth clubs went searching for their "Aryan" identity – the Jewish organizations offered a realm of peace as well as a forum for younger Jews to confront the new tendencies of the period.

These new tendencies were an ill omen for Berlin's Jews. Berlin was little different from the rest of Germany as, at the turn of the 1930s, Nazi election successes inspired large-scale anti-Semitic verbal and non-verbal force. Harassment became an everyday occurrence. In 1923 a pogrom was directed against *Ostjuden* in the *Scheunenviertel*. In September 1931 the National Socialists rioted on Rosh Hashanah (the Jewish New Year) brazenly doing so near Berlin's main shopping street, the Kurfuerstendamm. For over an hour they assaulted the Jewish prayer-goers of the Fasanenstrasse synagogue. When the police finally halted the goings-on, 63 instigators were arrested. The official representatives of the Centralverein congratulated the police for their effective work, but, behind closed doors, criticized them for coming much too late. Because of the fact that among the 15,000 policemen there were several hundred National Socialists, it was later admitted by the Minister of the Interior, Karl Severing, that sympathy with the thugs had probably prevented the police from arriving earlier.

A few years before this event, Walter Mehring had described in one of his most bitter satires a phenomenon that was yet to come. The Russian word *pogrom* had found itself a niche in the Berlin scene:

In the Ufa film
There's Emperor Wil'lm
The reaction hoists its flag on the cathedral
It has a swastika and blue-cross gas,
Monocle opposing the hooked nose,
Off to the pogrom,
At the hippodrome.

The anti-Jewish climate had many manifestations. Appeals to boycott Jewish shops

Above left: The actress Lucie Mannheim (1899–1976)
ca. 1929 in a still photograph from the play
Wet or Dry by Frank Green.
Photograph Schmidt.
Above right: The actor Max Pallenberg (1877–1934)
in a 1931 film still from the
The Brave Sinner, directed by Fritz Kortner.
Below left: Actress Elisabeth Bergner in a film still
from Miss Julie, 1924.
Below right: The actor Ernst Deutsch (1890–1969)
ca. 1930.

were louder and more frequent. Many such appeals incited mischief against the Jewish-owned department stores of Wertheim, Tietz, Schocken and the Kaufhaus des Westens. But there were entire professions whose members were attacked with anti-Semitic propaganda. This was especially true of doctors and lawyers, a striking 48 percent of whom were Jewish. It was still possible to react to these chilling manifestations with satire, as the cabarettist at "Tingel Tangel" Friedrich Hollaender did a few days after the 1931 incident near Kurfuerstendamm. To a melody from Bizet's *Carmen* he set the following text:

Whether it rains or hails,
whether it snows or there's lightning,
whether the sun goes down or it thunders,
whether one freezes or sweats,
whether it's nice or cloudy,
whether it thaws or pours,
whether it drizzles, whether it trickles,
whether you cough or whether you sneeze
For all of this the Jews are guilty.
The Jews are guilty of everything.

In contrast to Hollaender's song, which made light of "little Hitler," Jewish organizations such as the Centralverein and the Reich Union of Jewish Front Soldiers treated the manifestations with deadly seriousness. They reacted with increasingly vocal protests. None of these organizations, however, could halt the downfall of the Weimar Republic. When Hitler seized power on January 30, 1933, the worst fears of the German Jews had come true.

A few years earlier, the Berlin travel author Artur Landsberger had written a variation of the Viennese author Hugo Bettauer's bestseller *The City without Jews*. He called it *Berlin without Jews*. Today the words he put in the mouth of the speaker of the German Reichstag in 1925 seem prophetic: "The German Jews stand outside the constitution and can be considered foreign. Since the majority of the German people reject the Jews in their society, they must be considered a burden and driven from the country." In Landsberger's book, 97 older German Jewish patriots, who demand to be buried on German soil, commit mass suicide. Simultaneously, a tidal wave of hundreds of thousands of emigrants floods beyond Germany's borders. While the cultural and economic life of other European centers blooms, Berlin is down and out: "Berlin is dead!" It is difficult to find a doctor or a lawyer. The stock exchange is empty. The hoteliers Mr. and Mrs. Adlon greet each and every guest individually, and travelers at the railway station attempt to hail a cab but find nothing more than "a junk heap with a driver in tatters and a horse whose ribs are sticking out above his hide." It is no wonder that, as in Bettauer's Vienna (the original *City without Jews*), the hungry and disappointed population begs the Jews to return and removes the anti-Semitic government from power.

But it is only in the novel that the Jews return. Both Landsberger and Bettauer soon felt reality at their necks. Bettauer was murdered in his Vienna office in 1925 by a right-wing extremist after a film based on his book created a furor. And, like the 97 "German citizens of Jewish faith" in his novel, Landsberger took his own life in 1933. His dystopian vision had been usurped by reality. Landsberger could perceive only too clearly that the real fate of the German Jews would, in contrast to his novel, not have a happy end.

Michael Brenner

Left page:
Members of the Youth Clubs at the beginning
of the 1930s. Jews felt themselves excluded from the
many German youth clubs, which increasingly
emphasized Voelkisch (ethnic German) ideology.
They organized clubs of their own.
The Zionist "Blue-White" hiking club was created
in 1912. With 3,000 members it was the largest
Jewish youth organization in Germany.
In 1923 the Youth-Jewish Hiking Club with
Zionist-Socialist ideology was created, and in 1931,
the Haschomer Hazair (Young Watchman).
Other clubs were the Bund der Kameraden
(Club of Comrades), die Werkleute (the Working
People) and Addas Isroel's group, Esra.

Right page, above left:
A Berlin sporting ground photographed
by Abraham Pisarek in 1925.
Above right: Martel Jakob of the Bar Kochba sports
club and German javelin champion,
photographed in 1929.
Below: March of the Bar Kochba sports club
at the German Maccabi-championships
in Hamburg, 1930.

Max Liebermann during the spring 1932 elections for the Reichs President.
The candidates were Paul von Hindenburg, Ernst Thaelmann and Adolf Hitler.

Jews during the Period of National Socialism

Not only is an academic history of the Berlin Jews after 1871 still unwritten. There is also no adequate historical account of the years between 1933 and 1945, the most dramatic period in the existence of the Jews in Berlin. In 2000 in the New Synagogue on Oranienburger Strasse, the Centrum Judaicum created an exhibition on the history of Berlin's Jews during the part of the National Socialist regime of terror from 1938 to 1945. For the first time an exhibition was mounted from the point of view of Jews themselves – in the very place where so much had happened, where times of success, defeat, and cautious revival were so close to each other. The exhibition was accompanied by an illustrated catalogue.

According to statistics, 160,564 Jews lived in Berlin in 1933, 3.8 percent of the entire Berlin population. Twelve years later, on April 1, 1945, a mere 5,100 Jews remained.

The enormity of what happened to the Jews of Berlin at the hands of the Nazis could not be foreseen in 1933. The noose tightened ever so slowly, and the state policies of the National Socialists, the forced emigration, changed gradually into a policy to exterminate all the Jews of Europe.

One should try to avoid judging history from the vantage point of the present. For example, it is wrong to ask how it was possible for the Jewish Museum to open its doors on January 24, 1933, only to be forced to close them again after the pogrom of November 1938. It simply was possible. Until November 10, 1938, this and many other institutions of the Jewish Community had been able to withstand the increasingly threatening circumstances. And holding out was also a form of resistance.

The life of the Berlin Jews during the Third Reich seems easy to deal with as it concerns only a minority in one city and for only a short period of twelve years. In truth, however, we are faced with so many problems and aspects that – in order to avoid encyclopedic superficiality that in the end says nothing (positively stated: if we strive to paint an accurate picture) – we have to be more precise and limit our inquiry in many respects.

Let us begin with the problem of periodization. The Nazi period is generally divided into two periods of six years each. The first period was one of – highly tenuous – peace outside Germany's borders. The succeeding six years were a period of catastrophic war. Although this division was significant for Jews in Germany – and especially for those in Berlin – for their specific history, other dividing lines and other ways of perceiving the problems played a greater role.

Left Page:
above left: An appeal to boycott Jewish doctors and lawyers photographed ca. 1930.
Above right: Poster of the NSDAP (Nazi Party) for the Day of the Jewish Boycott, April 1, 1933. Photograph by Joe J. Heydecker.
Middle: A tourist steamer on the Havel River bears a slogan announcing: "Those who buy from Jews are stealing the people's property."
Below: 1933 boycott appeal on a shop window of the Kopp & Joseph drugstore at Koernerstrasse 5.

Right page:
Photographs of April 1, 1933.
Top: National Socialists paste boycott appeals on the shop window of a Jewish boutique.
Below: SA men with boycott appeals in front of a Jewish shop in Berlin.

JOACHIM PRINZ

WIR JUDEN

VERLEGT BEI ERICH REISS
BERLIN 1934

Title page of Prinz's 1934 book We Jews,
published in Berlin.

*Joachim Prinz (1902–88),
a liberal rabbi active in the Zionist movement.*

DEUTSCHJÜDISCHER WEG / EINE SCHRIFTENREIHE / NR. 1

WIR
DEUTSCHEN JUDEN

V O N

DR. PHIL. HANS JOACHIM SCHOEPS

V V

1 9 3 4

VORTRUPP VERLAG / BERLIN SW 29

*Below left: Hans-Joachim Schoeps (1909–80),
historian of religion and ideas (after his return from
exile in Sweden, professor in Erlangen).
Title page of his book* We German Jews,
*which appeared in 1934 in the Vortrupp publishing
house, of which he was the head.*

Right page: Title of the newspaper Juedische
Rundschau *of April 4, 1933, with the headline
of a remarkable article by Robert Weltsch,
"Tragt ihn mit Stolz, den gelben Fleck" (Wear it with
Pride, the Yellow Badge!)*

The Attempt to be Positive

How did Jewish Berliners conduct themselves in 1933? Robert Weltsch, editor-in-chief of the Zionist newspaper *Juedische Rundschau,* described in an editorial on April 4, 1933, the reaction to the Nazi boycott of Jewish shops of April 1, 1933, with the title: "Wear it with Pride, the Yellow Badge!" In printing this he was either showing or urging a new sort of Jewish self-image, a positive idea of Jewish identity. The issue sold so well that another 5,000 had to be printed. Alex Bein, the biographer of Theodor Herzl, commented on Weltsch's article fifty years later: "The essay, with its courageous but controlled pride, made a profound impression on all who read it, even on German Gentiles. I couldn't help notice the effects. . . . The essay is nevertheless a symptom of the cluelessness about the magnitude and systematic nature of the impending disaster." Ten years later Weltsch, now living in Palestine, regretted his naïveté and wrote: "Today [April 13, 1943] I would not dare – least of all from the safe haven here – to demand that Jews in a martyred Europe wear the 'yellow badge with pride.' Today it is this badge that is a sign of defeat [from September 1941 on, Jews had to wear a yellow 6-pointed star] – it was no longer a simple outward sign of one's belonging to Jewry, but now a stigma that identified its bearer as fair game in a gigantic, brutal hunt."

Twenty years later, in 1963, Weltsch looked back:

Then, in 1943, nobody knew of Auschwitz, but we felt that an earthquake was going on. We were witnesses to a performance nobody would have ever thought possible. What was going on in the Jewish soul? We were alternating between hope and despair. Everything seemed unreal, like a bad dream. Curiously and miraculously, however, it was not only fear and loathing within us, but an inexplicable feeling of superiority, even of triumph. The perpetrators who raged here [on April 1, 1933] revealed themselves to be a kind of underworld, and the persecuted were the moral victors. And it is a fact that the will to moral resistance then arose in the Jews. The echo of that editorial "Wear it with Pride, the Yellow Badge" in the *Juedische Rundschau* was a sign of the changed attitude.

It should be pointed out that the various committees of the Jewish Community did not take the political changes that took place on January 30, 1933, very seriously. Kurt Jakob Ball-Kaduri, who assembled a large collection of memoirs after his emigration,

On May 10, 1933, to protest "against the un-German spirit,"
National Socialist students burned the works of Jewish and politically disdained authors.
The autodafé took place at the square next to the opera house on Unter den Linden,
and Joseph Goebbels delivered a rabble-rousing speech.

has informed us: "On January 30, 1933, the day Adolf Hitler was named Reich Chancellor, the [liberal] board of the Berlin Jewish Community on Oranienburger Strasse was having a meeting. One of the agenda items was the budget and financing of the Jewish schools." All the school principals were present, and "a decision to close the primary schools was announced. The first school to be closed would be the [Zionist] school on Rykestrasse. . . . All protests were to no avail. Even the warning by Prof. Julius Guttmann [then lecturer on the Philosophy of the Jewish Religion at Hochschule fuer die Wissenschaft des Judentums] was rejected: 'Who knows if we might not be needing this school again very soon to take in the pupils from the public primary schools?' No sooner had Selma Schiratzki [principal of the Rykestrasse

school] told her colleagues this terrible message when the news came through that Hitler had just been appointed Chancellor."

The liberal board did not yet recognize the sign of the times. Later that evening a meeting took place at a café near Kurfuerstendamm to discuss the economic demands of Jewish craftsmen. An hour before the meeting began, the news of Hitler's rise to power was made known. "The first speaker," wrote Ball-Kaduri, "a liberal, limited his remarks to his prepared subject and put great stress on the opposing views among Jews. The second speaker was . . . [Hans] Tramer for the Zionists. He said: 'History has taken a major turn. Hitler has become Reich Chancellor. All differences among Jews are now senseless; we are all faced by the same danger.' His speech did not seem to impress anyone. All present thought he was painting too black a picture. There was no supportive response." Of course some liberals knew that Tramer's remarks were not exaggerated; nevertheless, in January 1933 many Jews still wanted to believe that Hitler's anti-Semitic ravings were nothing but election campaign tactics and that Hitler did not really mean what he was saying.

Right after the events of early 1933 Jews in Germany and especially in Berlin underwent a certain process described by Ernst Simon many years later as "building while sinking." Thus a blossoming of Jewish organizations and institutions of the Berlin Jewish Community can be identified between 1933 and 1938. The development of the Jewish Museum is only one of many possible examples. In this context the Jewish Kulturbund (Jewish Cultural League) should also be mentioned. Originally founded under the name Cultural League of German Jews, its first activities date from spring 1933 and it was dissolved on September 11, 1941. On October 1, 1933, the activities of the Kulturbund were inaugurated with a performance of Lessing's *Nathan der Weise*, as it were "a kind of credo of the liberal Jewish middle class" (Geisel and Broder).

The Kulturbund, as expressed in Paragraph 1 of its statutes, "has the aim of promoting the artistic and scholarly interests of the Jewish population and to assist Jewish artists and scholars in obtaining employment." "Finding work for Jewish artists and scholars driven out of theaters and concert and lecture halls" turned the Kulturbund, according to Herbert Freeden, into a "forced community with social functions." Mirjam Stern, daughter of Moritz Stern, was the first head of the library and art collection of the Jewish Community. She recalled the "beneficent institution, Kulturbund" in December 1992 in a letter to me: "In the three to four years of my membership I received an essential part of my education in culture and the arts." It was similar for an entire generation of young people whose access to German culture was disappearing.

By order of the Gestapo the Kulturbund was dissolved on September 11, 1941. One of the founders, Julius Bab, was able to emigrate via France to the United States in 1939, where, after the forced dissolution of the Kulturbund, he wrote: "Without doubt it is good that the Nazis' diabolical game is now over, in which they tried to show the world that Jews in Germany even had organizations for theater and the arts! For this reason only, Nazi authorities maintained the Kulturbund. . . . It is good that the lie is over."

Another example can be seen in the Jewish schools, which developed considerably after 1933. Consider the fate of the middle school of the Berlin Jewish Community, on Grosse Hamburger Strasse. The building was dedicated as a school on November 26, 1906. (Since the early 1990s, it is once again used as a school of the Berlin Jewish Community.) Thousands of children were educated at the school in the spirit of Mendelssohn, since it had been founded in 1826 as the successor to the Jewish Free School, which was opened in 1778 by Moses Mendelssohn and David Friedleander. As of late 1931 it was open to both boys and girls. We know from the memoirs of the school principal, Heinemann Stern, about what happened in the building as long as it served as a school. His book *Warum hassen sie uns, eigentlich?* (Why Do They Hate Us, Really?) was edited and published in 1970, long after his death.

After the Nazis came to power in 1933, many Jewish boys and girls left the general public schools for the safety of the Jewish schools. At its peak in 1935, the school on Grosse Hamburger was, with 1,025 pupils, bursting at the seams. After the pogrom of

Above:
In the office of the Juedische Rundschau.
Center: Editor-in-chief Robert Weltsch (1891–1982).
Left: Betty Frankenstein (1882–1960),
publisher beginning in 1933.
Photograph by Herbert Sonnenfeld,
1937.

Below:
Exhibition rooms at the Jewish Museum
on Oranienburger Strasse.
Photograph by Herbert Sonnenfeld,
ca. 1935.

Girls reading with a caretaker at the Baruch Auerbach orphanage.
Photograph by Abraham Pisarek, ca. 1935.

November 9, 1938, when many families managed to emigrate, the school started losing pupils. From spring 1939 until it was banned in the summer of 1942, it only had about 380 pupils. Even though today the school is open and Jewish life has returned, the name "Grosse Hamburger Strasse" still carries with it visions of horror, as the Jewish home for the aged next door had become a pre-deportation assembly camp under Nazi rule.

It should not be overlooked, however, that despite the apparent revival of Jewish culture the fate about to befall the Berlin Jews was clearly visible. In a 1933 essay commemorating Leo Baeck's sixtieth birthday (born May 23, 1873), published by the newspaper of the Central Association of German Citizens of the Jewish Faith, one could read: "This is not the time for German Jews to be celebrating."

Immediately after assuming power, the Nazis began excluding Jews from the civil service, cultural affairs, and business. Laws and edicts aimed to destroy their means of earning a living and to isolate them. Government and Nazi Party officials and business associations worked hand in hand to achieve these goals. In 1933 the so-called "Aryanization" of business started. Banks, prosperous businesses, department stores, and hotels were among the first to fall into greedy hands. Jewish entrepreneurs not willing to "sell" their businesses were put under legal pressure and faced financial ruin. On April 1, 1933, Jewish stores were boycotted, especially the "Jewish Department Stores": Hermann Tietz, Karstadt, Wertheim, and

Above:
Title pages of various Jewish newspapers with reports
on the Jewish Winter Relief.
At the middle (in the Star of David)
is an appeal to contribute.
Photograph and montage by Abraham Pisarek, 1937.

Below:
A concert given by a Jewish Youth orchestra
in the Pankow orphanage.
Photograph by Abraham Pisarek, ca. 1935.

Right page:
Kulturbund advertisement in the
Juedisches Gemeindeblatt *(Jewish Community*
newsletter) of September 4, 1938.

Der Kulturbund zeigte:

Oben von links: Elfriede Borodkin in „Er und Sie". — Hans Karl Rosenberg in dem Palästina-Schauspiel „Das Gericht". — Jenny Berstein-Schaffer in „Aresha". — Gina Friedmann in „Schabbatai Zwi".
Mitte von links: Rita Atlasz in der Oper „Don Pasquale". — Camilla Eisner-Spira in „Arm wie eine Kirchenmaus". — Max Ehrlich in „Schöne Helena".
Unten von links: Szene aus dem Palästina-Schauspiel „Das Gericht". — Alfred Berliner im gleichen Stück — Fritz Wisten in „Schabbatai Zwi".
Photos: Abraham; Montage: Szkolny

KaDeWe. In reality they were ruined through the efforts of the "Aryan" banks, which blocked their means of credit and forced their sale under unfavorable conditions.

The legal disenfranchisement of the Jews began in 1933 with the "Law to Re-establish Professional Civil Servants," which led to he dismissal of all Jews in public employment. On September 15, 1935, the so-called Nuremberg Race Laws were proclaimed at the Nazi Party convention. The notorious law "to protect German blood and German honor" prohibited German "Aryans" from marrying or having extramarital sexual relations with Jews. Before long the courts in the capital were handling dozens of trials against both sides. The "Reich Citizenship Law" deprived Jews of their civic equality and degraded them officially to second-class beings.

The "Decree on the Declaration of Jewish Property" followed on April 26, 1938, providing the foundation for extensive "Aryanization" of Jewish-held property. The Fourth Edict to the "Reich Citizenship Law" of July 25, 1938, rescinded Jewish doctors' rights to practice medicine, and the Fifth Edict made it impossible for Jewish lawyers to litigate. All these measures aimed to drive Jews to emigrate after they had been stripped of their financial assets. Despite this harassment, however, only 48,000 of 160,000 Jews in Berlin had decided to emigrate by 1937. For that reason in 1938 the Nazis developed a plan to force them to leave Germany.

A Security Service department (IV/2) memorandum to its chief, Reinhard Heydrich, dated May 24, 1934, said: "The goal of the policies regarding Jews must be to get all of them to leave Germany. . . . It is to restrict them of all means of livelihood – not only in an economic sense. For them Germany must cease to be their future – a land where the older generation dies off, and the young should not be able to live, so they will constantly feel the need to emigrate."

On June 10, 1938, Goebbels held a speech before 300 police officers in his Ministry of Propaganda, and he wrote in his diary: "I actually goad them. Not a trace of sentimentality. The law is not important. What is important is harassment. The Jews must leave Berlin. The police will help me to this end." This was the primer for a hate campaign against Jews, in the course of which their shops and the signs of doctors and lawyers were besmirched and, in the action of June 16, 1938, several thousand Jews were rounded up under the pretext that they were dealing in drugs. This "June Action" – discontinued after a few days because it was condemned in the foreign press – was a dress rehearsal for the pogrom that November.

The November Pogrom

The November Pogrom, known euphemistically as *Kristallnacht* or "The Night of Broken Glass," signaled a major break in the life of Jews all over Germany. Masses of Jewish citizens were arrested and put in concentration camps. They were threatened with mass murder in the newspaper *Schwarzes Korps* (Black Corps). Anti-Semitic attacks became a daily occurrence and, through the laws following the pogrom, Jews were systematically and virtually completely driven from all areas of life.

It is impossible now to find out when the November Pogrom was first called *Kristallnacht* or *Reichskristallnacht*. There is no evidence that the expression was first used by local Berliners. What is clear, however, is that the night of November 9, 1938, completely changed the life of Berlin's Jews. Any hopes held up to that time of coming to terms with the circumstances were destroyed once and for all. It must have been a terrible experience for the Berlin Jews to see their synagogues on fire. And, at first, it was "only" the synagogues that burned.

There are very few extant photographs of the shops that were destroyed, but the photograph showing the New Synagogue on Oranienburger Strasse burning is a postwar manipulation; the flames in the photograph were supplied by a skillful retoucher. This synagogue did *not* burn on the night of - November 9, but was severely damaged by Allied bombs in February 1943. In his book *Der beherzte Reviervorsteher* (The Stout-Hearted Policeman), Berlin writer Heinz Knobloch created a monument to Wilhelm Kruetzfeld, the policeman who prevented Nazi thugs from causing major damage to the synagogue that night.

Although it is difficult to ascertain how many shops and businesses were damaged or destroyed that night, it is known that most of the private synagogues and those of the Jewish Community were damaged, including the one on Fasanenstrasse. A detailed report about the damage was written by a former schoolboy, Ernest Guenter Frontheim:

The synagogue was one of the most beautiful I have ever seen, inside and out. As usual we went to school on November 10. Where we lived, in the Westend district, there were no Jewish shops. I didn't pass any synagogues, so I knew nothing about the pogrom going on. It was only when I arrived at school that I heard the terrible stories from my classmates, most of whom lived in Jewish neighborhoods; they were stories of broken windows and plunderings, of burning synagogues, prayer rooms, etc. When the bell rang at 8 AM not a single teacher appeared, nei-

ther in our class nor the parallel one – that was unique. We just sat depressed in our classroom, waiting.

Somewhat later – exactly when, I don't remember, perhaps a half-hour or less – the door to the teachers' room opened and they all came into the classrooms with worried expressions. Our teacher Dr. Wollheim came into the classroom, closed the door, and said that since the security of the school could not be guaranteed it would be closed immediately. He told us to go home and gave us the following instructions: Don't loiter, anywhere; go straight home so that our parents know we are safe; and only in groups of two, at most three; larger groups would only attract the attention of the Nazi hordes. We would be notified when it was safe again to attend classes.

The Adass School was near the Tiergarten rail station, and to get home from school I used the train from that station to the Heerstrasse station, which was only five minutes from where I lived. I looked out the train window, and between the Zoo and Savignyplatz stations I could see the synagogue on Fasanenstrasse. That was where I had had my bar mitzvah three years earlier. As the train passed, I saw a huge cloud of smoke rising from the middle cupola – the synagogue had three cupolas. I was so shocked that I forgot the advice Dr. Wollheim gave us and got off at the next stop, and then ran as fast as I could to see what was going on. On the sidewalk across the street, a crowd of people was standing, all being held back by the police. There was a lot of anti-Semitic shouting – I can't remember the details, but I heard such things as "Out with the Jews!"

I stood there in the middle, oblivious of the danger, I was so hypnotized by the sight of the burning synagogue – I couldn't think of anything else. All of a sudden somebody said that a Jewish family lived opposite the synagogue, in the building we were standing in front of. Then somebody shouted: "Get them out!" That really scared me. The people were evidently bored and wanted some more excitement. They all turned around and those who were closest to the house went in; within a few seconds I could hear loud banging on the door. Secretly I hoped the apartment door would withstand the blows, but then I heard the sound of the door breaking down, of wood splitting, of cries – cries of victory – and then complete quiet, not a sound.

Suddenly the crowd began to move, and I noticed how an elderly bald man was brutally beaten by the crowd. Fists pounded on him mercilessly until his face was covered with blood. From somewhere a man shouted: "What kind of cowards are you, so many against one!" Whereupon the crowd fell upon him. He kept shouting: "What incredible cowardice!" He was then pushed aside and the Jew was forced to go through the mill – you couldn't call it anything else – and shoved to the curb; mysteriously, a police van appeared. He was pushed into the van – that saved him – and driven off.

After I had seen that – I still had no sense that I myself might be in danger – I had seen enough and went back to the station and rode home. The Adass School, like most of the other Jewish schools, never re-opened. My parents thought it wise, for purposes of emigration, that I learn English as quickly as possible.

Resistance to the riots of November 9 was hardly possible, but some acts of resistance are known. Two boys were able to save the

Torah scrolls of the Temple of Peace, their synagogue on Markgraf-Albrecht-Strasse. The two boys were David Zwingermann, then 14, and his somewhat younger friend Horst Loewenstein. On the morning of November 10 they saw through the smoke and fire the heavy oak door of the Ark of the Covenant and discovered that the twelve Torah scrolls were still intact. Unnoticed they carried the heavy scrolls outside and were lucky to find a taxi driver who was willing to transport them. With the help of Zwingermann's mother the scrolls were sequestered in the storeroom of a Jewish English tea importer and later returned to the congregation. Elieser Ehrenreich, the man in the congregation responsible for religious affairs, was so moved by the courage of the boys that he tried to make arrangements for them to emigrate; he was only successful in the case of David Zwingermann, who left Germany for England with his parents on the first *Kindertransport*, on December 1, 1938. Horst Loewenstein was murdered in late 1941 in Riga.

There are also instances of resistance on a psychological level – especially by the Jewish press, whose mottoes could have been "One must get the truth out with tricks" (Bertolt Brecht) and "The only kind of satire that censors understand is bad satire!" (Karl Kraus). The November Pogrom meant the end of a long tradition of German-language Jewish press. All the newspapers were banned. Several days later the former editors of the two largest Jewish newspapers were summoned to the Ministry of Propaganda. As Clemens Maier writes:

They were informed that they had to organize the *Juedisches Nachrichtenblatt* within only a few days. They had at their disposal the facilities and money of the newspapers that had just been banned. The newspaper was to have the function

Portrait of Rabbi Leo Baeck by Ludwig Meidner, 1931.
Baeck (1873–1956), one of the most important representatives of liberal Judaism, was appointed
a rabbi in Berlin in 1912. He taught at the Hochschule fuer die Wissenschaft des Judentums
(College for the Study of Judaism) and belonged to the board of the Centralverein. After 1933 he held
the chair of the Reich Association of German Jews (RV). On January 26, 1943, Baeck was deported
to Theresienstadt, and belonged to the Council of Elders there. He survived, emigrated to
Great Britain and taught after 1948 at the Hebrew Union College in Cincinnati, Ohio.
He died on November 2, 1956, in London. Painting on permanent loan to the
Jewish Museum, Berlin, from the Israel Museum, Jerusalem.

of "disseminating news to the Jewish population in German territory" and as an information source for the increasingly disenfranchised minority. It was to be a source of highly censored information in order to get what the regime felt was important news to the remaining Jews in Germany.

This newspaper was able to outtrick the German censors – mainly with camouflage – in their report on the November Pogrom, though the readers understood the intended message. For instance there was a review of the film *Chicago* that had been shown at the Kulturbund:

> A city is on fire and the men of the fire brigade do nothing but stand idly by and watch. All the hoses are rolled out, the ladders are pointed in the right direction, the pumps are ready for action, but no one lifts a finger. All are waiting for orders that never come. Only after the city, which is larger than 500 morgens [1058 acres], has entirely burned down, does the order come. The fire department drives home. Is that a malicious invention? An ugly fairy tale? Not at all, it is the truth. And it happened in Hollywood.

In the course of the pogrom, 12,000 Jewish men from Berlin were arrested and taken to the Sachsenhausen concentration camp north of Berlin. Getting released from Sachsenhausen was in many cases equivalent to being rescued completely, since after that many Jewish foreign organizations started to help people emigrate. The story of the attorney Herbert Eger is a case in point. The Bne Briss lodge was able to help him and his family escape to England after his release. His son has retold the story:

> In November 1938 my father was called to the Gestapo, which was not really unusual, since he was the secretary of the [Pankow] Synagogue and it had happened frequently. Each time he went he took his toothbrush, soap, and a towel with him, just in case he was kept there – except this time! But he did not come home. Inquiries at the Gestapo office were of course not answered. We then heard rumors that he had been seen on a truck full of men being transported in the direction of Oranienburg. My mother thought they might have taken him to the Sachsenhausen concentration camp. A few days later she and I drove there to try to drop off a package for my father, but that was impossible. On the way we saw groups of prisoners who were being marched to the camp.

After several weeks Eger was released. His son continued: "He never told us much about his experiences in the concentration camp, but my mother told me after his death [in 1953] that he woke up almost every night screaming and that had to do with what he had gone through in the camp."

After the pogrom, the number of Jews wanting to emigrate rose enormously. There was a general storming of the foreign consulates, especially the US embassy and the British Passport Control Office. For a short time the British eased their immigration restrictions. The Palestine Office on Meinekestrasse (Charlottenburg district) had already organized courses so that people could be trained in skills that were needed in Palestine. Such training was prerequisite to get an immigration permit. For younger people, the Zionists organized many training facilities, in Germany and elsewhere. Several of these Hachshara camps, in which Jewish boys learned skills in the handicrafts and in farming, and in which Jewish girls learned housekeeping skills, were located near Ber-

*The synagogue on Fasanenstrasse immediately
after its destruction in the night of November 9–10, 1938.
Photograph by Herbert Hoffmann.*

Left page:
Regina Jonas (1902–44)
the first woman rabbi.
She was deported to Theresienstadt
on November 6, 1942, transferred
to Auschwitz on October 12, 1944,
and murdered there.

Above:
Children of the
Baruch Auerbach orphanage
attending a service.
Photograph by Abraham Pisarek, ca.
1935.

Below:
A family seder in Berlin,
ca. 1935.

lin. A total of 57,000 German Jews managed to emigrate both legally and illegally from Germany to Palestine.

The Beginning of the End

After the November Pogrom, laws and ordinances were intensified. On November 12, to add insult to injury, German Jewry was forced to make a "punitive payment" in the amount of one billion Reichsmarks for the damages suffered at the hands of the "Aryans." The "Decree on the Use of Jewish Assets" gave the authorities the opportunity to squeeze the Jews out of the business world entirely and to expropriate them. From November 15, Jewish children were no longer allowed to attend public schools. The harassment of Jews extended to all areas of public and private life. An ordinance was issued, for example, prohibiting Jews from having carrier pigeons. On December 3 Himmler issued an ordinance rescinding Jews' driver's licenses and automobile registrations. An ordinance of December 5 curtailed the pensions of former Jewish civil servants. The Berlin city government also actively supported the disenfranchisement measures. On December 5, a law came into effect barring Jews from entering cinemas, theaters, museums, exhibitions, sports grounds, public baths, parks, and the zoos; they were even banned from the city center, Vossstrasse, Wilhelmstrasse, and Unter den Linden.

An ordinance of December 8 excluded Jews from institutions of higher learning and from teaching or working in such schools and libraries. On January 17, 1939, all licenses for dentists, veterinarians, and pharmacists were revoked. These laws served to effectively bar German Jews from being professionally active in almost all areas of scholarship, culture, and business. They cut them off from any and all participation in public life.

All these laws and measures resulted in the progressive impoverishment of the German Jews. Their property had been de facto confiscated and they were banned from virtually all sources of income. The number of Jewish welfare cases increased rapidly and it was the Jewish Communities, impoverished as well, that had to shoulder them. On December 20, 1938, unemployed Jews were stipulated by law to take up forced work. Only a few days later an administrative office to coordinate the labor was established at Fontanepromenade 15 in the Kreuzberg district.

Conditions worsened radically after November 1938. Jews knew there was nothing more to build on, so that all that remained was to prepare for the worst. The majority now made plans to leave Germany. In the end, only 50,000 Jews, a small percentage of those willing, were able to leave. The reason more did not emigrate was due to the onerous requirements of the countries accepting immigrants. Only a few countries were willing to accept limited numbers of Jews, and frequently they demanded financial guarantees (affidavits from someone in the host country) or proof that the applicants had financial means of support. Most of the Jews had neither relations nor connections abroad nor financial assets – few could even afford the passage. For many, suicide was the last resort.

In 1939 there were 75,344 Jews left in Berlin; they huddled close to the Jewish Community. At the outset of the war, total repression became the rule. The telephone lines of the Jews were cut off, and they were no longer allowed to use public phones. In the autumn of 1940, Jews were prohibited from shopping for groceries except afternoons between 4 and 5 PM; there was also a nightly curfew for Jews. Jewish newspapers and magazines were prohibited, with the exception of the aforementioned *Nachrichtenblatt.* This was followed by the confiscation of radio receivers. Jews had to surrender works of art and carpets, and starting on September 1, 1941, the middle ages returned in full: all Jews six years of age and older were required to wear a yellow star. Later even Jewish homes and apartments had to be marked, and Jews were then prohibited from even leaving their communities. These measures helped pave the way for deportation to the extermination camps. The measures intensified. First Jews were denied rental protection, and then their apartments were taken away from them. Soon they were forced to live only on certain streets and in particular buildings. The concentration of Jews made it much easier for the Nazis deport them. It is hard to grasp a method to the evictions; in part, however, some of the evictions in the city center were part of Albert Speer's megalomaniac plans to transform Berlin into Germania, capital of the world.

In July 1941, long before the decisions taken at the Wannsee Conference of January 20, 1942, "The Final Solution of the Jewish Question" was started. Goering commissioned Heydrich to exterminate all the Jews in the Nazi-occupied countries of Eastern Europe. It was then that the mass deportation of the Jews to extermination camps set up in Poland began. For Berlin Jews, the destruction began in the fall of 1941. In October emigration was prohibited and in the same month the first transports left from the Grunewald station to the Łódz ghetto in Poland. By the end of January 1942, 10,000 Berlin Jews had been deported to "Litzmannstadt" (i.e., Łódz), Minsk, and Riga.

The transports followed one after another until, on February 27, 1943, the so-called

"Factory Action" took place. More than 11,000 Jews had been working in armaments factories. They were arrested on the job and deported. Berlin was now considered "free of Jews!" The expression comes from Goebbels, who needed a new success bulletin to take the people's minds off the defeat at Stalingrad. He entered into his diary: "The rest of Berlin's Jews are finally being forced to go; as of February 28, they will all be put in camps and then deported, up to 2,000 per day. My goal is to make Berlin completely free of Jews by mid- or at the latest the end of March."

The "Factory Action" was devastating for Berlin's Jews. There were 35,642, roughly 17,000 of whom were doing forced labor, arrested not only at their place of work, but also at employment offices and sites where they could obtain food ration cards. On the streets there were literally manhunts. Those rounded up were assembled camps at the Levetzowstrasse synagogue or the former Jewish home for the aged on Grosse Hamburger Strasse. Deportations to Auschwitz started at the end of February 1943; the total for March 1943 was 8,658 Jews. By March 1945 a total of about 50,000 Berlin Jews had been deported in 122 transports.

*Above left: Recha Freier
(1892–1983), initiator of the
Youth Alijah, which enabled some
8,000 Jewish children and
adolescents to leave Germany.
In 1941 Freier herself reached
Palestine in safety.
Photograph by Walter Zadek, 1934.*

*The Association to Help Jews in Germany providing advice on emigration.
On the right hangs a poster requesting that people not speak about politics. Photograph by Abraham Pisarek, 1936.*

*Above:
Martin Buber speaks
in Philharmonic Hall
during "Palestine Week"
in February 1935.
Photograph by
Abraham Pisarek,
1935.*

*Left page, right:
Hebrew lessons
for children about to
emigrate to Palestine.
Photograph by
Abraham Pisarek,
1935.*

*The Berlin Zionist Movement commemorates Joseph Trumpeldors (1880–1920), a settler in Palestine
who was murdered there by Arabs in 1920. At the lectern is Seew Orbach. Photograph by Abraham Pisarek, ca. 1935.*

After the November Pogrom in 1938, the English government permitted Jewish children from Germany to come to Great Britain. The photograph shows a luggage sticker from the sixteenth Kindertransport. *From November 1938 to November 1939, some 11,000 German Jewish children and adolescents were able to emigrate from Germany to England.*

Racial Madness and its Results

Who is actually Jewish? Who was considered Jewish at the time? This is a not an easy question to answer. According to the Nuremberg laws even baptized Jews, i.e., people who were practicing Christians, were considered non-Aryans and were thus targeted for persecution. Since racial and biological traits were obviously impossible to ascertain, the religion of the suspect's grandparents became a Nazi criterion. Of course, reasonable people don't lump together Jews and baptized Jews for two reasons. In the first place, it is absurd to distinguish people according to pseudo-scientific racial theories. To judge people by their race is both immoral and just plain nonsense. Secondly – and this is hardly less important – it has to be clear that, from a sociological and psychological point of view, Jews and former Jews who converted

to Christianity are two completely different groups.

If we look at those who were persecuted not only as the objects of history but also as acting and reacting subjects (no matter how limited their ability to act was), it is clear that Jews and converts saw themselves in completely different situations. Jews could view their fate within the continuum of Jewish history. They could see their suffering as part of the history of persecution of their people since the Diaspora after the destruction of the Temple. And this could give them a sense of support. For converts however, suddenly alienated from society and persecuted, left to fend for themselves by their Church, the misfortune came like a natural disaster. (The resistance of Christian groups and individuals was an exception to official Church policy.)

I define Jews as people who profess their belonging to a Jewish community. I have consciously avoided calling them "Jews by belief" because not all those who consider

The childrens' choir
of the old synagogue
on Heidereutergasse,
1942.
Photograph
by Rotholz, 1942.

themselves Jews are also believers. Loyalty to the Jewish community can be based on an awareness of belonging to this historic community or to a national minority.

In a metropolis like Berlin, capital of the Nazi regime, even during the period of the harshest persecution, which aimed for a *judenfreies* Berlin, a shadow of Jewish life was still possible. In a large city, the residents, including the Jews, lived in anonymity. A Jew could go to a different district and move around without the yellow star and not be recognized or denounced. And in large cities there were always more intelligent, skeptical, or critical people – especially liberal-minded workers, but also opponents of the regime from other social strata – than in the country and small towns. People who were persecuted could find refuge there, and they had a better chance of finding a courageous friend ready to help, sometimes even braving great dangers. And for those friends willing to resist, the big city offered the anonymity they

needed as well. For those reasons the capital and the provinces were totally different worlds for Jews during the Nazi regime.

And so Jews came in large numbers to Berlin. They came as refugees. In Berlin they could breathe more freely since they were not continuously harassed. They could be on the streets without being attacked, insulted, or beaten. And in Jewish institutions they found help and advice; the large Jewish Community offered the refugees – at least for a while – support and a safe haven. At first many came to arrange their emigration, which was much easier to do from Berlin than from a small town. In 1941 however this became a vain hope, and before long the new arrivals were sharing the same fate as their Berlin brethren. Since the flood of refugees could not be accounted for, it is very difficult to offer any figures.

To illustrate the situation of the Jews in Berlin and the actions of large groups of Berliners I would like to relate the following

Kaethe Schoeps (1886–1944) and Julius Schoeps (1864–1942), physician and military doctor.
In June 1942 J. Schoeps was deported to Theresienstadt, where he died at the age of 78.
His wife, who came with him, was deported to Auschwitz in 1944 and was murdered there.

The synagogue on Levetzowstrasse was misused as a pre-deportation assembly camp.
Berlin Jews had to go on foot from there to the loading ramp at the Putlitzstrasse station.
This photograph of 1935 was taken before the deportations.

The Putlitzstrasse station in the Tiergarten district.
The deportation trains left from here and went straight to the extermination camps and ghettos
in the occupied countries of Eastern Europe.

Early morning roll call at the Sachsenhausen concentration camp. Only a few kilometers
north of Berlin, 250,000 people were incarcerated there between 1936 and 1945.
About 116,000 of them died or were murdered there.

Transport Nr.	Datum	Zahl
98.	15. 11. 43	50
99.	10. 1. 44	351
100.	21. 1. 44	63
101.	9. 2. 44	100
102.	23. 2. 44	74
103.	10. 3. 44	56
104.	19. 4. 44	50
105.	4. 5. 44	26
106.	26. 5. 44	30
107.	16. 6. 44	28
108.	13. 7. 44	27

Transport Nr.	Datum	Zahl
109.	11. 8. 44	32
110.	5. 9. 44	27
111.	13. 10. 44	30
112.	27. 10. 44	50
113.	24. 11. 44	37
114.	8. 12. 44	22
115.	5. 1. 45	19
116.	2. 2. 45	38
117.	27. 3. 45	19
	gesamt	14 797

Osttransporte

Nr.	Datum	Bestimmungsort	Zahl
1.	18. 10. 41	Lodz	1013*)
2.	24. 10. 41	Lodz	1024
3.	27. 10. 41	Lodz	1009
4.	1. 11. 41	Lodz	1033
5.	14. 11. 41	Minsk	
6.	17. 11. 41	Kowno	3715*)
7.	27. 11. 41	Riga	
8.	13. 1. 42	Riga	907
9.	19. 1. 42	Riga	579
10.	25. 1. 42	Riga	905
11.	28. 3. 42	Twarnici b. Lubl.	972
12.	2. 4. 42	Twarnici b. Lubl.	728
13.	2. 4. 42	Twarnici b. Lubl.	642
14.	14. 4. 42	Twarnici b. Lubl.	72
15.	13. 6. 42	Osten	748
16.	26. 6. 42	Osten	201
17.	11. 7. 42	Auschwitz	210
18.	15. 8. 42	Riga	1004
19.	5. 9. 42	unbekannt	790
20.	3. 10. 42	unbekannt	816
21.	19. 10. 42	unbekannt	944
22.	26. 10. 42	unbekannt	800
23.	29. 11. 42	Auschwitz	980
24.	9. 12. 42	Auschwitz	1000
25.	14. 12. 42	Auschwitz	811
26.	12. 1. 43	Auschwitz	1190
27.	29. 1. 43	Auschwitz	1000
28.	3. 2. 43	Auschwitz	952
29.	19. 2. 43	Auschwitz	1000
30.	26. 2. 43	Auschwitz	913
31.	1. 3. 43	Auschwitz	1862
32.	2. 3. 43	Auschwitz	1592
33.	3. 3. 43	Auschwitz	1732
34.	4. 3. 43	Auschwitz	1143
35.	6. 3. 43	Auschwitz	657
36.	12. 3. 43	Auschwitz	946

Nr.	Datum	Bestimmungsort	Zahl
37.	19. 4. 43	Auschwitz	338
38.	17. 5. 43	Auschwitz	395
39.	28. 6. 43	Auschwitz	319
40.	4. 8. 43	Auschwitz	99
41.	24. 8. 43	Auschwitz	50
42.	10. 9. 43	Auschwitz	53
43.	28. 9. 43	Auschwitz	74
44.	14. 10. 43	Auschwitz	74
45.	29. 10. 43	Auschwitz	49
46.	8. 11. 43	Auschwitz	50
47.	7. 12. 43	Auschwitz	55
48.	20. 1. 44	Auschwitz	48
49.	22. 2. 44	Auschwitz	32
50.	9. 3. 44	Auschwitz	32
51.	18. 4. 44	Auschwitz	30
52.	3. 5. 44	Auschwitz	27
53.	19. 5. 44	Auschwitz	24
54.	15. 6. 44	Auschwitz	29
55.	12. 7. 44	Auschwitz	30
56.	10. 8. 44	Auschwitz	38
57.	6. 9. 44	Auschwitz	39
58.	12. 10. 44	Auschwitz	31
59.	24. 11. 44	Auschwitz	28
60.	8. 12. 44	Auschwitz	15
61.	5. 1. 45	Auschwitz	14
62.	5. 1. 45	Bergen-Belsen	6
	2. 2. 45	M. Sachsenhausen	14
	2. 2. 45	F. Ravensbrück	11
63.	M. f. Sachsenhausen vorgesehen		11
	F. f. Ravensbrück vorgesehen		13
		gesamt	35 738

Nach Theresienstadt verschleppt		14 797
nach dem Osten verschleppt		35 738
	insgesamt:	50 535

*) Transportlisten nicht vorhanden. Ziffern nach den Transportnummern ermittelt.

story as told by a person who lived through it. A Jew named Adolf Pogoda had to get something done kilometers away from where he lived on Prenzlauer Strasse. Since Jews were not allowed to use public transportation, he removed his yellow star, put it in his pocket and got on a subway. During the trip he had to sneeze, so he reached into his pocket for a handkerchief. In doing so, he also pulled out his star, and it flew through the subway car in a high arch. He was therefore "discovered." And what happened? A high-ranking officer bent down, picked it up, and with an elegant bow handed it back to its owner with the following words: "Allow me to return this object to you, as you will certainly need it later." Laughter broke out in the crowded subway car. Nothing else happened. Evidently, not a single fanatic Nazi was present. That was possible in Berlin! I would dare to say that it was possible only in Berlin!

Which Jews stayed in Berlin throughout the war? There were three categories: The first category consisted of Jews who were living in a so-called mixed marriage, that is, a marriage in which one of the partners was an "Aryan"; The children of these marriages, whom the Nazis called "first order *mischlings*" belonged to the second category. The last category was filled by Jews as they were defined in the Nuremberg laws. This last

Left page:
This list of deportation trains was published
in 1959 – a chilling documentation of the
"Prussian love of orderliness." It was only by a lucky
accident that the list was not destroyed.
The document speaks for itself. It shows
the train number, date, destination and number
of victims on board.
Source: Hans Gerd Sellenthin:
Geschichte der Juden in Berlin,
Berlin 1959, p. 85.

group was, starting in 1941, subject to deportation, and individuals were only able to avoid a terrible fate by living "illegally" in the underground; the first two groups, at least according to existing laws, managed to survive legally.

The group of those who lived in mixed marriages can be broken down into other sub-groups, those of "privileged" and "non-privileged" mixed marriages. If the husband was Jewish and the wife "Aryan" then the marriage was considered "privileged" – the privilege was mostly that the partner did not have to wear the yellow star. The same was true of children who were not raised as Jews, or if an only son had fallen in World War I. The privilege remained even if the marriage had been terminated. If an "Aryan" man however was married to a Jewish woman, the marriage, even without children, was considered "privileged" only as long as it held. Non-privileged mixed marriages, on the other hand, were marriages in which the male partner was a Jew and there were either no children or the children were raised Jewish – according to the terminology they were *Geltungsjuden*, or "treated as Jews"; both husband and children had to wear the yellow star.

Thus there were members of the Jewish Community who, either because they wore the star or because they were excused from wearing it because of their "privileged" marriage, survived legally in Berlin throughout the war. It is however quite certain that they too would have been deported had the end of the war not prevented it. The psychological burden they suffered was enormous. They lived through difficult years, always worried about what the future would bring.

In contrast to these "legal" Jews were the Jews who lived "illegally" – in Berlin the number was relatively high. It is estimated that 1,400 survived illegally, but the numbers vary considerably. Often, no difference is made between those who survived in Berlin as "illegals" underground, and those who tried to escape deportation by going into hiding (estimates are about 5,000), and who, because of an unlucky accident or due to employed Jewish "snatchers" – the most notorious of them was Stella Kuebler – were caught, arrested, deported again, and finally murdered.

One "illegal" was Hans Rosenthal (1925–1987), later one of the most famous and beloved of German television hosts. From the end of March 1943 until the liberation he lived "illegally." It is quite unfortunate that the terminology of "legal" and "illegal" Jews, stemming from the Nazis, has remained in use. In a moral sense it is reprehensible to use their vocabulary. A legal system that denied human beings the right to exist without a trial and without the option of a legal defense, and murdered them without even the evidence that a crime or misdemeanor had been committed – such a system was itself criminal, not the attempt to escape it.

Those who resisted getting sent to their deaths by going underground referred to themselves as having "gone under." In Vienna one spoke of "submarines" using the same metaphor. The expression "illegals," however, was frequently used by the hunted themselves. The expression survived liberation and is used in literature on the subject.

The Life of "Legal" Jews

How did the "legal" Jews in Berlin live or, rather, "vegetate"? The conditions were, to say the least, "precarious." Many had been evicted from their dwellings as of 1938. Those without a residence had to be quartered together with Jews who still had their residences. Thus it happened that in many large apartments each room was taken up by an entire family. Living under such conditions was hell. Such problems arise wherever too many people are herded into too little space. Arguments about using the kitchen, toilet, and bathroom ensued. Nervousness due to insecurity and fear brought about by persecution led to touchiness, and living in close quarters just exacerbated the problems. This made life even more unbearable.

On top of this, partners in mixed marriages and "half-Jews" had ration cards with a "J" stamped on them, so they were entitled only to reduced rations. During the war, the great majority of the population went to bed hungry; the Jews virtually starved. Getting groceries on the black market was difficult because the necessary cash was lacking. Most Jews were impoverished and received only pitiful wages. Regardless of their training they were forced to accept the most menial work. Berlin Jews were forced to work in more than 230 different Berlin enterprises, many in the armaments industry. In 1941, 19,000 Berlin Jews were employed in industries considered vital to the German war effort. For a while it spared them deportation. They performed the most onerous and menial tasks. A dentist was put to work at the sewage fields and later had to pick up papers in a public park. Jewish girls had to clean railway cars.

The worst part of life for those living legally in Berlin was the fear that in the end

*Right: Herbert Baum (1921–1942),
leader of a Communist resistance group named
after him. After his arrest in May 1942,
he allegedly committed suicide in jail.*

*Above: memorial stone for the "anti-fascist
resistance group" in the Berlin Lustgarten, erected
in 1981 in East Berlin.*

*Right: A Nazi poster designed by Axster-Heudtlass
advertising the 1942 anti-Soviet propaganda
exhibition,* The Soviet Paradise. *The show was
sabotaged by Herbert Baum and his group,
which led to their arrest.*

they too would be deported. These were not irrational fears based on rumors, which do abound in bad times, but bitter acknowledgement of reality. It can safely be said that partners in mixed marriages and "half-Jews" only survived because the Allied armies were quicker than the murderous machinery of the Nazis.

There was an attempt – which failed – to deport the Jewish husbands of non-Jewish wives. During the aforementioned "Factory Action" of February 1943, when the last of those Jews who worked in armaments factories were rounded up, many Jews from mixed marriages were also arrested and detained for deportation in a building on Rosenstrasse, in the middle of the city. Gestapo headquarters were located close by, on Burgstrasse, a street name that says little to us today, but which struck terror in the inhabitants of Berlin then. Nevertheless, the wives of the arrested men were courageous enough to camp outside the building on Rosenstrasse, staying day and night and chanting, "Give us back our husbands!"

The Nazis were undecided about shooting German women on an open street, especially after the defeat at Stalingrad. The general mood was quite poor. War enthusiasts could be found only among fanatics. The demonstration was successful. The men were released and were able to return home. That was the only demonstration during the entire Nazi period. It was led and carried out by women, and it was successful! "Academic research has evaluated this event as proof that public protest against the responsible Nazi institutions led the Nazis to quickly retreat" (Diana Schulle). How many women took part in this protest is unfortunately not known. However, according to reports, many women were relieved by relatives, neighbors and friends, considering the demonstration lasted several days and nights.

And many of the "Aryan" wives arrived with a group of friends and acquaintances as reinforcement.

The non-Jewish wives were constantly pressured to divorce their Jewish husbands, but very few succumbed, thereby sending their husbands to their deaths. Most non-Jewish men married to Jewish women behaved the same way. Those who refused to divorce by 1944 were forced to perform hard labor under extremely adverse conditions in one of the camps of the notorious "Organization Todt" (O.T.).

Some of the "legal" Jews in Berlin worked for Jewish institutions. It was only here that Jewish life could exist, greatly weakened and always endangered; Jewish life continued in the most modest way. It was those in mixed marriages and "half-Jews" who were most outstanding in this effort. Jews in the underground were of course unable to be very active.

Six months before the November Pogrom of 1938 the status of the Jewish Community as a public institution was revoked. It continued to exist as a registered association whose members had to join in a formal manner. The Nazis had the perfidious idea to have a central Jewish organization coordinate the Jewish emigration, including its financing. To that end the Reich Association of Jews in Germany (Reichsvereinigung, or RV) was founded and placed under the responsibility of the Gestapo and the Reich Security Main Office. "For all practical purposes, the Reichsvereinigung was becoming the first of the Jewish Councils, the Nazi-controlled Jewish organizations that, in most parts of occupied Europe, were to carry out the orders of their German masters regarding life and death in their respective communities" (Saul Friedlaender). In 1938 and 1939, 16,000 Berlin Jews emigrated annually, almost all with the aid of the services of Jewish organizations. In addition to the Reich Association in Berlin, the Jewish Community formally existed until January 1943; it had been forced to change its name in the spring of 1941 to the Jewish Religious Association (Kultusvereinigung), and its offices were located in the building complex of the New Synagogue on Oranienburger Strasse. In February 1943 it was incorporated into the RV of Germany by the Nazis and struck from the official register of associations. It nevertheless was able to maintain its independence, no less than the Jewish Communities in Hamburg, Munich, and Frankfurt am Main.

The Reich Association (RV) had its headquarters in Berlin. At first its employees seemed to be protected because of their activities for the pre-deportation assembly camps and their preparations for the "relocation." But on June 10, 1943, the Gestapo appeared at the Kantstrasse office, arrested the few Jews still working there who were not related to "Aryans" and confiscated the property of the institution. Similar actions took place at the Berlin Jewish Community and the district offices of the RV throughout Germany. The board of the Berlin Jewish Community, also leading figures in the RV, had been deported in 1942, together with their chairman Heinrich Stahl. Soon after June 10, 1943, a new RV was founded. It had its offices in the administrative offices of the Jewish Hospital in the district of Wedding. Walter Lustig, first government counselor and chief medical officer of the hospital, was installed as its director. Lustig remains a very controversial figure. Unfortunately no biography of this "notorious director" of the Jewish Hospital, who lived in a mixed marriage, has been written. According to Hildegard Henschel he was, "although a great capacity in his field, an anti-Semite without conscience." Even though many scholars have

been researching for decades, very little material on him has been found.

It is known that he was born in Ratibor on August 10, 1891, and had been employed in Berlin since the end of the 1920s. In October 1929, as the chief medical examiner of the police, he became the head of the Berlin municipal health services. Although he had little interest in Jewish matters and played not the slightest role in the Jewish Community, the Jewish address book of 1929–30 lists him as an "outstanding Jewish personality." Lustig's career in public service also ended in 1933. Consequent to the law reinstating professional civil servants he was "retired" on October 19, 1933, shortly after having turned 42. In 1934, as author of many medical books, he entered the service of the Berlin Jewish Community, where he not only administered the health program but was also active on the board of the Jewish Hospital. In early 1938 no less a personality than Leo Baeck wrote a brilliant reference about him: He has "distinguished" himself "highly," wrote Baeck, who praised his "great expertise, broad knowledge, and organizational skills . . . and his untiring devotion to duty." Baeck characterized him as a man whom the Jewish Community "could always rely on."

It appears that Lustig remained in the service of the Jewish Community during the following years. In October 1942 – the deportations had been going on for a year – he became the director of the Jewish Hospital. Before that he had led the investigation section for transport claims, an important position in efforts to defer deportations. In June 1943, however, when the RV was officially dissolved, Lustig was the only person spared. He became the new chairman of the new association, whose offices in the Jewish Hospital were known as the "Forecourt to Hell." "Not only were sick people treated here, but

A hastily scribbled message by Klaus Scheurenberg to his father relating that the Nazis picked him and his mother up and put them in the assembly camp on Grosse Hamburger Strasse. Scheurenberg, an employee of the synagogue congregation, was spared for a while, but the family was deported to Theresienstadt in May 1943.

all other persons detained whose family background the Nazis felt merited clarification" (Beate Meyer).

It is clear that Lustig's role as executor of Gestapo orders is more than controversial. He appears as one of the most dubious figures of that era and is presumed to have been shot in 1945 by the Soviet authorities, with whom he had attempted to ingratiate himself. Not until 1954 did his family have his date of death determined as December 31, 1945. It has been impossible so far to find even a photo of Lustig, and therefore the descriptions of him, despised by so many survivors, are somewhat contradictory. In the exhibition *Jews in Berlin 1938–45* at the Centrum Judaicum, we tried to clearly depict the lack of a photo by leaving an empty frame in the showcase. A niece of Lustig visited the exhibition and allowed us to use a photo she had of her uncle in a doctor's smock, wearing the yellow star, although many witnesses have maintained that as head of the hospital he did not have to wear it.

The Jewish Hospital, although directly subject to the Gestapo and its whims, was a functioning Jewish organization and therefore a center of Jewish life, responsible for those living in mixed marriages, those "treated as Jews," and the very small number of Jews not yet deported from Berlin.

The care of cemeteries and organization of funerals were among the RV's responsibilities, which meant there was a second center of Jewish life: the cemetery in the Weissensee district of Berlin. Burials continued there as late as May 6, 1945. This was the workplace of the Jewish preacher (and later Chief Rabbi of East Germany) Martin Riesenburger, who was installed there on June 10, 1945. He had been protected because his wife was not Jewish. About twelve people were employed at the cemetery after June 1943. The head of the cemetery was the lawyer Arthur Brass. His great service to the Jewish Community was hiding many Torah scrolls in the cemetery, thereby saving them from destruction. In his memoirs, which appeared in 1960, Riesenburger wrote: "We saved these sacred objects from the deepest night of inhumanity, so that they were there for the – unfortunately very few – returnees to the Berlin Community."

The end of the Berlin Jewish Community has yet to be adequately researched. One of the few extant sources are Riesenburger's memoirs:

The grand demise of the Berlin Jewish Community took place here at the cemetery, but under all the ash, we few kept the fire going against all odds. What we saw here at the cemetery was unbelievably terrible. Day after day we received the bodies of those who preferred suicide to the endless torment, torture, and abuse. All kinds of poison were especially popular. There were weeks in which there were so many suicide victims that we had to conduct funerals well into the evening.

Even in 1944 Riesenburger made a Jewish calendar so Jews could follow the holidays. Secret prayer services were held in the cemetery, and sometimes "illegals" participated. Hidden deep in the cemetery a *sukkah* was even built in 1944. The cemetery remained a center of Jewish life; many "illegals" were able to hide there; some used the tomb of the singer Joseph Schwarz, which had the inscription, "Lord, You have been our refuge in each and every generation." For them the inscription was filled with new meaning.

The Life of the "Illegals"

This is a group made up of individual destinies. If I speak of a group it is just to collect post facto people who took the same path – namely toward the underground – after they had escaped deportation. But they did not take this path together. They were not at all a group held together by something. The fact that they were mostly individuals does not, however, rule out the existence of a small number of groups that dared the leap into the unknown. There were small groups of friends and old acquaintances who were in the same situation and sometimes met by exercising extreme caution. There they discussed their problems and gave each other courage to continue. That was, however, the exception.

One group deserves special mention; it is a group largely of adolescents which called itself *Chug Chaluzi* (the Circle of [Palestine] Pioneers)." The *Chug* was a sub-group of the *Hechaluz* (Hebrew: Pioneer), a worldwide Zionist organization established in 1917 to build up Palestine. It had spread a wide net for rescuing Jews by arranging their escape to Palestine. Its members were Zionists and therefore had a common goal and an illegal organization, which was necessary in order to help each other obtain lodging, food, and other necessities. The first leader of the *Chug* was Jizchak Schwersenz, a teacher. After he was able to escape to Switzerland, leadership passed to Gerhard (Gad) Beck. Ferdinand Kroh wrote a book about this resistance group: *David kaempft: vom juedischen Widerstand gegen Hitler* (David Fights: On Jewish Resistance to Hitler). Gad Beck's memoirs of this period have been published in English as *An Underground Life: Memoirs of a Gay Jew in Nazi Berlin.*

The number of Jews in the Berlin underground in the summer of 1943 is estimated at 3,000–4,000; by early February 1944 it was about 2,000. More young people than old went underground. And more women than men survived living "illegally." Men were in greater danger, since there were frequent round-ups to locate deserters from the army. It was difficult to get military IDs and other documents that made it legal to be in Berlin out of uniform. It was easier to get forged papers for women. Something else favored women; due to the war, the number of household helpers had greatly dwindled. A family that took on a Jewish housekeeper solved two problems, their housecleaning one and that of the girl.

It is impossible to categorize the people who helped Jews. They came from all social strata and classes and distanced themselves from the Nazi-supporting masses in different ways. Helpers who hid people from the Nazis included laborers, office workers, small

Der Niedergang der jüdischen Bevölkerung Berlins in Zahlen

Alter Jahre	am 16. Juni 1933 gesamt Zahl	%	männlich Zahl	%	weiblich Zahl	%	am 14. Mai 1939 gesamt Zahl	%	männlich Zahl	%	weiblich Zahl	%	am 1. November 1946 gesamt Zahl	%	männlich Zahl	%	weiblich Zahl	%
unter 6	6 654	4,1	3 356	2,1	3 298	2,0	1 699	2,3	829	1,1	870	1,2	216	3.0	99	1,3	117	1,7
über 6-10	15 122	9,4	7 656	4,8	7 466	4,6	1 334	1.8	680	0,9	654	0,9	105	1,4	47	0.6	58	0.8
„ 10-14							2 169	2,9	1 105	1.6	1 064	1.3	143	2,0	65	0.9	78	1,1
„ 14-16	2 104	1,3	1 045	0,6	1 059	0,7	1 427	1,9	707	0,9	720	1,0	77	1,1	39	0.6	38	0,5
„ 16-18	2 379	1,5	1 174	0,7	1 205	0,8	1 340	1,8	545	0,7	795	1,1	41	0.6	19	0,3	22	0,3
„ 18-20	3 785	2,3	1 838	1,1	1 947	1,2	1 278	1,7	546	0,7	732	1.0	196	2,7	115	1,6	81	1,1
„ 20-21	10 709	6,7	5 206	3,3	5 503	3,4	281	0,4	113	0,1	168	0,3	83	1,1	46	0.6	37	0,5
„ 21-25							1 305	1,7	485	0,6	820	1,1	336	4,6	143	1,9	193	2,7
„ 25-30	12 474	7,8	5 899	3.7	6 575	4,1	2 741	3,7	1 001	1,3	1 740	2,4	355	4,9	181	2,5	174	2,4
„ 30-35	29 145	18,2	14 130	8,9	15 015	9,3	3 795	5,0	1 532	2,0	2 263	3.0	399	5,5	179	2,5	220	3.0
„ 35-40							5 007	6.6	2 042	2,7	2 965	3,9	508	7.0	283	3,9	225	3,1
„ 40-45	13 939	8,7	6 753	4,3	7 186	4,4	6 382	8,5	2 476	3,3	3 906	5,2	643	8,8	287	3,9	356	4,9
„ 45-50	13 659	8,5	6 619	4,2	7 040	4,3	6 958	9.2	2 741	3,6	4 217	5,6	832	11,4	391	5,4	441	6,0
„ 50-55	25 118	15,7	12 258	7,6	12 860	8,1	7 888	10,4	3 371	4,5	4 517	5,9	850	11.8	396	5,5	454	6,3
„ 55-60							7 918	10,4	3 477	4,6	4 441	5,8	720	9,9	366	5,0	354	4,9
„ 60-65	9 368	5,8	4 384	2,6	4 984	3,2	8 120	10,8	3 621	4,9	4 499	5,5	670	9,2	400	5,5	270	3,7
„ 65	16 108	10.0	6 383	3,9	9 725	6,1	15 702	20,9	6 054	8,1	9 648	12,8	1 100	15,0	576	7.9	524	7,1
Zusammen	160 564	100,0	76 701	47,8	83 863	52.2	75 344	100,0	31 325	41,6	44 019	58,4	7 274	100,0	3 632	49,9	3 642	50,1
Familienstand																		
ledig	68 617	42,7	35 084	21,9	33 533	20,8	25 185	33,4	10 468	13,9	14 717	19,5	1 756	24,1	876	12,0	880	12,1
verheiratet	71 685	44,6	37 233	23,2	34 452	21,4	34 121	45,3	17 455	23,2	16 666	22,1	4 278	58 8	2 446	33,6	1 832	25,2
verwitwet	16 127	10,0	2 771	1,6	13 356	8,4	12 651	16,8	2 117	2,8	10 534	14,0	962	13,2	226	3 1	736	10,1
geschieden	4 135	2,7	1 613	1,1	2 522	1,6	3 387	4.5	1 285	1,7	2 102	2,8	278	3,9	84	1.2	194	2,7
Zusammen	160 564	100 0	76 701	47,8	83 863	52.2	75 344	100,0	31 325	41,6	44 019	58,4	7 274	100,0	3 632	49,9	3 642	50,1
Sektoren																		
Britisch	66 631	41,5	31 095	19,4	35 536	22,1							2 123	29.2	1 062	14,6	1 061	14,6
Französ.	4 615	2,9	2 243	1,4	2 372	1.5							744	10.2	343	4,7	401	5,5
Sowjetisch	56 181	35,0	27 546	17,1	28 635	17,9							2 442	33.6	1 229	16,9	1 213	16,7
Amerik.	33 137	20.6	15 817	9,9	17 320	10 7							1 965	27,0	998	13,7	967	13 3
Zusammen	160 564	100.0	76 701	47,8	83 863	52.2							7 274	100,0	3 632	49,9	3 642	50,1

Statistics on the "Decline of the Jewish Population of Berlin" from June 16, 1933 to November 1, 1946, from 160,564 to 7,274. Published in Der Weg, *December 13, 1946.*

shopkeepers, members of the nobility, the military, prostitutes, criminals, intellectuals, and even a few farmers. Some people helped for political reasons. Foremost among them were Communists and Social Democrats, but there were also Liberals and Conservatives, and even individual National Socialists who disagreed with their party's policy of mass murder. Others had religious motives for becoming helpers. Catholics and Protestants as well as members of other religions helped to save lives.

There were people who helped Jews in the underground out of purely humanitarian reasons – independent of ideology, religion, or politics. Many helpers sacrificed a great deal and were willing to risk their freedom – even their lives. But there were also ambivalent helpers. Some hid their "illegals" and then robbed them, or demanded hard work from them in exchange for a night's lodging in the coal bins.

Of the 160,000 Jews living in Berlin in 1933, 90,000 had emigrated by the war's end. Another 55,000 had been murdered, and 7,000 committed suicide. Aside from those who emigrated, only about 8,000 of Berlin's Jews survived.

Hermann Simon

National Socialist Laws and Decrees against Jews
(A Selection)

April 7, 1933: Law to Re-establish the Professional Civil Service: "§ 3 Civil servants who are not of Aryan descent are to be retired." For the time being, Jewish soldiers who fought on the front are exempt.

September 22, 1933: Law to Establish the Reich Chamber of Culture: Jews are excluded from membership, which is required to pursue a career in culture.

January 24, 1934: Law on the Organization of National Labor: "Non-Aryan" employees can no longer fill responsible functionary positions in the National Labor Front.

March 5, 1934: New license requirements for physicians and dentists: "Non-Aryans" are no longer permitted to take the required tests.

July 22, 1934: "Aryan" descent is now a requirement to take lawyers' examinations.

December 8, 1934: Pharmacist Decree: "Non-Aryans" can no longer take the pharmacist exam.

December 13, 1934: *Habilitation* Decree: Post-doctoral *Habilitation* is henceforth dependent upon being "Aryan." (This effectively bars all Jews from obtaining professorships.)

July 25, 1935: Decree on Military Service: "Non-Aryans" cannot serve on active military duty.

Summer 1935: Signs with "Jews not wanted here" are seen with increasing frequency at the entrance to towns, shops and restaurants.

September 6, 1935: Decree by the President of the Reich Chamber of the Press: selling Jewish newspapers on the street is forbidden.

September 15, 1935: The Nuremberg Race Laws are passed: "Reich Citizenship Law" and the "Law for the Protection of German Blood and German Honor." In the first, § 2 (1) says: "Citizen of the German Reich must be a citizen of German or related blood, who by his conduct proves that he is willing and able to loyally serve the German people and Reich." In the second law, §1 (1) says that "marriages between Jews and citizens of German or related blood are prohibited. Marriages contracted despite this prohibition are null and void, even if they were concluded outside the German Reich to circumvent this law. § 2 Extra-marital sexual relations between Jews and citizens of German or related blood are prohibited. § 3 Jews may not employ in their homes citizens of German or related blood who are younger than 45. §4 Jews are prohibited from hoisting the Reich and National flags or to show the colors of the Reich."

November 14, 1935:   Decree No. 1 to the Reich Citizenship Law: §4 (1): A Jew cannot be a citizen of Germany. He has no right to vote in political matters; he may not hold public office. (2) Jewish civil servants shall be retired as of December 31, 1935. This holds also for Jewish soldiers who fought on the front.

December 13, 1935:   Reich Physician Decree: "The license to practice medicine is to be withheld if the candidate, because of either his or his spouse's descent, is prohibited from being a civil servant and the proportion of physicians of non-German blood among all physicians exceeds the proportion of people of non-German blood in the general population."

April 15, 1937:   Jews of Germany are barred from obtaining a doctorate.

March 28, 1938:   Law on the Legal Conditions of Jewish Cultural Associations: The Jewish Community of Berlin loses its position as a public corporation.

April 26, 1938:   Decree on the Declaration of Property to prepare the expulsion of Jews from businesses.

June 9, 1938:   Jews are no longer allowed to audit classes at universities.

June 16, 1938:   Arrest of all Jews who have criminal records.

July 25, 1938:   Jewish physicians lose their license to practice. They are no longer allowed to treat non-Jews or to call themselves "Doctors." Henceforth they must call themselves "Caretakers of the Sick."

August 17, 1938:   Decree No. 2 to the Application of the Law on Changing First and Family Names: "§1 Jews are only allowed to have first names that are listed in the guidelines on having a first name issued by the Reich Minister of the Interior. §2: inasmuch as Jews bear names other than those they are permitted, they must assume a second first name: men the name Israel, and women the name Sara."

September 27, 1938:   Jewish lawyers may no longer practice law. Henceforth they can advise only Jews and are to be called "consultants."

October 5, 1938:   Jewish passports are stamped with the letter "J."

November 12, 1938:   Decree on the punitive payment, "*Suehneleistung*", to be paid by Jews: "The Jews of German citizenship must collectively pay to the German Reich a contribution of one billion Reichsmarks."

Introduction of the "Aryanization" of Germany via the Decree to Eliminate Jews from the German Economy. § 1: "From January 1, 1939, Jews are prohibited from operating small businesses, mail-order businesses, order agencies and the independent operation of trades and crafts" [professions such as plumber and electrician].

November 15, 1938: Jewish children are no longer allowed to attend public schools.

November 28, 1938: Police Decree on the Appearance of Jews in Public. "The government presidents in Prussia, Bavaria, and in the Sudeten German areas may frame regulations about the times and places Jews of German citizenship and stateless Jews are allowed in public; these regulations can stipulate that such persons cannot be seen in certain places and at certain times."

December 3, 1938: The drivers' licenses and automobile registrations of Jews are declared invalid and must be surrendered.

December 6, 1938: Jews are no longer permitted to attend theaters, cinemas, cabarets, public concerts, reading halls, museums, variety theaters, exhibition halls, sports grounds and ice-skating rinks, or public and private bathing facilities. Furthermore, in Berlin, Jews are not permitted to set foot on the Wilhelmstrasse from Leipziger Strasse to Unter den Linden; Wilhelmplatz; Vossstrasse as far as Wilhelmstrasse (in front of the Reich Chancellery); or the northern side of Unter den Linden from the University to the Arsenal Building. For this measure, the term *Judenbann* (off-limits for Jews) shall be coined.

Decree on the Use of Jewish Assets to settle the forced sales of Jewish property. "§ 1 Jews can be ordered to either close or sell their businesses within a designated period." Certain stipulations can be attached to such orders. "§11 Within one week of the publication of this order, Jews must deposit all their shares, bonds, coupons, fixed-interest loans and other valuable papers in a depot of a commercial bank." . . . "§ 14 Jews are prohibited from selling, buying, or pawning objects of gold, platinum, or silver and precious gems and pearls . . ."

December 8, 1938: Jews are excluded from attending universities.

February 21, 1939: Further forced sales: Jews of German citizenship must deliver all objects of gold, silver, or platinum and precious gems and pearls within two weeks to public purchase sites. Only wedding rings are excluded from this measure.

July 4, 1939: Tenth Decree to the Reich Citizenship Law: "§1 (1) Jews are hereby joined together as the Reich Association [RV]. (2) The Reich Association is an association based on public law. It bears the name Reichsvereinigung der Juden in Deutschland [Reich Association of Jews in Germany] and has its headquarters in Berlin. § 2 (1) The major goal of the Reich Association is to further the emigration of Jews."

September 23, 1939:   Decree by local police stations for Jews to surrender their radios.

October 22, 1939:   Decree by the Reich Minister for Education: Citing works by Jewish authors in a dissertation is permitted only when this is absolutely necessary for scholarly purposes. Such authors must be expressly identified as Jews.

July 4, 1940:   Jews in Berlin are permitted to purchase groceries only between the hours of 4 and 5 PM.

July 29, 1940:   The telephones of Jews are to be deactivated by September 30, 1940. Exceptions are to be made for "caretakers of the sick," "treaters of teeth," "consultants" and Jewish organizations.

September 21, 1940:   Decree by the President of Berlin Police Concerning Air-raid Shelters: "If Jews live in the same building as non-Jews, special air-raid shelters have to be made for Jews so that they can be separated from the others living in the building."

September 1, 1941:   Police decree ordering distinguishing marks for Jews (Yellow Star obligatory as of Sept. 19, 1941).

October 10, 1941:   Jews are no longer permitted to change their address without permission from the police.

December 26, 1941:   Jews who are obliged to wear the Yellow Star are prohibited from using public telephones.

January 10, 1942:   Jews must surrender all their furs and woolens.

May 15, 1942:   Jews are prohibited from having house pets.

July 7, 1942:   Jews are prohibited from using waiting rooms, restaurants, and other facilities of the public transportation company. All Jewish schools shall be closed.

September 18, 1942:   Further limitations on Jews in obtaining groceries. They can no longer obtain ration cards for meat, clothing, dairy products, tobacco products, white bread, or other scarce items.

March 11, 1943:   Decree by the Reichssicherheitshauptamt (Reich Security Main Office): "After serving a sentence for a criminal offence, Jews must be transported for a life sentence to the concentration camps of Auschwitz or Lublin. In the case of Jews, the severity of the crime for which they have been imprisoned makes is irrelevant."

July 1, 1943:   Jews have no protection under German courts of law. Jews are placed exclusively under police law.

FROM 1945 TO THE PRESENT

On May 6, 1945, four days after Berlin capitulated and two days before the downfall of the Nazi regime, it was possible to hear – among the ruins of the city – the sound of a *shofar*. According to biblical legend, this same sound caused the walls of Jericho to come tumbling down. The Polish chief Rabbi, who had entered Berlin with the soldiers of the Red Army, blew the ritual ram's horn at a "liberation service" held at Kantstrasse, 158 in Charlottenburg. In attendance were several Jewish Red Army soldiers and several Jews who had survived underground in Berlin.

A short time later, a service was held in the synagogue on Lothringer Strasse, at the entrance to the Weissensee cemetery, in a waiting room used for funerals. Martin Riesenburger, from 1933 a preacher and pastor at the Jewish Community's home for the aged, wrote:

> Just after the capitulation, we began – as well as we could under the circumstances – to repair the windows of our tiny synagogue. On Friday evening, May 11, 1945, we held the first public prayer service. We tried to have it announced on the radio. Several people came, people who were emerging for the first time from the underground – into the daylight – where they had hidden for so many years.

Those attending belonged to the approximately 8,000 Jews of Berlin who had survived the horrors of the Holocaust – in one way or another. In concentration camps. In hiding. In *Mischehen* (mixed marriages). Before the war some 135,000 Jews had lived 3in Berlin. About 56,000 of them had been murdered.

How the official Jewish Community in Berlin came to be reconstituted is a story worth telling. There is a letter dated December 12, 1945, from the head of the Jewish Community to the Soviet Central Command, in addition to some files from the Berlin Jewish Community's North East Office. One may assume that early on several institutions were established on the sites of former synagogues that had been destroyed. Only slowly, with the establishment of a general infrastructure in the "rubbish heap outside Potsdam" (as Bertolt Brecht called Berlin in 1948), was it possible to create a reunified Jewish Community. The December letter provides a general description of what happened:

> After the entry of the victorious Red Army into Berlin, Lieutenant General Bersarin met at the Reichstagbuilding with the Jewish dentist, Dr. Martin Blum. Bersarin urged Blum to rebuild the Jewish Community, which the Hitler regime had abolished. Dr. Blum gathered the following persons around him: Dr. med. Leo Hirsch, . . ., Arnold Peymer, . . . and Erich Mendelsohn, . . . , and these men con-

Interior of the vandalized synagogue on Thielsch-Ufer (today Fraenkel-Ufer), in the Kreuzberg district. Photograph 1945.

Above: Employees of the Jewish hospital in 1946 at a memorial ceremony for the victims of fascism. Photograph by Abraham Pisarek.
Left: People waiting in line to get help from the "Joint."
Photograph by F. Eschen, 1946.
Below: A Jewish "returnee" in a make-shift dwelling.
Photograph by F. Eschen, 1947.

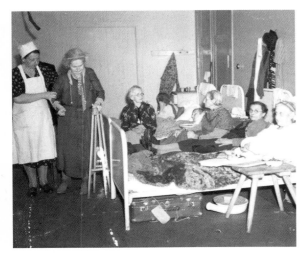

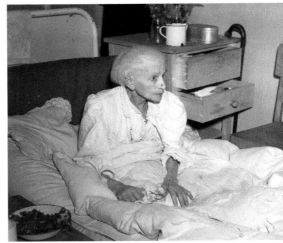

ducted the reorganization of the Jewish Community of Berlin during the months of June and July 1945. Just after the war was over, district communities had been established, and these were organized into a single Jewish Community of Berlin.

The letter noted that Jewish Community headquarters were located at Oranienburger Strasse, 28, and that its board was composed of Erich Nelhans, Hans Muenzer, Hans-

Erich Fabian, Leo Loewenstein, Karl Busch and Julius Meyer.

Some lines (not cited above) of the letter indicate how it came to be written. They mention that the Jewish Community was supported by several foreign non-political organizations that had helped Jews during the Nazi regime to obtain ration cards, among other things. Specifically named were the United Nations Relief and Rehabilitation Administration (UNRRA) and the American

Joint Distribution Committee (colloquially known as "the Joint"). It is clear from the letter that the Jewish Community in the Soviet sector had already become embroiled in the onsetting Cold War; the Soviets were suspicious of any western organizations getting involved. It is possible to interpret the letter as a proclamation that the Community's reorganization was due the efforts of Bersarin, the Soviet Commandant. (It must be added, that he died on June 16, 1945, after a motorcycle accident.)

The earliest documents on the rebuilding of the Jewish Community in the days after the war ended have to do with the miserable situation in which the Jews found themselves, particularly with their difficulty obtaining food. Some things changed with the entry of the Americans into Berlin on July 4, 1945. It was then that the UNRRA was able to begin its work helping millions of non-German Displaced Persons (DPs). Although these included thousands of Jews from European countries occupied by the Germans, German Jews were excluded. The UNRRA established camps for the DPs and, if the DPs were also Jews, it was able in a position to help them emigrate to Palestine and other countries.

As a result of brutal pogroms in Poland in the fall of 1945, a large number of Jewish refugees from Poland arrived in Germany and in the UNRRA camps that November. Rabbi Herbert Friedman, US Army chaplain, commandeered a US-Army truck at night in order to accept DPs and take care of them. Those who were capable of bearing arms were taken in by the Bericha, an organization that heeded the wishes of Ben Gurion and was active between 1944 and 1948 in bringing Jews to Palestine over the Berlin camps.

As the flood of Jewish refugees waned, the UNRRA camps lost the character of mere transit stations. Educational programs were started, and the refugees got medical help, with the help of qualified DPs. A theater group was formed, the Baderech, and there was also a regular newspaper, *Undser Leben, Irgun fun di befreite Jidin in Berlin.*

The first Jewish-American aid organization in Berlin was the aforementioned

*Left page:
Photos for a magazine report with the title "How the Berlin Jews are plagued."
Photographs by Frederick Remage, 1945.*

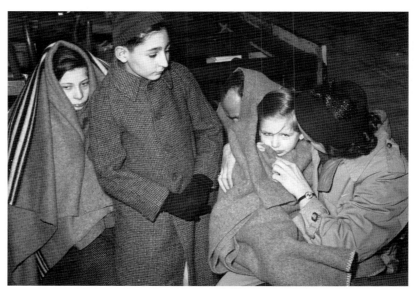

*GDR-refugees on a truck.
Photograph by A. C. Lassberg, 1953.*

Die Kandidaten der Liste 1

1. Dr. Hans-Erich Fabian

geb. am 22. 9. 1902 in Bromberg.

Landgerichtsrat. 1943—1945 KZ Theresienstadt. Seit 1919 für die Interessen des Judentums in führenden Stellungen tätig. Früher Generalsekretär der Lehranstalt für die Wissenschaft des Judentums. Vorstandsmitglied der Jüdischen Gemeinde zu Berlin. Mitglied der Arbeitsgemeinschaft der jüdischen Gemeinden Deutschlands. Herausgeber der Zeitschrift „DER WEG". Vorstandsmitglied der VVN Groß-Berlin. Im Ausschuß OdF Wilmersdorf.

2. Heinz Galinski

geb. am 28. 11. 1912 in Marienburg/Westpreußen.

Stellvertretender Leiter des Hauptamtes Opfer des Faschismus, Abt. Nürnberger Gesetzgebung. Vorsitzender der VVN Groß-Berlin. 3 Jahre Zwangsarbeit bei Siemens. 3 Jahre KZ Auschwitz, Dora, Bergen-Belsen. Seit Anfang 1946 Repräsentant der Jüdischen Gemeinde zu Berlin. In verschiedenen Kommissionen tätig, u. a. Joint-Kommission. Innerhalb des Hauptamtes OdF und der Vereinigung der Verfolgten des Naziregimes Eintreten für die Forderungen a l l e r rassisch Verfolgten. Ständiger Mitarbeiter am WEG.

3. Richard May

geb. am 19. 5. 1886 in Berlin.

Bis zum Pressegesetz Chefredakteur an großen Zeitungen, dann 5 Jahre Zwangsarbeit, Sternträger, Redakteur am WEG. Bisher Repräsentant der Jüdischen Gemeinde zu Berlin. Vorstandsmitglied der VVN Groß-Berlin. Im Ausschuß OdF Wilmersdorf.

4. Jeannette Wolff, geb. Cohen

geb. am 22. 6. 1888 in Bocholt/Westfalen.

Stadtverordnete in Groß-Berlin. Vorsitzende einer Entnazifizierungs-Kommission in Berlin-Neukölln. Seit 1911 in der jüdischen Jugend- und Frauenbewegung tätig. Mitarbeiterin der liberal-jüdischen Vereinigung in Deutschland (Mitarbeiterin von Rabb. Dr. Leo Baeck). 1933 verhaftet. Nach Freilassung illegale Arbeit. Ab 1941 KZ Riga, Mühlgraben/Lettland, Stutthof/Danzig. Repräsentantin der Jüdischen Gemeinde zu Berlin, Vorsitzende der Jüdischen Frauengruppe Groß-Berlin. Mitglied der Joint-Kommission.

5. Fritz Sachs

geb. am 5. 5. 1881 in Kattowitz/Oberschlesien.

Kaufmann. Seit 1938 Zwangsarbeit. Seit langem in der Jüdischen Gemeinde zu Berlin tätig. Leiter der Bezirksstelle der Jüdischen Gemeinde im britischen Sektor und der Auswanderungsabteilung. Besondere Betreuung der nichtjüdischen Ehepartner. Vorsteher der Synagoge Pestalozzistraße und Repräsentant der Jüdischen Gemeinde zu Berlin.

Left page:
Information list for the elections to the Jewish Assembly of Representatives in January 1948. Those candidates listed here represented a liberal attitude – "without consideration of 'all-Jewish' or 'mixed-marriage' Jews." The first name on the list is that of Hans-Erich Fabian, survivor of Theresienstadt, who became the Community leader. Heinz Galinski is second on the list.

Right:
Sabbath ceremony in the American Chaplain Center on Huettenweg in Berlin. Estrongo Nachama, first cantor of the Jewish Community (left), and Chaplain Aromovicz. Photograph, 1965.

Below: A Chanukkah-party photographed by A. C. Lassberg, ca. 1955.

"Joint," which was not only the major point of support for DPs but for German Jews as well. In its reports, the "Joint" complained repeatedly that the German Jews were not permitted in UNRRA camps and were being treated as enemy Germans – although they had barely survived Nazi rule, either in hiding or in concentration camps. The help of the "Joint" also led to curiosities, as Robert Weltsch wrote in a report from Berlin in January 1946:

> Recently there have been many applications to join the Jewish Community from people who had earlier left it. The reasons given are possibly sentimental or personal, but the real reason is the delivery of food parcels by the American Joint Distribution Committee. All the recipients of these parcels praise their contents. Those who don't receive them complain that they, as 'non-Aryans' in Germany [during Nazi rule], had carried the full burden and should now be given advantages. Everyone is interested in only one thing: obtaining extra rations. Food, lodging, heating and perhaps cigarettes are the main concerns. Judaism is now not seen as a source of spiritual nourishment but as a way of obtaining the greatly desired 'Joint-parcels.'

The situation of the European Jews who had survived the Holocaust was also a major problem for the US Army. For that reason General Eisenhower appointed an American military chaplain, Rabbi Judah Nadich, to be his special advisor and asked him to write up a report about the special situation of the Jews in occupied Germany. Nadich visited the UNRRA collecting points in the American Zone of Occupation and looked at the Berlin camps as well.

Nadich's report mentions that the Jewish Community had 3,500,000 marks (blocked) on its accounts and that the elections for the Jewish Community were scheduled for October 1, 1945. It also mentions that the Jewish Community had property in all four sectors of Berlin, but that only in the American sector was there any attempt at restitution underway. The report continues:

> A direct problem is the influx of 250-300 Jewish DPs of Polish origin who refused to be repatriated to Poland. In the collection points (Rykestrasse and Iranische Strasse) most of the inhabitants are young and are living in very poor conditions. Both camps or points need repairs to their windows, roofs and ceilings. Rykestrasse has [only] 140 beds and 80 blankets for 180 persons, and there are primitive wooden barracks without window panes, each holding 20 persons. The food ration amounts to 300g of bread, one bowl of soup, a cube of margarine per week and, once in a while, a tomato.

Nadich also mentions Rabbi Isidore Breslauer, apparently the first military chaplain for the American soldiers in Berlin and also one of the first to contact the Jews in the Berlin Jewish Community.

On March 1, 1946, the first issue of *Der Weg* (The Way) appeared. The Berlin magazine was devoted to questions about Judaism and helped generate a discussion within the Jewish Community about the future. Was the Jewish Community in 1945 the legal successor to the Jewish Community that had been abolished by the Nazis? Or was it a new creation? Should the fledgling organization establishing itself in Berlin exist in perpetuity or should it only care for Jews until they had found a new place to live?

On August 29, 1947, *Der Weg* reported the arrival in Berlin of 295 Jews from Shanghai, where they had found refuge after the Nazi pogrom of November 9, 1938 (also called *Kristallnacht*). This was the first large group of former Berliners to return to their old home. In the meantime, Hans-Erich Fabian, who had been head of the Jewish Community's section on finance and property, returned to Berlin. He had been deported to Theresienstadt in 1943 and then forced back by the Gestapo in 1944 to profitably organize the Nazi confiscation of Jewish property nation-wide. Now, in 1945, he succeeded Erich Nelhans as head of Berlin's postwar Jewish Community. Fabian welcomed back the Shanghai returnees to Berlin but himself decided to emigrate to the US with his family in April 1949. His successor was Heinz Galinski, who served without a break as head of the Berlin Jewish Community for four decades, until his death on July 19, 1992.

There was much tension between the Jews living in the DP camps and those within the Jewish Community of Berlin. This was not only due to the better care provided within the camps. Those in Berlin proper had chosen to stay and to attempt a new beginning in the city, while those in the DP camps were sitting on their luggage waiting to leave. Nevertheless the DPs attracted public attention through a number of political activities. For instance at the end of September 1947, they protested a concert by the violinist Yehudi Menuhin with Wilhelm Furtwaengler at Berlin's Titania Palast. They considered it wrong for a Jewish soloist to perform with a conductor who had been active during the Third Reich.

After the proclamation of the State of Israel "thousands of DPs assembled in the 'abduction' camps to joyously greet the day." Heinz Galinski, visiting the camp at Berlin-Wittenau, expressed the Berlin Jewish Community's commitment to the young Jewish state.

About one month after the start of the Berlin airlift (June 26, 1948) the UNRRA began to evacuate its camps in the western zone of occupation. Until August 16, about 5,400 people were flown out. The empty UNRRA camps were returned to the administration of the US Army. But even after the action was over – and most of the DPs had been flown out of Berlin on the same planes that had been used to bring in supplies – about five hundred DPs remained and took up residence in the city.

Politically, the DPs appeared as a group one more time, in late 1949. A film of apparent anti-Semitic content was being shown at a movie theater in Charlottenburg. Riots broke out in front of the theater, and 25 DPs were injured, four of whom had to be hospitalized. Thirty Berlin policemen and many British Military Police tried to quell the disturbance, but the crowd had grown to about 1,500. When the screening began, the curtain had been torn down, the screen itself ruined by hurled rocks and the chairs demolished.

By 1951 the Jewish Community had seven synagogues, two rabbis, three preachers, four cantors and more than four schools for teaching religion, but there were still few Jewish textbooks or prayer books available for the Community's religious life.

On the Road to Division

The Cold War did not stop at the doors of the Berlin Jewish Community. Inasmuch as the UNRRA was active only in the western sectors of Berlin, the Community's activities were somewhat geared toward the west as well. Julius Meyer, however, maintained contact with the occupying Soviet power until 1953. A prominent member of the Jewish Community's board (and a co-chairman alongside Heinz Galinski from 1949 to 1953), Meyer was also a member of the VVN – the

Vereinigung der Verfolgten des Naziregimes (Association of Those Persecuted by the Nazi Regime) – a parliamentary group within the East German Volkskammer. In 1948, the following was published in issue 43 of *Der Weg*.

Congratulations upon the thirty-first anniversary of the Great Socialist October Revolution. In the following we publish the congratulatory address sent by the chairman of the board of the Berlin Jewish Community to the Russian Central Command: . . . Upon the occasion of the thirty-first anniversary of the Great Socialist Revolution we send you the most cordial congratulations. We are aware of the fact that it was the Soviet Army that liberated Berlin and the members of our Community. The basis for the glorious deeds of the Army was established in the October revolution. . . .

With the expression of our preferred respect,

The Board of the
Jewish Community

After the division of Berlin in 1948, there was much competition in matters of compensation among the municipal governments of East Berlin and West Berlin and the government of the Federal Republic of Germany. In the end, both Galinski (for the West) and Meyer (for the East) were able to arrive at solutions that were codified in the laws of compensation for victims of the Nazi regime.

The Jewish Community in the eastern sector, however, had to face a new wave of anti-Jewish propaganda stemming from the Stalinist show trials then taking place in Hungary and in Czechoslovakia. In these trials the ruling powers tried to prove that certain Jews in the eastern bloc had links to Jewish-American organizations. To Stalinists, this was tantamount to having contacts with Zionists or the CIA. The propaganda campaign, combined with Bolshevism's traditional principle of atheism, resulted in the demand that East Germany's Jewish Communities be disbanded. Practicing Jews were, for the most part, reviled. *Neues Deutschland*, the newspaper of East Germany's ruling communist Party (the SED), sent its own correspondent to cover the Slansky trial in Prague. Slansky's "confession" was printed in the November 22, 1952 issue, and alongside it was the remark that it signaled "to more attentive readers that this trial will not be without effects within the GDR" (the German Democratic Republic).

The situation was untenable. In the spring of 1953 West Berlin's Rabbi Nathan Peter Levinson called for Jews to leave the GDR. Many did. By the end of April, a specially erected collection point was entrusted to the Jewish Community to care for 570 refugees. Another 260 were flown straight to the Federal Republic of Germany. Meyer himself fled to West Berlin in January 1953. His membership in the SED was cancelled and his seat in the Volkskammer was vacated. According to legend, Meyer was reproached by Galinski for having collaborated with the wrong side; now he was receiving his comeuppance. Galinski is said to have thrown Meyer out of the West-Berlin office on Joachimsthaler Strasse. Meyer emigrated to Brazil in the spring of 1954.

The split can be seen in retrospect to have occurred between January and June in 1953. Galinski had, in addition to his office in the Community's headquarters on Oranienburger Strasse (in East Berlin), long since established another office (in West Berlin), at Joachimsthaler Strasse 13. He did not have the slightest difficulty leading the administration from the West since most of the Community's administration had already settled there as a result of the city's division into four sectors. Moreover, many properties of

Heinz Galinski (1912–1992), survivor of Auschwitz, Dora and Bergen-Belsen,
served from 1949 until his death in 1992 as chairman of the Berlin Jewish Community.
Left: The foundation-stone ceremony for the House of the Jewish Community on Fasanenstrasse. Behind Galinski
are, at right, Mayor Willy Brandt, and Ernst Lemmer, Minister for All-German Affairs. Photograph 1957.
Right: Heinz Galinski at his desk in 1953. Photograph by Hans Schaller.

Heinz Galinski with US Secretary of State Henry Kissinger on a May 1975 visit
to the Jewish Community House on Fasanenstrasse.

the Jewish Community were still intact in West Berlin.

The Treaties of Luxembourg (September 10, 1952) recognized that those properties then being used as synagogues and Community houses by the Jewish Communities in the Federal Republic of Germany (and in the western sectors of Berlin) would be transferred to the Jewish Communities themselves. Those buildings that were not in use could be sold off and the proceeds divided 70:30 between the Jewish Claims Conference and the Jewish Communities. Accordingly, in the following years, the Claims Conference vacated several Berlin synagogues and sold the properties to West Berlin's municipal government. A parking lot was planned for the property at Fasanenstrasse 79–80. In 1957, however, the Jewish Community approached the city Senate and asked to have the property to erect a Community House. The proposal was accepted, and in November 1957 Mayor Willy Brandt laid the foundation stone. At the beginning, the Jewish Community received the property as a hereditary lease. Later, on January 8, 1971, it was returned completely to the Jewish Community.

Because the Jewish cemetery was in Weissensee (in East Berlin), burials were affected by the events that took place in East Berlin on June 17, 1953. (A major worker's revolt was quashed with the help of Soviet tanks.) Thereafter, very few Jews living in West Berlin could use or even visit the Weissensee cemetery, and when the wall was built 1961, it became virtually impossible for them to do so. A new Jewish cemetery was therefore laid out in West Berlin on Scholzplatz (in Charlottenburg) in 1959. Between 1953 and 1959 Jewish burials were held in a non-Jewish cemetery. The remains of those interred there were later transferred to Charlottenburg.

Community Life After the Division

After 1953, almost all of the Jewish Community's activities took place in West Berlin. The small number of Jews in East Berlin were cared for by Rabbi Martin Riesenburger and soon became subject to the political authorities.

In West Berlin, the laying of the foundation stone for the *Gemeindehaus* (Community House) was proof enough that the Jewish Community was in Berlin to stay. The person of Heinz Galinski (1912–92) is inseparable from the Community's transformation from a state of near liquidation to reconstruction. Galinski, who had survived the concentration camps of Auschwitz, Dora and Bergen-Belsen, favored the integration of the Jews into a democratic Germany. At the same time he was a Zionist and never tired of resisting assimilationist tendencies. Because of his indefatigable insistence that Germans be reminded of the Holocaust, he became an important figure in the political life of Berlin and the Federal Republic of Germany.

In 1962 the Jewish School for Adult Education was founded, thereby helping the Jewish Community expand its influence and the understanding of Jewish history and culture beyond the Community's immediate radius. In 1971 the West Berlin Senate and the Jewish Community reached an agreement wherein the municipal government pledged to support the Community, which had been greatly decimated by Nazi lawlessness. In November 1993 a formal "State Treaty" was signed.

Since East and West Berlin were ruled and administered by two completely different and in many ways antithetical systems, the Jewish Community, like the Church, had little choice but to accommodate itself to both systems. This is clearly seen in the different ways that the ravages of National Socialism were remembered. In East Berlin ceremonies in memory of Herbert Baum and his resistance group took place at the Weissensee cemetery. There were ceremonies commemorating the Rosenstrasse Protest and annually the anniversary of the November pogrom of 1938. In West Berlin, on Yom Hashoa – a holy day commemorating the Shoah – the Jewish Community remembered the Warsaw Ghetto Uprising. It, too, commemorated *Kristallnacht* in November. Ceremonies were held in the large hall of the *Gemeindehaus* on Fasanenstrasse. All governing mayors, parliament presidents and a great many Federal ministers made speeches and laid wreaths at the Fasanenstrasse Shoah monument. They professed Germany's obligation to teach German youth about the Holocaust, about responsibility for the past and for the future. They also gave the leader of the Jewish Community a platform for protesting right-wing radicals, neo-Nazis and, from the 1970s on, outbreaks of xenophobia, both in Berlin and in Germany at large.

A watchman in 1948 guards the Jewish Community office on Joachimsthaler Strasse.

New Considerations of Culture

The exhibition *Achievement and Destiny – 300 Years of the Jewish Community in Berlin* opened in 1971 to mark the tricentennial of the Community's founding in 1671. This exhibition was the first postwar attempt at an inclusive recollection of Berlin's Jewish history. It led to the establishment of The Jewish Museum, initially a department within Stadtmuseum Berlin (City Museum of Berlin). In addition, a growing number of exhibitions about the Jews, their world and their history started to appear throughout the city. Perhaps the most elaborate of these was held in

1992 at the Martin-Gropius Bau, *Juedische Lebenswelten* (Jewish Worlds). During its three-month run, the exhibition was seen by three hundred thousand visitors, and two hundred thousand more attended various related events. *Juedische Lebenswelten* led to an ever more effective revival of Jewish cultural events in the city. A festival of "Jewish Cultural Days" has been taking place annually since 1987. Before reunification this West Berlin festival coincided with East Berlin's "Days of Yiddish Culture." The two festivals were combined after the fall of the wall, and the Juedische Kulturtage are still going strong.

Before reunification (1990), East Berlin's only synagogue was on Rykestrasse. West Berlin's Jewish Community maintained four synagogues: one Orthodox, one conservative and two liberal. From 1980 there were two rabbis and six cantors in West Berlin. Rabbi David Weisz headed the Orthodox congregation from 1961 to 1995. The liberal rabbis during the 1960s were Professor Dr. Cuno Lehrmann, and, toward the end of the decade, Rabbi Uri Themal. The congregation

The Jewish Community's Simchat-Torah-Ball in 1975 in West Berlin.
Below: Heinz Galinski is third from the left.

Performances by children of West Berlin's Jewish Community.
Photographs by Helga Simon, 1975.

*Memorial ceremony on November 9, 1965 at the Jewish cemetery in Weissensee (in East Berlin)
for the victims of the November pogrom of 1938. From the left: Heinz Schenk, chairman of East Berlin's Jewish
Community, Itzek Davidowitcz, cantor from West Berlin, and Siegfried Wexberg, member of the board.*

*Memorial ceremony on November 8, 1970 at the Jewish Community House on Fasanenstrasse.
Mayor Klaus Schuetz stands in front of the monument. Photograph by Klaus Lehnartz.*

was then led by Rabbi Manfred Lubbiner (1972–80), Rabbi Ernst Stein (1980–97), and today Rabbi Dr. Chajim Rozwaski.

The 1960s initiated a period of intensive dialogue between the Christian churches and the Jewish Community. This dialog extended beyond the framework of Jewish-Christian meetings held during the "Week of Brotherhood." The high point of these meetings took place during the Six-Day War of 1967. Monsignore Clausener and Protestant Bishop Scharf attended an intercessory prayer service in the Pestalozzistrasse synagogue. The East German paper *Neues Deutschland* simultaneously printed a protest by GDR-citizens of Jewish origin against Israel's policy.

The solidarity of the West Berlin Jews with Israel was visible through the presence of such Israeli organizations as the KKL (Jewish National Fund) and the Keren Hajessod as well as Zionist organizations such as the WIZO. These organizations were prepared to reach out to the non-Jewish public. For example, since the 1960s the spouse of Berlin's Mayor has served as honorary chairperson of the annual March WIZO bazaar, the proceeds of which go to the "Theodor-Heuss Home for Convalescing Mothers" near Tel Aviv.

To celebrate the Community's tricentennial in the early 1970s, then-Mayor Klaus Schuetz inaugurated a program in which Berlin's former Jews were invited back to the city (at Berlin's expense) for a week's visit. Berlin was the first German city to introduce this successful program.

Jewish Institutions

The Jewish Community has maintained a kindergarten since 1946. In 1986 a primary school was opened on Bleibtreustrasse. A large building on Waldschulallee designed by the Israeli architect Zvi Hecker is its new home, and today it has almost three hundred pupils. Not all of the students are Jewish, which underscores the Jewish Community's integrative character. In 1993 the primary school was augmented by two high schools: a classical *Gymnasium* and a *Realschule*.

With only 6,000 members in 1963, it had become difficult for the Jewish Community to maintain its own four hundred-bed hospital – the Jewish hospital, founded in 1754 and, after June 1914, located in the district of Wedding. The hospital became a public foundation in 1963. Today the Senate and the Jewish Community are jointly responsible for the institution, which continues to operate in the tradition of Jewish medicine. It is currently being enlarged and modernized.

Toward the end of the 1980s the government of the GDR realized that the Jewish Community of East Berlin could serve as a useful instrument of foreign policy. Erich Honecker, head of the SED and also of the State Council of Ministers, was of the opinion that, with the support of Jewish organizations – and by raising the specter of Nazi lawlessness – he could keep Germany divided. Thus, on November 9, 1988 – the fiftieth anniversary of the November pogrom – a public memorial ceremony was held in the Volkskammer in the Palace of the Republic. Heinz Galinski, among others, was presented with a golden "Star of Friendship of Peoples." Furthermore, the Jews were welcomed to revive the Orthodox Community of Adass Jisroel in East Berlin. This congregation had once been legally considered a *Gemeinde* in its own right and had been independent of the larger Jewish Community of Berlin. After the city was reunified, there was therefore some controversy between Galinski's Jewish Community of Berlin and Adass Jisroel. At the same time, a long legal battle was taking

Artists at the "Days of Jewish Culture" festival,
which has taken place annually since 1987.
Photographs by Hans D. Beyer.

Charity auction in 1980 for the WIZO at the House of the Jewish Community, hosted by the TV-personality Hans Rosenthal (left) and the actor Wolfgang Voelz. Rosenthal (1925–1987) had survived the National Socialist regime underground in Berlin and was for many years the chairman of the Assembly of Representatives of the Berlin Jewish Community.

place with Berlin's municipal government. The Senate refused to reinstate Adass Jisroel or recognize it as the legal successor to the old congregation (that is, as an entity entitled to taxes and subsidies, and with legal responsibilities of its own). In 1997, the German Supreme Administrative Court recognized it as the legal heir to the Adass Jisroel Community that had existed prior to World War II.

On his seventieth birthday in 1982 Galinski formulated his fears and hopes for the future of the Jewish Community:

Right-wing radicalism has become more active and brutal. Even today it is possible to import right-wing and anti-Semitic hate-literature from abroad. Even now these holes have not been plugged. That means that our [Jewish] Community has to be even more active. It means that we have to position ourselves against radicalism from both the left and the right, against terrorism in the Federal Republic, and against international terrorism. . . . We have to make Judaism more transparent, help to break down barriers, prejudices and mistrust and, simultaneously, combat radicalism and terrorism wherever

we can. Another central point in our life is to support secure borders for the Jewish state.

Galinski's speech, in keeping with his long service at the head of the Jewish Community, stressed the necessity of taking a position:

The Jewish Community here does not live in an ivory tower. History will not pass us by. What I wish for is inner peace in this country and in this city. I wish further that the controversies – the political controversies – be conducted soberly, without attacks on persons or things, and that only a fair discussion determine the best political goal. I also want this Community to participate in all that happens in this country. It is good that we are represented in the municipal "Commission on Foreigners" and that we always take a stand against xenophobia. We know, of course, what it means to be a minority, to be outcast.

Galinski's declaration was made long before the distressing new wave of anti-Semitism and xenophobia of the 1990s. His position against xenophobia was important to his successor as well. After Galinski died, his deputy, Jerzy Kanal, served as head of the Community until 1997. For reasons of age he declined to run for a second term.

The Jewish Community after Reunification

With German Reunification in 1990, the Jewish Community of Berlin was reunited to include East Berlin's 200 members. A particular circumstance, however, made the work much more difficult: starting in the 1970s, a small number of Soviet Jews had been allowed to emigrate to East Germany. Now, with the demise of the Soviet Union, what had once been a trickle became a mighty river, and this presented major problems for the Jewish Community. Old rules for accommodating immigrants were quickly scrapped, and by the end of the year 2000 there were over 11,000 Jews in the Jewish Community, many of them from the former Soviet Union. Like the other *Bundeslaender* (German states) the city of Berlin was expected to take a certain quota. This quota was filled long ago.

On November 9, 1988, the East German government solemnly pledged to rebuild the New Synagogue on Oranienburger Strasse (originally dedicated in 1866). The restored building was re-dedicated in 1995 as a synagogue but as a house of Jewish Culture, the Centrum Judaicum. The reconstruction was made possible by the then East German Minister for Culture, Schirmer, who shortly before political reunification, in September 1990, had been able to set aside seventy million Deutschmarks from the party coffers of the former SED. Today the Centrum Judaicum houses the permanent exhibition *Tuet auf die Pforten* (Open the Gates!) as well

as a small synagogue (inaugurated in May 1998) with eighty seats, where egalitarian services are held.

In addition to the Jewish Community and the Community of Adass Jisroel, there is a Jewish Cultural Association (established in 1988) as well as such other institutions as the sporting club Makkabi, the Anti-Defamation Forum, and offices of international Jewish organizations such as B'nai B'rith Youth, Magen David Adom (for hospital work in Israel), Friends of the Hebrew University and Friends of the Bar Ilan University. There is also an association to help the Jewish hospital, an organization of Jewish physicians and psychologists, a Jewish student union and numerous self-help groups.

From 1991 on, Israel maintained a General Consulate in Berlin. After the German government moved from Bonn to Berlin in 1999, the consulate became an embassy. The new quarters, designed by architect Orit Willenberg-Giladi, were dedicated in the spring of 2001 in the presence of Israeli Foreign Minister Shimon Peres, German Foreign Minister Joschka Fischer and over one thousand invited guests.

No less important are the many sites that commemorate the important events in the positive but also tortured history of the Jews in Germany: the House of the Wannsee Conference (established in 1992) and the Topography of Terror (established in 1987). As capital of the Federal Republic of Germany, Berlin has become the seat of many international Jewish organizations, among them the Ronald Lauder Foundation (1997), the American Jewish Committee (1998), the European Jewish Congress (1999) and the Central Council of Jews in Germany, whose Berlin headquarters moved into the building of the former Institute for the Science of Judaism on Tucholskystrasse. The same building houses the *Allgemeine Juedische Wochen-*

Above: The new Israeli Embassy. Architect: Orit Willenberg-Giladi. Photograph by Guenter Schneider.
Below: The Heinz-Galinski school, dedicated in 1995, designed by Zvi Hecker. Photograph by Elke Nord.

Above right: Cantor Avital Gerstetter.
Photograph by Margrit Schmidt.
Above left: Rabbi Itzak Ehrenberg, teaching.
Photograph by Burkhard Peter.

Below left: Arkady Fried, librarian at the Jewish
Community House on Fasanenstrasse.
Photograph by Burkhard Peter.
Below right: In the synagogue on Joachimsthaler
Strasse. Photograph by Burkhard Peter.

Demonstration against right-wing extremism and xenophobia in front of the New Synagogue on Oranienburger Strasse. November 9, 2000. Photograph by Margit Billeb.

zeitung (the General Jewish Weekly Newspaper).

On September 9, 2001, Berlin's Jewish Museum was opened with a speech by the President of Germany, Johannes Rau. In early 1998, after several heated controversies about the museum, its mission (three hundred years of Jewish history in Berlin) and its leadership, W. Michael Blumenthal was chosen to be director. The former US Secretary of the Treasury in the Carter administration was born in Oranienburg and had been among the Shanghai exiles. He supervised the completion of the new building and expanded the museum's mission to include the history of Jews in all of Germany from its beginnings – around 2000 years ago – through to the present day. The new building's design by architect Daniel Libeskind has made it an icon of contemporary architecture. Even when it stood empty, it was visited by thousands. Now, with its exhibitions, it has become one of Berlin's star attractions.

Jewish life in Berlin today is characterized by the tradition of the political Community founded and led by Heinz Galinski. It is not political in the sense of being partial to a party, but in the sense that it has committed itself to democracy, tolerance and to combating neo-nazism, right-wing radicalism and xenophobia. It has also been involved in the long controversy surrounding the provision of an adequate memorial to the murdered Jews of Europe, and it publicly denounces disturbing signs of brutal right-wing radicalism. Berlin is also home to an independent cultural Jewish life that continues to grow and attract admirers from all over Germany and the world. The beginnings of a revival of Jewish urban culture are to be seen in the neighborhood of the New Synagogue, around the Hackesche Markt. It will have to prove, however, that it is not just a guidebook attraction but also a genuine part of the life of the Jewish Community of Berlin.

Andreas Nachama

A tank in front of the Jewish Community House on Fasanenstrasse.
Photograph by S. Nowak, 1994.

Above:
Bird's-eye view of the Jewish Museum Berlin,
designed by architect Daniel Libeskind.

Below:
The interior of the Jewish Museum.
Photographs by Hans D. Beyer.

APPENDIX

Chronology

From the Beginnings until 1789

1244	First trace of Jewish history in the Berlin area: a gravestone in Spandau.
1295	First official mention of Jews in Berlin.
1349	Persecution of the Jews during the black death.
1354	Construction of the *Kleiner Judenhof*. Six Jewish families settle in Berlin.
1446	First expulsion of the Jews from Brandenburg.
1447	Jews are readmitted into Berlin
1510	The "Desecration of the Host" Trial. On July 19, 38 Jews are burned at the stake and all Jews are expelled from the city.
1539	Elector Joachim II repeals the prohibition against Jews immigrating to the region.
1556	Joachim II appoints his coiner Lippold, as overseer of all Jews in the Mark Brandenburg.
1564	Berlin's Jews apply for permission to construct a new synagogue.
Easter 1571	Elector Johann Georg bans Jews "for all time" from Brandenburg.
January 28, 1573	After Lippold's trial and public execution, Jews are once again expelled.
May 21, 1671	Edict giving protection to fifty Jewish families from Vienna, with the stipulation that they are not allowed to build a synagogue.
September 12, 1671	Letters of privilege (*Schutzbriefe*) issued to the first two Jewish families. A Jewish community is started.
1672	Land purchased for a Jewish cemetery on the Grosse Hamburger Strasse. (Cemetery used until 1827).
1688	Installation of the first *Judencommission* (Jew Commission).
1700	Edict banning the Jewish Prayer Alenu.
January 1, 1714	Dedication of the first official synagogue on Heidereutergasse.
May 20, 1714	Confirmation of rights conferred by the 1671 Edict of Acceptance.
1722	The internal organization of the Jewish Community of Berlin begins with the publication of the "Regulations for the Superior and Other Elders of the Berlin Jewish Citizenry."
September 29, 1730	General privileges and regulations. Limitations on the rights conferred in 1714.
1737	King Frederick Wilhelm decrees that 584 Jewish families must leave Berlin.

April 17, 1750	The "Revised States of General Privilege and Regulations about the Jewry of the Kingdom of Prussia" further limits the rights of Jews.
1755	Opening of the new Jewish hospital on Oranienburger Strasse.
1767	Moses Mendelssohn's *Phaedon: Or on Immortality in Three Dialogues.*
1778	Opening of the Juedische Freyschule (Jewish Free School) initiated by David Friedlaender and Isaac Daniel Itzig. Jewish children are taught in German for the first time.
1780–83	Moses Mendelssohn translates the Old Testament's Pentateuch, the Five Books of Moses into German with Hebrew characters.
1781	Publication of *On the Civic Improvement of the Lot of the Jews* by Christian Wilhelm Dohm. Beginning of the emancipation of the Jews in Prussia.

The Process of Adaptation (1790–1870).

1792	The Gesellschaft der Freunde (Society of Friends) is founded.
1799	Publication of David Friedlaender's *Sendschreiben.*
March 11, 1812	Edict of Emancipation: Jews become citizens of Prussia.
1819	Association for the Culture and Science of the Jews is founded.
1822	Jews are deprived of the right to hold high military positions and positions in schools and other institutions of learning.
1827	Jewish cemetery on Schoenhauser Allee (in use until 1880).
1845	Sigismund Stern founds the Cooperative for the Reform of Judaism.
1847	The Jewish Community of Berlin acquires legal status.
January 1, 1850	Under Article Four of the revised Prussian constitution all citizens of Prussia, including the Jews, are equal before the law. (These provisions are transferred to the states of the North German confederation in 1869 and in 1871 to the German Reich.)
May 23, 1861	Adoption of the statutes for the Jewish Community of Berlin.
1866	Dedication of the New Synagogue on Oranienburger Strasse.
1869	Founding of the Orthodox religious community of Adass Jisroel.

The Imperial Era (1871–1918)

1872	The High School for the Science of Judaism is founded. Sara and Moritz Reichenheim establish the first Jewish orphanage.
1873	Esriel Hildesheimer opens the Orthodox rabbinical seminary.
1879–81	The Berlin Anti-Semitism Dispute, provoked by Heinrich von Treitschke. Anti-Semitic agitation by bourgeois-conservative groups.
September 9, 1880	Opening of the Jewish cemetery in Weissensee.
1882	Hermann Makower establishes the second Jewish orphanage.
1885	Prussian state legally recognizes the Adass Jisroel congregation.
1890	Founding of the Association to Ward off Anti-Semitism.
1893	Founding of the Centralverein.
1898	Founding of the Bar Kochba sports club.
1902	Founding of Jewish Community's old-age home on Exerzierstrasse.

1903	Founding of the Association of Jewish Women.
1904	Founding of the Association of German Jews.
1908	Founding of the Association for Liberal Judaism in Germany.
1911	Transfer to Berlin of the World Zionist Organization headquarters.
August 26, 1912	Dedication of Fasanenstrasse synagogue in Charlottenburg.
1915	Founding in Berlin of the Committee for the East.
1916	*Judenzaehlung* (Census of Jews in the military).
1917	Foundation of the Central Welfare Office of German Jews in Berlin.

The Weimar Years (1919–32)

1922	Establishment of the Jewish Welfare Agency (fusion of the committees for the care of the destitute, orphans, etc.).
1925	Opening of the Yiddish-speaking YIVO (Institute Jewish Scientific Institute) in Berlin.
1930	The completion of the Prinzregentenstrasse synagogue.
January 24, 1933	Opening of the Jewish Museum next door to the New Synagogue on Oranienburger Strasse.

The Period of National Socialism (1933–45)

January 30, 1933	Hitler becomes chancellor. 160,000 Jews are living in Berlin (about one-third of all Jews in Germany).
February 27, 1933	Reichstag fire. First wave of arrests of political opponents.
February 28, 1933	"Decree to Protect the People and the State." Many civil rights suspended.
March 23, 1933	Reichstag passes the "Enabling Law." The first concentration camps for political enemies are erected.
April 1, 1933	Boycott against shops owned by Jews.
May 10, 1933	Nazi's burn "un-German" books.
October 27–28, 1938	"Polenaktion" (Action against Poles); about 15,000 Jews from Eastern Europe are arrested and deported.
November 9–10, 1938	State-organized Pogrom (so-called *Kristallnacht*). Arrest and murder of Jewish citizens. Almost all synagogues in Germany are plundered and burned. Shops owned by Jews are also plundered.
September 1, 1939	World War II begins. Since 1933, 236,000 Jews have managed to leave Germany – about one half of the Jewish population. About 80,000 Jews are still living in Berlin.
February 10–12, 1940	First deportations of Jews from the districts of Stettin, Stralsund and Schneidemuehl to Poland.
July 1941	Reinhard Heydrich is ordered by Goering to take all necessary preparations for a "complete solution of the Jewish question in those areas of Europe controlled by Germany."

October 18, 1941	First deportation of about 1,000 Berlin Jews to Lodz, in Poland. About 60,000 Jews are still living in Berlin.
January 1, 1942	Wannsee Conference and the formulation of "The Final Solution of the Jewish question.": "In order to reach a final solution, the Jews, under appropriate directions shall be made to do hard work in the East. They will be herded into large groups of laborers, men will be separated from women. Those Jews who are able, will be put to work building streets and roads in these areas, whereby a large portion will be sorted out through natural reduction."
January 1942	Beginning of the deportations to Theresienstadt.
July 11, 1942	Beginning of the deportations to Auschwitz. In 1942, over 800 Jews commit suicide to escape deportation.
February 27, 1943	The so-called "Factory Action": Jews working in Berlin's armaments factories are deported to Auschwitz.
June 10, 1943	Dissolution of the Reich Association of Jews [RV] in Germany.
July 1943	Leading members of the Reich Association are deported to Theresienstadt.
1944	The Jewish inmates of neurological clinics are brought to Berlin from all over Germany and then deported to Auschwitz.
March 1945	The last deportation trains leave Berlin for Ravensbrueck and Sachsenhausen.
	Of the 160,000 Jews living in Berlin in 1933, 55,000 were murdered in concentration camps, 7,000 died by suicide. 90,000 managed to emigrate, and only about 8,000 Jews remained in Berlin to see the liberation. The majority of these survived in "mixed marriages." A smaller number lived "underground." Only a few survived the concentration camps.

From 1945 to the Present

May 2, 1945	Liberation of Berlin by the Red Army.
May 6, 1945	First Jewish services, held at Kantstrasse 158.
May 11, 1945	First public services, held near the Jewish cemetery in Weissensee.
Summer 1945	Jews from Poland flee to Berlin because of pogroms there. The Americans establish camps for Displaced Persons (DPs).
February 1946	The Jewish Community in Berlin is re-established and legally recognized by the authorities.
March 1, 1946	First issue of the magazine *Der Weg*.
August 1947	Some 295 refugees return from exile in Shanghai.
July 23 – August 16, 1948	"Berlin Airlift." DPs are flown out of Berlin to camps in the western zones of occupation.
September 10, 1952	The Treaties of Luxemburg.
1953	Berlin's Jewish Community splits into eastern and western Communities.

February 2, 1952	Julius Meyer flees East Germany.
November 1955	Opening of the Jewish cemetery in West Berlin.
September 27, 1959	Dedication of the Jewish Community House on Fasanenstrasse.
March 12, 1962	Re-opening of the Jewish Adult Education School.
January 1, 1971	Agreement on the Regulation of Questions Concerning both Parties between the Jewish Community and the municipal Senate.
September 10, 1971	Ceremony marking the three hundredth anniversary of the founding of the Jewish Community of Berlin.
September 22, 1980	Limitations in East Berlin on the immigration of Jews from the Soviet Union.
January 16, 1982	Bomb explosion in the Israeli restaurant Mifgash Israel. A baby is killed and 25 people are injured.
1982	With the Israeli invasion of Lebanon, the police step up their patrols outside Jewish institutions in West Berlin.
July 1986	In East Berlin, the restored cemetery of Adass Jisroel re-opens.
September 1986	In West Berlin, the opening of a Jewish elementary school.
January 1987	The first "Days of Yiddish Culture" are celebrated in East Berlin.
May 1987	The "Days of Jewish Culture" are celebrated in West Berlin.
1988	Foundation of the Association for Jewish Culture (Juedischer Kulturverein).
October 3, 1990	Jewish Community of Berlin is reunified.
1991	Israeli General Consulate opens in Berlin.
July 19, 1992	Death of Heinz Galinski, Community chairman, 1948–92.
1992	Exhibition "Juedische Lebenswelten" (Jewish Worlds of Living) at the Martin-Gropius Bau.
1992	Opening of the Moses Mendelssohn Center for European Jewish studies in Potsdam.
August 1993	Opening of the Jewish High School on Grosse Hamburger Strasse.
1995	State treaty between the Jewish Community and the State of Berlin.
May 7, 1995	Opening of the Centrum Judaicum in the restored New Synagogue.
Beginning of 1997	Opening of the Berlin representation of the American Jewish Committee, Mosse House on Leipziger Platz.
End of 1998	Opening of the Lauder Teaching House at the Rykestrasse synagogue.
1999	The Central Council of Jews in Germany (Zentralrat der Juden in Deutschland) moves to the former building of the Academy for the Science of Judaism (Hochschule fuer die Wissenschaft des Judentums) on Tucholskystrasse.
June 21, 2000	First class of pupils graduates from the Jewish High School.

Selected Bibliography

General Works

Adler, H. G.: Die Juden in Deutschland. Von der Aufklärung bis zum Nationalsozialismus, München
1987.

Albertz, J. (Hg.): ›Judenklischees‹ und jüdische Wirk-
lichkeit in unserer Gesellschaft, Wiesbaden 1985.

Am Wedding haben sie gelebt. Lebenswege jüdischer
Bürgerinnen und Bürger. Hg. Berliner Geschichtswerkstatt, Berlin 1997.

Battenberg, Friedrich: Das europäische Zeitalter der
Juden. Zur Entwicklung einer Minderheit in der
nichtjüdischen Umwelt Europas, 2 Bde., Darmstadt
1990.

Bein, Alex: Die Judenfrage. Biographie eines Weltprob-
lems, 2 Bde., Stuttgart 1980.

Blumenthal, W. Michael: Die unsichtbare Mauer. Die
dreihundertjährige Geschichte einer deutsch-jüdischen Familie, München 1999.

Carlebach, Julius (Hg.): Zur Geschichte der jüdischen
Frau in Deutschland, Berlin 1993.

Christoffel, Udo (Hg.): Berlin Wilmersdorf. Die Juden.
Leben und Leiden, Berlin 1987.

Deutsche Juden – Juden in Deutschland. Hg. Bundes-
zentrale für politische Bildung, o.O. o.J.

Dick, Jutta/Sassenberg, Marina: Jüdische Frauen im 19.
und 20. Jahrhundert. Lexikon zu Leben und Werk,
Reinbek 1993.

Domke, Petra: Synagogen in Berlin, Berlin 1996.

Eckhardt, Ulrich/Nachama, Andreas: Jüdische Orte in
Berlin, Berlin 1996.

Eckhardt, Ulrich/Nord, Elke: Der Moses Mendelssohn
Pfad. Eine Berliner Zeitreise oder Wanderwege in
eine versunkene Stadt, Berlin 1987.

Endlich, Stefanie/Lutz, Thomas: Gedenken und Lernen an historischen Orten. Ein Wegweiser zu Ge-
denkstätten für die Opfer des Nationalsozialismus
in Berlin, Berlin 1995.

Etzold, Alfred u. a.: Die Jüdischen Friedhöfe in Berlin,
4., verb. u. erw. Aufl. Berlin 1991.

Gay, Ruth: Geschichte der Juden in Deutschland. Von
der Römerzeit bis zum Zweiten Weltkrieg, München 1993.

Geiger, Ludwig: Geschichte der Juden in Berlin. Fest-
schrift zur zweiten Säkular-Feier. Anmerkungen,
Ausführungen, urkundliche Beilagen und zwei
Nachträge, [zuerst Berlin 1871–90 2 Bde.], 2. Aufl.
Berlin 1989.

Gottschalk, Wolfgang: Die Friedhöfe der Jüdischen Gemeinde zu Berlin, Berlin 1992.

Graupe, Heinz Moshe: Die Entstehung des modernen
Judentums. Geistesgeschichte der deutschen Juden
1650–1942, 2. Aufl. Hamburg 1977.

Günther-Kaminski, Michael/Weiss, Michael: »… als
wäre es nie gewesen«. Juden am Ku'damm, 2., überarb. Aufl. Berlin 1989.

Hartung-von Doentinchem, Dagmar/Winau, Rolf
(Hg.): Zerstörte Fortschritte. Das Jüdische Krankenhaus in Berlin 1756–1861/1914–1989, Berlin
1989.

Hübner, Barbara u. a.: Juden in Hohenschönhausen.
Eine Spurensuche, Berlin 1988.

Jersch-Wenzel, Stefi/John, Barbara (Hg.): Von Zuwan-
derern zu Einheimischen. Hugenotten, Juden, Böh-
men, Polen in Berlin, Berlin 1990.

Die Juden in Berlin 1671–1945. Ein Lesebuch. Mit
Beiträgen von Annegret Ehmann u.a., Berlin 1988.

Juden in Kreuzberg. Fundstücke…Fragmente…Er-
innerungen. Hg. Berliner Geschichtswerkstatt, Berlin 1991.

Juden in Treptow. Sie haben geheißen, wie ihr heißt.
Hg. Kulturbund e.V. Berlin-Treptow, Berlin 1993.

Juden in Weißensee. »Ich hatte einst ein schönes Vaterland«. Hg. Kulturamt Weißensee, Berlin 1994.

Jüdische Lebenswelten. Bd. 1: Essays. Hg. Andreas
Nachama/Julius H. Schoeps/Edward van Voolen;
Bd. 2: Katalog [der Ausstellung]. Hg. Andreas
Nachama/Gereon Sievernich, Frankfurt am Main
1991–1992.

Jüdisches Leben in Pankow. Eine zeitgeschichtliche Dokumentation. Hg. Bund der Antifaschisten Berlin-
Pankow e. V., Berlin 1993.

Kaulen, Alois/Pohl, Joachim: Juden in Spandau vom
Mittelalter bis 1945, Berlin 1988.

Kaznelson, Siegmund (Hg.): Juden im deutschen Kul-
turbereich, Berlin 1959.

Kisch, Guido: Judentaufen. Eine historisch-biogra-
phisch-psychologisch-soziologische Studie be-
sonders für Berlin und Königsberg, Berlin 1973.

Knobloch, Heinz: Berliner Grabsteine, 4., erw. Aufl.
Berlin 1991.

Köhler, Rosemarie/Kratz-Whan, Ulrich: Der jüdische
Friedhof Schönhauser Allee, Berlin 1992.

Kolland, Dorothea (Hg.): Zehn Brüder waren wir gewesen … Spuren jüdischen Lebens in Berlin-Neukölln,
Berlin 1988.

Lammel, Inge: Jüdische Lebensbilder aus Pankow. Familiengeschichten, Lebensläufe, Kurzporträts, Berlin 1996.

Leistung und Schicksal. 300 Jahre Jüdische Gemeinde zu Berlin. Dokumente, Gemälde, Druckgraphik, Handzeichnungen, Plastik, [Ausstellungskatalog] Berlin 1971.

Lowenthal, Ernst G.: Die Juden in Preußen. Ein biographisches Verzeichnis. Ein repräsentativer Querschnitt, 2. Aufl. Berlin 1982.

Lüdersdorf, Gerd: Es war ihr Zuhause. Juden in Köpenick, Berlin 1998.

Mattenklott, Gert (Hg.): Jüdische Städtebilder: Berlin, Frankfurt am Main 1997.

Melcher, Peter: Weißensee. Ein Friedhof als Spiegelbild jüdischer Geschichte in Berlin, Berlin 1986.

Meyer, Michael A. (Hg.): Deutsch-jüdische Geschichte in der Neuzeit, 4 Bde., München 1996–1997.

Meyer, Michael A.: Jüdische Identität in der Moderne, Frankfurt am Main 1992.

Mosse, Georg L.: Jüdische Intellektuelle in Deutschland. Zwischen Religion und Nationalismus, Frankfurt am Main 1992.

Müller, Ernst: Die Juden Berlins. Nach historischen Quellen, Berlin 1882.

Mun, Richard: Die Juden in Berlin, Leipzig 1924.

Nachama, Andreas/Simon, Hermann (Hg.): Jüdische Grabstätten und Friedhöfe in Berlin. Eine Dokumentation, Berlin 1992.

Orte des Erinnerns. Bd. 1: Das Denkmal im Bayerischen Viertel, Bd. 2: Jüdisches Alltagsleben im Bayerischen Viertel. Hg. Kunstamt Schöneberg in Zusammenarbeit mit der Gedenkstätte Haus der Wannsee-Konferenz, Berlin 1994.

Philo-Lexikon. Handbuch des jüdischen Wissens, Nachdruck der Ausgabe Berlin 1935 Frankfurt am Main 1992.

Rennert, Jürgen/Riemann, Dietmar: Der Gute Ort in Weißensee. Bilder vom jüdischen Friedhof und eine Sammlung jüdischer Stimmen zu Vergehen und Werden, Bleiben und Sein, Berlin 1987.

Richarz, Monika: Bürger auf Widerruf. Lebenszeugnisse deutscher Juden 1780–1945, München 1989.

Runge, Irene: Vom Kommen und Bleiben. Osteuropäische jüdische Einwanderer in Berlin, Berlin 1992.

Rürup, Reinhard (Hg.): Jüdische Geschichte in Berlin. Essays und Studien, 2 Bde., Berlin 1995.

Schoeps, Julius H.: Deutsch-jüdische Symbiose oder Die mißglückte Emanzipation, Berlin 1996.

Schoeps, Julius H.: Das Gewaltsyndrom. Verformungen und Brüche im deutsch-jüdischen Verhältnis, Berlin 1998.

Schoeps, Julius H. (Hg.): Juden als Träger der bürgerlichen Kultur in Deutschland, Sachsenheim 1989.

Schoeps, Julius H. (Hg.): Neues Lexikon des Judentums, Gütersloh 1998.

Schoeps, Julius H. (Hg.): Zionismus. Texte zu seiner Entwicklung, 2., überarb. Aufl. Dreieich 1983.

Sellenthin, Hans Gerd: Geschichte der Juden in Berlin und des Gebäudes Fasanenstraße 79–80. Festschrift anläßlich der Einweihung des jüdischen Gemeindehauses, Berlin 1959.

Simon, Hermann: Die Neue Synagoge Berlin. Geschichte, Gegenwart, Zukunft, Berlin 1991.

Simon, Hermann (Hg.): Erbe und Auftrag. Eine Ausstellung aus Anlaß des 325jährigen Bestehens der Jüdischen Gemeinde zu Berlin, Berlin 1996.

Sinasohn, Max M.: Die Berliner Privatsynagogen und ihre Rabbiner 1671–1971. Zur Erinnerung an das 300jährige Bestehen der Jüdischen Gemeinde zu Berlin, Jerusalem 1971.

Stern, Selma: Der Preußische Staat und die Juden, 7 Bde., Tübingen 1962–1971.

Synagogen in Berlin. Zur Geschichte einer zerstörten Architektur, [Ausstellungskatalog] 2 Bde., Berlin 1983.

Tetzlaff, Walter: 2000 Kurzbiographien bedeutender deutscher Juden des 20. Jahrhunderts, Lindhorst 1982.

Toury, Jacob: Die politischen Orientierungen der Juden in Deutschland. Von Jena bis Weimar, Tübingen 1966.

Vogel, Rolf: Ein Stück von uns: Deutsche Juden in deutschen Armeen 1813–1976, Mainz 1977.

Volkov, Shulamit: Die Juden in Deutschland 1780–1918, München 1994.

Volkov, Shulamit: Jüdisches Leben und Antisemitismus im 19. und 20. Jahrhundert, München 1990.

Von Juden in Steglitz. Beiträge zur Ortsgeschichte. Hg. Initiative Haus Wolfenstein, 2. Aufl. Berlin 1990.

Wolbe, Eugen: Geschichte der Juden in Berlin und in der Mark Brandenburg, Berlin 1937.

Zielenziger, Kurt: Juden in der deutschen Wirtschaft, Berlin 1930.

Zivier, Georg/Huder, Walter: 300 Jahre Jüdische Gemeinde zu Berlin, Berlin 1971.

From the Beginnings until 1789

Bruer, Albert A.: Geschichte der Juden in Preußen 1750–1820, Frankfurt am Main 1991.

Davidsohn, Ludwig: Beiträge zur Sozial- und Wirtschaftsgeschichte der Berliner Juden vor der Emanzipation, Berlin 1920.

Dohm, Christian Konrad Wilhelm von: Über die bürgerliche Verbesserung der Juden, Nachdruck der Ausgabe Berlin 1781–83, Hildesheim 1973.

Fehrs, Jörg H.: Von der Heidereutergasse zum Roseneck. Jüdische Schulen in Berlin 1712–1942, Berlin 1993.

Feilchenfeld, Alfred (Hg.): Denkwürdigkeiten der Glückel von Hameln, Nachdruck der 4. Auflage Berlin 1923, Bodenheim 1999.

Heise, Werner: Die Juden in der Mark Brandenburg bis zum Jahre 1571, Nachdruck der Ausg. Berlin 1932, Vaduz 1965.

Hensel, Sebastian (Hg.): Die Familie Mendelssohn 1729–1847. Nach Briefen und Tagebüchern, [zuerst Berlin 1879] Frankfurt am Main 1995.

Knobloch, Heinz: Herr Moses in Berlin. Auf den Spuren eines Menschenfreundes, Frankfurt am Main 1996.

Meisl, Josef (Hg.): Protokollbuch der jüdischen Gemeinde Berlin 1723–1854, Jerusalem 1962.

Meyer, Michael A.: Von Moses Mendelssohn zu Leopold Zunz. Jüdische Identität in Deutschland 1749–1824, München 1994.

Richarz, Monika: Der Eintritt der Juden in die akademischen Berufe. Jüdische Studenten und Akademiker in Deutschland 1678–1848, Tübingen 1974.

Sorkin, David: The Berlin Haskalah and German Religious Thought. Orphans of Knowledge, London 2000.

Virnich, Carl-Joseph: Die Berliner Hofjuden. Jüdische Lebensläufe im 17. und 18. Jahrhundert, [Microfiches] Marburg 1997.

The Process of Adaptation (1790–1870)

Arendt, Hannah: Rahel Varnhagen. Lebensgeschichte einer Jüdin aus der Romantik, 10. Aufl. München 1990.

Aschheim, Steven E.: Brothers and Strangers. The East European Jew in German and German Jewish Conciousness 1800–1923, Madison 1982.

Awerbuch, Marianne/Jersch-Wenzel, Stefi (Hg.): Bild und Selbstbild der Juden Berlins zwischen Aufklärung und Romantik, Berlin 1992.

Bering, Dietz: Der Name als Stigma. Antisemitismus im deutschen Alltag 1812–1933, Stuttgart 1987.

Erb, Rainer/Bergmann, Werner: Die Nachtseite der Judenemanzipation. Der Widerstand gegen die Integration der Juden 1780-1860, Berlin 1989.

Freund, Ismar: Die Emanzipation der Juden in Preußen, unter besonderer Berücksichtigung des Gesetzes vom 11. März 1812. Ein Beitrag zur Rechtsgeschichte der Juden in Preußen, 2 Bde., Berlin 1912.

Gilbert, Felix (Hg.): Bankiers, Künstler und Gelehrte. Unveröffentlichte Briefe der Familie Mendelssohn aus dem 19. Jahrhundert, Tübingen 1975.

Grab, Walter/Schoeps, Julius H. (Hg.): Juden im Vormärz und in der Revolution von 1848, Stuttgart 1983.

Hertz, Deborah: Die jüdischen Salons im alten Berlin, Frankfurt am Main 1998.

Holdheim; Samuel: Geschichte der Entstehung und Entwicklung der jüdischen Reformgemeinde in Berlin, Berlin 1857.

Jacobson, Jacob: Die Judenbürgerbücher der Stadt Berlin 1809–1851, Berlin 1962.

Jersch-Wenzel, Stefi: Juden und ›Franzosen‹ in der Wirtschaft des Raumes Berlin/Brandenburg zur Zeit des Merkantilismus, Berlin 1978.

Jersch-Wenzel, Stefi: Jüdische Bürger und kommunale Selbstverwaltung in preußischen Städten 1808–1848, Berlin 1967.

Katz, Jacob: Die Hep-Hep-Verfolgungen des Jahres 1819, Berlin 1994.

Katz, Jacob: Zur Emanzipation und Assimilation der Juden in Deutschland, Darmstadt 1982.

Kleßmann, Eckard: Die Mendelssohns. Bilder aus einer deutschen Familie, München 1990.

Liebeschütz, Hans/Paucker, Arnold (Hg.): Das Judentum in der deutschen Umwelt 1800–1850. Studien zur Frühgeschichte der Emanzipation, Tübingen 1977.

Lowenstein, Steven M.: The Berlin Jewish Community. Enlightment, Family and Crisis 1770–1830, New York 1994.

Die Mendelssohns in Berlin. Eine Familie und ihre Stadt. Bearb. Rudolf Elvers/Hans-Günter Klein, [Ausstellungskatalog] Wiesbaden 1983.

Mosse, Werner E./Pohl, Hans: Jüdische Unternehmer in Deutschland im 19. und 20. Jahrhundert, Stuttgart 1992.

Pulzer, Peter: Jews and the German State. The Political History of a Minority 1848–1933, Oxford and Cambridge Mass. 1992.

Rönne, Ludwig von/Simon, Heinrich: Die früheren und gegenwärtigen Verhältnisse der Juden in den sämmtlichen Landestheilen des Preußischen Staates, Breslau 1843.

Schoeps, Julius H.: Bürgerliche Aufklärung und liberales Freiheitsdenken. A. Bernstein in seiner Zeit, Stuttgart 1992.

Sorkin, David: The Transformation of German Jewry 1780–1840, New York 1987.

Toury, Jacob: Soziale und politische Geschichte der Juden in Deutschland 1847–1871, Düsseldorf 1977.

The Imperial Era (1871–1918)

Adler-Rudel, Shalom: Ostjuden in Deutschland 1880–1940. Zugleich eine Geschichte der Organisationen, die sie betreuten, Tübingen 1959.

Auerbach, Leopold: Das Judenthum und seine Bekenner in Preußen und in anderen deutschen Bundesstaaten, Berlin 1890.

Bendt, Vera/Galliner, Nicola (Hg.): »Öffne deine Hand für die Stummen«. Die Geschichte der Israelitischen Taubstummen-Anstalt Berlin-Weißensee 1873 bis 1942, Berlin 1993.

Benjamin, Walter: Berliner Kindheit um 1900, Frankfurt am Main 1987.

Bilski, Emily u. a.: Berlin Metropolis. Jews and the New Culture 1890–1918, [Ausstellungskatalog] Berkely and Los Angeles 1999.

Boehlich, Walter (Hg.): Der Berliner Antisemitismusstreit, Frankfurt am Main 1988.

Breuer, Mordechai: Jüdische Orthodoxie im Deutschen Reich 1871–1918. Sozialgeschichte einer religiösen Minderheit, Frankfurt am Main 1986.

Bronsen, David: Jews and Germans from 1860 to 1933: The Problematic Symbiosis, Heidelberg 1979.

Eloni, Yehuda: Zionismus in Deutschland. Von den Anfängen bis 1914, Gerlingen 1987.

Geiger, Ludwig: Die deutschen Juden und der Krieg, Berlin 1916.

Girardet, Cella-Margaretha: Jüdische Mäzene für die Preußischen Museen zu Berlin. Eine Studie zum Mäzenatentum im Deutschen Kaiserreich und in der Weimarer Republik, Engelsbach 1998.

Hamburger, Ernest: Juden im öffentlichen Leben Deutschlands. Regierungsmitglieder, Beamte und Parlamentarier in der monarchistischen Zeit, Tübingen 1968.

Heuberger, Georg/Spiegel, Paul (Hg.): Zedaka. Jüdische Sozialarbeit im Wandel der Zeit. 75 Jahre Zentralwohlfahrtsstelle der Juden in Deutschland 1917–1992, Frankfurt am Main 1992.

Honigmann, Peter: Die Austritte aus der Jüdischen Gemeinde Berlin 1873–1941. Statistische Auswertung und historische Interpretation, Frankfurt am Main 1988.

Jöhlinger, Otto: Bismarck und die Juden, Berlin 1921.

Jungmann-Bradt, Tutti: Die Bradts. Jüdische Familiengeschichte aus Berlin 1870–1999, Konstanz 1999.

Kampe, Norbert: Studenten und ›Judenfrage‹ im deutschen Kaiserreich, Göttingen 1988.

Kaplan, Marion A.: Die jüdische Frauenbewegung in Deutschland. Organisation und Ziele des Jüdischen Frauenbundes 1904–1938, Hamburg 1981.

Ladewig-Winters, Simone: Wertheim, ein Warenhausunternehmen und seine Eigentümer. Ein Beispiel der Entwicklung der Berliner Warenhäuser bis zur ›Arisierung‹, Münster 1997.

Lichtblau, Albert: Antisemitismus und soziale Spannung in Berlin und Wien 1867–1914, Berlin 1994.

Mosse, Werner E./Paucker, Arnold (Hg.): Deutsches Judentum in Krieg und Revolution 1916–1923, Tübingen 1971.

Mosse, Werner E./Paucker, Arnold (Hg.): Juden im Wilhelminischen Deutschland 1890–1914. Ein Sammelband, 2., erg. Aufl. Tübingen 1998.

Offenberg, Mario (Hg.): Adass Jisroel. Die Jüdische Gemeinde in Berlin (1869–1942). Vernichtet und Vergessen, Berlin 1986.

Poppel, Stephen M.: Zionism in Germany 1897-1933. The Shaping of a Jewish Identity, Philadelphia 1976.

Pulzer, Peter: The Rise of Political Anti-Semitism in Germany and Austria, London and New York 1988.

Reinharz, Jehuda: Fatherland or Promised Land. The Dilemma of the German Jews 1893–1914, Ann Arbor Mich. 1975.

Segall, Jacob: Die beruflichen und sozialen Verhältnisse der Juden in Deutschland, Berlin 1912.

Simmenauer, Felix: Die Goldmedaille. Erinnerungen an die Bar Kochba-Makkabi Turn- und Sportbewegung 1898–1938, Berlin 1989.

Simon, Hermann (Hg.): »Tuet auf die Pforten«. Die Neue Synagoge 1866–1995, [Ausstellungskatalog] Berlin 1995.

Sinasohn, Max M. (Hg.): Adass Jisroel Berlin. Entstehung, Entfaltung, Entwurzelung 1869–1939, Jerusalem 1966.

Sprengel, Peter: Populäres jüdisches Theater in Berlin von 1877 bis 1933, Berlin 1997.

Sprengel, Peter: Scheunenviertel-Theater. Jüdische Schauspielgruppen und jiddische Dramatik in Berlin (1900–1918), Berlin 1995.

Zechlin, Egmont: Die deutsche Politik und die Juden im Ersten Weltkrieg, Göttingen 1969.

The Weimar Years (1919–1933)

Benz, Wolfgang/Paucker, Arnold/Pulzer, Peter (Hg.): Jüdisches Leben in der Weimarer Republik, Tübingen 1998.

Bernstein, Reiner: Zwischen Emanzipation und Antisemitismus. Die Publizistik der deutschen Juden am Beispiel der ›C.V.-Zeitung‹, Organ des Centralvereins deutscher Staatsbürger jüdischen Glaubens 1924–1933, Phil.Diss. Berlin 1969.

Brenner, Michael: The Renaissance of Jewish Culture in Weimar Germany, New Haven 1996.

Dunker, Ulrich: Der Reichsbund jüdischer Frontsoldaten 1919–1939. Geschichte eines jüdischen Abwehrvereins, Düsseldorf 1977.

Führer durch die jüdische Gemeindeverwaltung und Wohlfahrtspflege 1932–1933, Berlin o. J.

Geisel, Eike: Im Scheunenviertel. Bilder, Texte und Dokumente, Berlin 1981.

Grab, Walter/Schoeps, Julius H. (Hg.): Juden in der Weimarer Republik, Bonn 1986.

Jonas, [Regina] Fräulein Rabbiner: Kann die Frau das rabbinische Amt bekleiden? Eine Streitschrift. Hg. Elisa Klapheck, Teetz 1999.

Jüdisches Adressbuch für Groß-Berlin. Ausgabe 1931. Mit einem Vorwort von Hermann Simon, Berlin 1994.

Klein, Brigitte: Die C.V.-Zeitung der Jahrgänge 1925-1935. Zum Problem des Selbstverständnis deutscher Juden, Phil.Diss. Frankfurt am Main 1969.

Knütter, Hans-Helmuth: Die Juden und die deutsche Linke in der Weimarer Republik 1918-1933, Düsseldorf 1971.

Liepach, Martin: Das Wahlverhalten der jüdischen Bevölkerung in der Weimarer Republik. Zur politischen Orientierung der Juden in der Weimarer Republik, Tübingen 1996.

Maurer, Trude: Ostjuden in Deutschland 1918–1933, Tübingen 1986.

Meyer, Bernhard (Hg.): Berliner jüdische Ärzte in der Weimarer Republik, Berlin 1996.

Meyhöfer, Rita: Gäste in Berlin? Jüdisches Schülererleben in der Weimarer Republik und im Nationalsozialismus, Hamburg 1996.

Mosse, Werner E./Paucker, Arnold (Hg.): Entscheidungsjahr 1932. Zur Judenfrage in der Endphase der Weimarer Republik, 2., rev. und erw. Aufl. Tübingen 1966.

Neiss, Marion: Die jiddische Presse in Berlin 1919–1925, Phil.Diss. Berlin 2000.

Niewyk, Donald L.: The Jews in Weimar Germany, Manchester N.H. 1980.

Paucker, Arnold: Der jüdische Abwehrkampf gegen Antisemitismus und Nationalsozialismus in den letzten Jahren der Weimarer Republik, 2. verb. Aufl. Hamburg 1969.

Pross, Christian/Winau Rolf (Hg.): »Nicht mißhandeln!« Das Krankenhaus Moabit: 1920–1933 ein Zentrum jüdischer Ärzte in Berlin. 1933–1945 Verfolgung – Widerstand – Zerstörung, Berlin 1984.

Richarz, Monika (Hg.): Jüdisches Leben in Deutschland. Selbstzeugnisse zur Sozialgeschichte 1918–1945, 3 Bde., Stuttgart 1976–1982.

Das Scheunenviertel. Spuren eines verlorenen Berlins. Hg. Verein Stiftung Scheunenviertel, 2., durchges. Aufl. Berlin 1996.

Scholem Gershom: Von Berlin nach Jerusalem. Jugenderinnerungen. Erweiterte Ausgabe, Frankfurt am Main 1997.

Silbergleit, Heinrich: Die Bevölkerungs- und Berufsverhältnisse der Juden im Deutschen Reich. Bd 1: Freistaat Preußen, Berlin 1930.

Stern, Heinemann: Warum hassen sie uns eigentlich? Jüdisches Leben zwischen den Kriegen. Erinnerungen, Düsseldorf 1970.

Walk, Joseph: Kurzbiographien zur Geschichte der Juden 1918–1945, München 1988.

Jews during the Period of National Socialism

Adler, H. G.: Der verwaltete Mensch. Studien zur Deportation der Juden aus Deutschland, Tübingen 1974.

Adler-Rudel, Shalom: Jüdische Selbsthilfe unter dem Naziregime 1933–1939 im Spiegel der Berichte der Reichsvertretung der Juden in Deutschland, Tübingen 1974.

Angress, Werner T.: Generation zwischen Furcht und Hoffnung. Jüdische Jugend im Dritten Reich, Hamburg 1985.

Ball-Kaduri, Kurt Jakob: Das Leben der Juden in Deutschland im Jahre 1933. Ein Zeitbericht, Frankfurt am Main 1963.

Ball-Kaduri, Kurt Jakob: Vor der Katastrophe. Juden in Deutschland 1934–1939, Tel Aviv 1967.

Barkai, Avraham: Vom Boykott zur ›Entjudung‹. Der wirtschaftliche Existenzkampf der Juden im Dritten Reich 1933–1943, Frankfurt am Main 1988.

Benz, Wolfgang (Hg.): Dimension des Völkermords. Die Zahl der jüdischen Opfer des Nationalsozialismus, München 1991.

Benz, Wolfgang (Hg.): Die Juden in Deutschland 1933–1945. Leben unter nationalsozialistischer Herrschaft, München 1988.

Busemann, Hertha Luise/Daxner, Michael/Fölling, Werner: Insel der Geborgenheit. Die Private Waldschule Kaliski. Berlin 1932 bis 1939, Stuttgart 1992.

Deutschkron, Inge: Berliner Juden im Untergrund, Berlin 1980.

Deutschkron, Inge: Ich trug den gelben Stern, Köln 1978.

Elkin, Rivka: Das Jüdische Krankenhaus in Berlin zwischen 1938 und 1945, Berlin 1993.

Fabarius, Hans-Werner: Juden in Marienfelde. Schicksale im Dritten Reich, Berlin 1990.

Fölling, Werner: Zwischen deutscher und jüdischer Identität. Deutsch-jüdische Familien und die Erziehung ihrer Kinder an einer jüdischen Reformschule in Berlin im ›Dritten Reich‹, Opladen 1995.

Freeden, Herbert: Jüdische Presse im Dritten Reich, Frankfurt am Main 1987.

Freeden, Herbert: Jüdisches Theater in Nazideutschland, Frankfurt am Main 1985.

Gedenkbuch Berlins der jüdischen Opfer des Nationalsozialismus. »Ihre Namen mögen nie vergessen werden«. Hg. Zentralinstitut für sozialwissenschaftliche Forschung der Freien Universität Berlin, Berlin 1995.

Geisel, Eike/Broder, Henrik M.: Premiere und Pogrom. Der jüdische Kulturbund 1933–1941, Berlin 1992.

Geschlossene Vorstellung. Der Jüdische Kulturbund in Deutschland 1933–1941. Hg. Akademie der Künste, Berlin 1992.

Ginzel, Günther: Jüdischer Alltag in Deutschland 1933–1945, Düsseldorf 1984.

Gross, Leonard: Versteckt. Wie Juden in Berlin die Nazi-Zeit überlebten, Reinbek 1983.

Gruner, Wolf: Judenverfolgung in Berlin 1933–1945. Eine Chronologie der Behördenmaßnahmen in der Reichshauptstadt, Berlin 1996.

Die Grunewald-Rampe. Die Deportation der Berliner Juden. Hg. Zentrum für audio-visuelle Medien, 2., korr. Aufl. Berlin 1993.

»Hier ist kein Bleiben länger«. Jüdische Schulgründerinnen in Wilmersdorf. Hg. Wilmersdorfer Museum, [Ausstellungskatalog] Berlin 1992.

Hildesheimer, Esriel Erich: Jüdische Selbstverwaltung unter dem NS-Regime. Der Existenzkampf der Reichsvertretung und Reichsvereinigung der Juden in Deutschland, Tübingen 1994.

Holzer, Willi: Jüdische Schulen in Berlin. Am Beispiel der privaten Volksschule der jüdischen Gemeinde Rykestraße, Berlin 1992.

Jäckel, Eberhard/Longerich, Peter/Schoeps, Julius H. (Hg.): Enzyklopädie des Holocaust. Die Verfolgung und Ermordung der europäischen Juden, 3 Bde., Berlin 1993.

Jochmann, Gernot: Frauenprotest in der Rosenstraße. »Gebt uns unsere Männer wieder«, Berlin 1993.

Koberstein, Thea/Stein, Norbert: Juden in Lichtenberg mit den früheren Ortsteilen Friedrichshain, Hellersdorf und Marzahn, Berlin 1995.

Krach, Tillmann: Jüdische Rechtsanwälte in Preußen. Über die Bedeutung der freien Advokatur und ihre Zerstörung durch den Nationalsozialismus, München 1991.

Kreutzer, Michael (Hg.): »Die Gespräche drehten sich auch vielfach um die Reise, die wir alle antreten müssen«. Leben und Verfolgtsein der Juden in Berlin-Tempelhof. Biographien und Dokumentation, Berlin 1988.

Kulka, Otto Dov (Hg.): Deutsches Judentum unter dem Nationalsozialismus, Tübingen 1997.

Kwiet, Konrad/Eschwege, Helmut: Selbstbehauptung und Widerstand. Deutsche Juden im Kampf um Existenz und Menschenwürde 1933–1945, Hamburg 1984.

Ladewig-Winters, Simone: Anwalt ohne Recht. Das Schicksal jüdischer Rechtsanwälte in Berlin nach 1933, Berlin 1998.

Löhken, Wilfried/Vathke, Werner (Hg.): Juden im Widerstand. Drei Gruppen zwischen Überlebenskampf und politischer Aktion, Berlin 1939–1945, Berlin 1993.

Meyer, Beate/Simon, Hermann (Hg.): Juden in Berlin 1938 bis 1945, [Ausstellungskatalog] Berlin 2000.

Pätzold, Kurt/Schwarz, Erika: Tagesordnung: Judenmord. Die Wannsee-Konferenz am 20. Januar 1942, Berlin 1992.

Paucker, Arnold (Hg.): Juden im nationalsozialistischen Deutschland/The Jews in Nazi Germany 1933–1945, Tübingen 1986.

Paucker, Arnold: Jüdischer Widerstand in Deutschland. Tatsachen und Problematik, Berlin 1989.

Philo-Atlas. Handbuch für die jüdische Auswanderung. Reprint der Ausgabe von 1938 mit einem Vorwort von Susanne Urban Fahr, Bodenheim o.J.

Rewald, Ilse: Berliner, die uns halfen, die Hitlerdiktatur zu überleben, 4. Aufl. Berlin 1985.

Rogge-Gau, Sylvia: Die doppelte Wurzel des Daseins. Julius Bab und der Jüdische Kulturbund Berlin, Berlin 1999.

Rosenstrauch, Hazel (Hg.): Aus Nachbarn wurden Juden. Ausgrenzung und Selbstbehauptung 1933–1942, 2. Aufl. Berlin 1991.

Rürup, Reinhard (Hg.): Topographie des Terrors. Gestapo, SS und Reichssicherheitshauptamt auf dem ›Prinz-Albrecht-Gelände‹. Eine Dokumentation, 10., verb. Aufl. Berlin 1995.

Schilde, Kurt: Vom Columbia-Haus zum Schulenburgring. Dokumentation mit Lebensgeschichten von Opfern des Widerstandes und der Verfolgung von 1933 bis 1945 aus dem Bezirk Tempelhof, Berlin 1987.

Schoenberner, Gerhard: Der gelbe Stern. Die Judenverfolgung in Europa 1933–1945, durchges., erw. Neuausg. Frankfurt am Main 1998.

Schönfeld, Martin: Gedenktafeln in Ost-Berlin. Orte der Erinnerung an die Zeit des Nationalsozialismus, Berlin 1991.

Schönfeld, Martin: Gedenktafeln in West-Berlin, Berlin 1993.

Schoeps, Hans-Joachim: »Bereit für Deutschland!«. Der Patriotismus deutscher Juden und der Nationalsozialismus, Berlin 1970.

Schwersenz, Jizchak: Die versteckte Gruppe. Ein jüdischer Lehrer erinnert sich an Deutschland, Berlin 1988.

Simon, Ernst: Aufbau im Untergang. Jüdische Erwachsenenbildung im nationalsozialistischen Deutschland als geistiger Widerstand, Tübingen 1959.

Simon, Hermann: Das Berliner Jüdische Museum in der Oranienburger Straße. Geschichte einer zerstörten Kulturstätte, wesentl. veränd. Neuausgabe, Teetz 2000.

Simon, Hermann: »Und lehrt sie: Gedächtnis!« Eine Ausstellung des Ministeriums für Kultur und des Staatssekretärs für Kirchenfragen in Zusammenarbeit mit dem Verband der Jüdischen Gemeinden in der DDR zum Gedenken an den faschistischen Novemberpogrom vor 50 Jahren, Berlin 1988.

Tichauer, Erwin R.: Totenkopf und Zebrakleid. Ein Berliner Jude in Auschwitz, Berlin 1999.

Tuchel, Johannes: Am Großen Wannsee 56–58. Von der Villa Minoux zum Haus der Wannsee-Konferenz, Berlin 1992.

Verfolgte Berliner Wissenschaft. Ein Gedenkwerk, zus.gest. von Rudolf Schottlaender, Berlin 1988.

Walk, Joseph (Hg.): Das Sonderrecht für die Juden im NS-Staat. Eine Sammlung der gesetzlichen Maßnahmen und Richtlinien. Inhalt und Bedeutung, 2. Aufl. Heidelberg 1996.

Wippermann, Wolfgang: Steinerne Zeugen. Stätten der Judenverfolgung in Berlin, Berlin 1982.

From 1945 to the Present

Breidenbach, Barbara: Lernen jüdischer Identität. Eine schulbezogene Fallstudie, Weinheim 1999 [zugl. Phil.Diss. Hagen: Jüdische Schulen in Deutschland. Ort des Lernens jüdischer Identität untersucht am Beispiel der Galinski-Grundschule, Berlin].

Brenner, Michael: Nach dem Holocaust. Juden in Deutschland 1945–1950, München 1995.

Brumlik, Micha u.a. (Hg.): Jüdisches Leben in Deutschland seit 1945, Frankfurt am Main 1988.

Deutschkron, Inge: Unbequem … Mein Leben nach dem Überleben, Köln 1992.

John, Barbara (Hg.): Von Aizenberg bis Zaidelmann. Jüdische Zuwanderer aus Osteuropa in Berlin und die Jüdische Gemeinde heute, Berlin 1995.

Der jüdische Kindergarten in Berlin 1946–1996. Festschrift anläßlich des 50jährigen Bestehens des jüdischen Kindergartens in Berlin, Berlin 1996.

Königseder, Angelika: Flucht nach Berlin. Jüdische Displaced Persons 1945–1948, Berlin 1998.

Münch, Ragnhild: Das Jüdische Krankenhaus in Berlin 1945–1965, Berlin 1997.

Nachama, Andreas/Schoeps, Julius H. (Hg.): Aufbau nach dem Untergang. Deutsch-jüdische Geschichte nach 1945, Berlin 1992.

Roth, Andrew/Frajman, Michael: Das jüdische Berlin heute. Ein Wegweiser, Berlin 1999.

Schoeps, Julius H./Jasper, Willi/Vogt, Bernhard (Hg.): Ein neues Judentum in Deutschland? Fremd- und Eigenbilder der russisch-jüdischen Einwanderer, Potsdam 1999.

Schoeps, Julius H. u.a. (Hg.): Russische Juden in Deutschland. Integration und Selbstbehauptung in einem fremden Land, Weinheim 1986.

Strauss, Herbert A./Grossmann, Kurt R. (Hg.): Gegenwart im Rückblick. Festgabe für die Jüdische Gemeinde zu Berlin 25 Jahre nach dem Neubeginn, Heidelberg 1970.

Wegweiser durch das jüdische Berlin. Geschichte und Gegenwart, Berlin 1987.

About the Authors

Michael Brenner was born in Weiden in 1964. A professor of Jewish history and culture at the University of Munich since 1997, he previously taught at Brandeis University. His numerous publications on German-Jewish history include *Nach dem Holocaust* and *Jüdische Kultur in der Weimarer Republik*. Brenner is, among other things, co-editor of *Deutsch-Jüdische Geschichte der Neuzeit* (in four volumes) and *Wissenschaft vom Judentum: Annäherungen nach dem Holocaust*. Because the present article was written in 1996, it does not reflect material published since.

Claudia-Ann Flumenbaum was born in Berlin in 1965. She studied ancient and modern history and political science at the Freie Universität Berlin and received her M.A. in 1995. Her thesis focused on controversies in German-Jewish journalism in the 1870s and 1880s. She has co-curated several exhibitions and cultural projects and has acted as event manager. She has worked as a coordinator for conferences and interpreters since 1997.

Andreas Nachama was born in Berlin in 1951. He studied history and Judaic studies in Berlin, where he received his Ph.D. in 1981. He was ordained as a rabbi in 2000. From 1981 to 1993 he served as head of the Berliner Festspiele and from 1992 to 1999 as Artistic Director of the Jüdische Kulturtage in Berlin. He has been Executive Director of the Topographie of Terror Foundation since 1994 and served as Chairman of Berlin's Jewish Community between 1997 and 2001. Nachama curated the exhibition *Jüdische Lebenswelten* and has co-curated various other exhibitions. He has authored numerous publications on German-Jewish history, on Prussian history, and in the field of cultural studies.

Julius H. Schoeps was born in Djursholm/Sweden in 1942. Since 1991 he has been a professor of modern history at the University of Potsdam, where he also directs the Moses Mendelssohn Center for European Jewish Studies. From 1993 to 1997 he served as founding director of The Vienna Jewish Museum. Among his numerous publications on German-Jewish history are *Theodor Herzl 1860–1904*, 'Wenn ihr wollt, ist es kein Märchen', and *Deutsch-jüdische Symbiose oder Die missglückte Emanzipation*. He has co-edited various publications, including: *Neues Lexikon des Judentums*, *Enzyklopädie des Holocaust*, *Menora. Jahrbuch für deutsch-jüdische Geschichte*.

Chana C. Schütz was born in Berlin in 1956 and studied art history and history in Berlin, Jerusalem, and Bonn. She received her Ph.D. in 1988 with a thesis on *Preußen in Jerusalem*. She is Vice-Director and Research Associate of the New Synagogue, Berlin – Centrum Judaicum Foundation and has curated various exhibitions. She is the author of numerous articles on German-Jewish art history and on the history of the Jews in Berlin.

Hermann Simon was born in Berlin in 1949. He studied history and oriental studies at Humboldt-University in Berlin, and undertook a post-graduate study in Prague in oriental numismatics, receiving his Ph.D. in 1976 with a thesis on medieval-oriental coins. From 1977 to 1988 he worked in this field at the Staatliche Museen zu Berlin. From 1988 to 1995 he directed the reconstruction of the New Synagogue as Centrum Judaicum. He has directed the New Synagogue Berlin – Centrum Judaicum Foundation since July, 1988. He directed various exhibitions, most notably *Juden in Berlin 1938–45* (with Beate Meyer). His publications include *Das Berliner Jüdische Museum in der Oranienburger Straße* and numerous articles on numismatic subjects and the history of the Jews in Germany.

Picture Credits

Archives du Centre de Documentation Juive Contemporaine, Paris 182 M.

Bildarchiv Abraham Pisarek 87 u., 189, 190 o., 190 u., 191.

Bildarchiv Preußischer Kulturbesitz, Berlin 2, 10, 14, 15 l., 15 r.o., 20/21, 24 o., 27, 28, 30 l., 30 r., 35 o., 42 o.l., 42 u.l., 43, 46 u., 47, 49 o., 49 u.l., 49 u.M., 49 u.r., 50 o.l., 50 o.r., 50 u., 51 o.r. 51 u.l., 51 u.M., 54 o., 54 u., 55, 60 o.l., 60 o.r., 60 u., 62, 63 o.l., 63 o.M., 63 M.l., 63 u.r., 63 u.M., 63 u.r., 70 o., 70 u., 71 o., 73 o.l., 73 o.r., 74, 75 o.l., 75 o.r., 75 u., 76, 77, 78/79, 81, 82, 83, 84, 89, 92 o.l., 92 o.r., 92 u., 93, 95 o., 95 u., 100 o.l., 100 u.l., 101, 104/105, 108 o., 109 o.l., 109 o.r., 109 u., 110, 112, 115 o.l., 115 u.r., 116 l.119 o.l., 119 o.r., 122 o., 122 u., 129 o., 129 u., 131, 138, 139, 140, 141 o., 141 u.l., 141 u.M., 141 u.r., 143 o., 143 u.r., 146, 148 o., 148 u.l., 148 u.r., 149, 153 o.l., 153 o.r., 153 u.157 o.l., 157 u.l., 157 r., 160 o.l., 160 u., 162 o., 162 u., 164 o., 168/169, 173 o., 173 u., 176 o.l., 176 o.r., 176 u.l., 176 u.r., 179 o.l., 179 o.r., 179 u., 182 o.r., 182 u.l., 183 o., 183 u., 185, 186, 197, 202 o.l.202 o.r., 202 u., 203 o., 203 u., 199 o., 199 u., 204, 207 o., 207 u., 211 l., 211 o.r., 211 u.r., 223 o., 231 o.r., 236 u.

Bundesarchiv Berlin 184 o.r.

Central Archives for the History of the Jewish People, Jerusalem 101 o.

Hulton Deutsch Collection, London 224 o.l., 224 o.r., 224 u.l., 224 u.r.

Jüdische Kulturtage Berlin 238 o.r., 238 M.l., 238 M.r., 238 u.l., 238 u.r., 239 o.r., 239 M.l., 239 M.r., 239 u.l., 239 u.r.

›Jüdisches Berlin‹, Redaktionsarchiv 243 o.l., 243 u.l., 243 u.r., 246 o., 246 M., 246 u.

Landesarchiv Berlin 206 u.

Moses Mendelssohn Zentrum für europäisch-jüdische Studien, Potsdam 9, 15 r.u., 16, 18, 24 u., 25, 26, 31, 35 u.l., 35 u.r., 65 r., 73 u.,

85, 87 o.r., 103, 106, 115 u.l., 117, 134 o., 145, 152, 160 o.r., 164 u.l., 164 u.M., 164 u.r., 165 r., 172, 182 o.l., 184 o.l., 184 u.r., 188 o., 188 u., 208, 216, 226, 227 o.231 o.l., 231 u., 233, 236 o., 240

Elke Nord, Berlin 242 u.

Sächsische Landesbibliothek, Dresden 223 u.l., 223 u.r.

Salomon Ludwig Steinheim Institut für deutsch-jüdische Geschichte, Archiv N. Gidal, Duisburg 6, 42 r., 51 o.l., 51 o.M., 51 u.r., 58, 63 o.r., 63 M.l., 65 o.l., 65 u.l., 71 u., 72 o.l., 72 o.r., 72 u.l., 72 u.r., 86 o., 86 u., 87 o.l., 96, 97, 100 o.l., 100 u.r., 108 u., 119, 121, 123 o., 123 u.l., 123 u.r., 125 o., 125 u., 134 u., 143 u.l., 147

Sammlung Julius H. Schoeps, Berlin 178 o., 178 u., 184 u.l., 206 o.l., 206 o.r.

Sammlung Hermann Simon, Berlin 130

Schiller-Nationalmuseum Deutsches Literaturarchiv, Marbach 115 o.r., 116 l.

Margrit Schmidt, Berlin 243 o.r.

Staatsbibliothek zu Berlin Preußischer Kulturbesitz 32 o.

Stiftung Jüdisches Museum Berlin 66/67, 195, 242 o.

Stiftung Neue Synagoge Berlin – Centrum Judaicum 198, 214, 225, 227 u., 234 o., 234 u., 235 o., 235 u., 244

Stiftung Stadtmuseum Berlin 32 u.l., 32 u.r.

Suhrkamp Taschenbuch Verlag Frankfurt a. M. 159 l.

Der Tagesspiegel, Berlin 245

Ullstein-Bilderdienst, Berlin 46 o., 113, 159 r., 165 l., 180

YIVO Institute for Jewish Research, New York 222

Unfortunately, the publisher was unable to contact the owners of rights to some of the pictures reproduced here. Please direct any existing demands regarding permissions to the publisher.

Index